The Structure of the Ordinary

The MIT Press · Cambridge, Massachusetts · London, England

The Structure of the

# Ordinary

Form and Control in the Built Environment
N. J. Habraken · edited by Jonathan Teicher

This book was set in Scala and Frutiger by Graphic Composition, Inc. and was printed and bound in the United States of America.

Library of Congress Cataloging-in-Publication Data
Habraken, N. J.
    The structure of the ordinary : form and control in the built environment / N. J. Habraken ; edited by Jonathan Teicher.
      p.    cm.
    Includes bibliographical references and index.
    ISBN 0-262-08260-8 (alk. paper)
    1. Architecture—Composition, proportion, etc.  2. Form
(Aesthetics)  3. Architecture—Environmental aspects.  I. Teicher,
Jonathan.  II. Title.
NA2760.H33  1998
720'.1—dc21
                              97-24601
                               CIP

Contents

## Illustrations

xiii

*To arrive at the simplest truth . . . requires years of contemplation. Not activity. Not reasoning. Not calculating. Not busy behavior of any kind. Not reading. Not talking. Not making an effort. Not thinking. Simply bearing in mind what it is one needs to know.*

G. Spencer-Brown, *Laws of Form*

Readers familiar with my earlier work will not fail to observe that the present book is rooted in applied research, begun in the 1960s in the Netherlands, on the distinction of support and infill levels in housing design.

That early work evolved while developing the tools for a new design approach, one based not on static program but on inevitable change over time. Over the years, a steadily growing international body of professionals, in various ways and in various places, contributed to the evolving body of "Open Building" knowledge—in theory, method, design, and actual implementation in practice. As projects pursuing open-ended design grew in number and sophistication, research into ways of designing for complexity and change continued.

It had been clear from the beginning that the issues we were exploring led far beyond housing, touching on the fundamental nature of built environment in general. At the newly founded SAR research foundation and the still newer Department of Architecture at Eindhoven, our practical applied research kept raising impractical philosophical questions, leading us to speculate on the broadest general principles of environmental structure that might lie behind our pragmatic solutions. And rightly so: mass housing, which we sought to remedy, was a pathology produced by unprecedented shifts in environmental structure.

In accepting the very naturalness of our point of departure—the conviction that individ-

## Sources and Acknowledgments

ual responsibility for one's own environment represents an essential precondition for environmental health—we sought continuity rather than revolution: Might separation of support and infill be expressing some constant principle? Might the range of levels of intervention in the environment be broader than expected? Could vestigial evidence of vanished levels be found within contemporary environment? Before long, our research extended upward in scale. We began to analyze historic urban tissues and, eventually, we examined general principles for design on that level.

It eventually dawned on me that the support/infill idea made us examine the environment as shaped by acts of transformation, which in turn revealed what was constant. What could be learned about environmental structure from observing change? Subsequently, after joining the extraordinarily diverse and inquisitive faculty and talented international student body at MIT's Department of Architecture, I came to participate intensively in studio and classroom teaching. This was an ideal setting in which to explore the relationship of transformation and continuity in form.

Through all of these years, the question of this relationship persistently arose, although it seldom took center stage. It helped frame my applied research, teaching, designing and managing, reading, and traveling. It called attention to facts and details that would otherwise have escaped me, compelling me to digest them. Soon, the same question would gradually reappear in the background, obliquely, in a different way.

**0.1**  *Cairo—Housing project, viewed from within.*

The reader may appreciate the implications of this method or, more accurately, lack thereof. Although all I did was ultimately colored by questions about change and form, there is no unified body of research on which this book reports. Although many individuals have contributed—often unwittingly—to this study, no single group brought it to fruition. Slowly, compellingly, observation and research revealed the three-part structure described in this book. And, as I reluctantly and painfully had to learn, no single discipline could easily accommodate it.

These circumstances explain the long period of gestation that produced the present book, shaping its contents as well as its format. Such a sustained reflection of many decades, presented in heavily condensed form, cannot hope to adequately pinpoint the wealth of impressions that have informed it.

In this work, I do not present writing that builds on other texts, footnote by footnote, to fill in blank spots in the map of our knowledge. Rather, in looking at what is already known— the more common the example, the better— I attempt to demonstrate a particular way of seeing. Naturally, I have strived to identify the origins of specific facts utilized. Most important, it behooves me to credit the sources that broadly nurtured my search. These fall into three often overlapping categories: people, places, and texts. A select bibliography limited to writings that have directly informed the present work, stimulating and informing my thinking (sometimes by opposition), has accordingly been added. Some of them the reader may want to peruse. In the footnotes, simple recognition due primary sources is occasionally the goal. Beyond that, there exists no conventional format for the listing of people and places as sources of information.

Hence I improvise:

**Places:** Built environment is ubiquitous. Yet to recognize its structure, fabric, and character requires deliberate search. To know it, one must stray from the familiar beaten path of airports, freeways, and conference centers. Its understanding lies far removed from the professional circuit leading to monuments and acclaimed locations. The back streets of cities; their apartment buildings, tenements, and townhouses; their suburbs and enclaves of the wealthy are no less fascinating. Among other places, Tokyo, Osaka, Kyoto, Suzhou, Beijing, Taiyuan, Tianjin, Hangzhou, Seoul, Hawhoe, Tainan, Djakarta, Bandung, Houston, San Francisco, Los Angeles, Boston and Cambridge, Montreal, Mexico City, Santiago de Chile, Buenos Aires, Cairo and Alexandria, Dammam, Jerusalem and Haifa have left memorable impressions of environmental types and patterns of streets, houses, and their parts.

So-called informal sectors are best explored with guides, particularly absent any language in common with their inhabitants. I have had the good fortune to visit some in Mexico City and Monterrey, Djakarta, Santiago de Chile, and Cairo. They were sometimes failing, often successful, always struggling. At times, but for experiencing the pride and energy of their inhabitants, I would have found it impossible to understand these locations as emerging urban fabric. The same forces can be witnessed in rural areas. For example, there are newly built houses in an age-old vernacular in the Chinese countryside, the Indonesian kampongs, and the brick-and-plaster villages of the Nile delta. I recall new houses emerging in villages in Croatia and Bosnia during Tito's reign: one year, a floor was built; perhaps another followed several years later, with money earned by labor in Germany or Italy.

Traditional urban environments too must first be experienced in their common fabric, before churches, palaces, and plazas can be understood. Here, the historic Dutch fabric, particularly in Delft and Amsterdam, as well as historic fabrics of other European towns—particularly Paris, London, Edinburgh, Venice, Urbino, Bologna, Rome, and Florence—have greatly stimulated my thinking. (Their turn-of-the-century neighborhoods—harbingers from recent history of things to come—are explicitly discussed.)

Likewise, Mediterranean hill towns, in all their wide variety but equally undeniable kinship, are mandatory places of pilgrimage for the student of urban fabric, as are the French bastide towns. Equally fascinating are the North American suburbs, at all levels of income. Compared to their European, South American, and Asian counterparts, they are often an irresistible mixture of innocence and sophistication.

It takes relatively little effort to walk the streets and observe the townscape. But gaining entry to houses is more difficult, frequently a result of circumstance. Such random samples of interiors are inevitably biased. To surprise life as it is lived, only unexpected visits are worth making. In some cultures this is simply not possible. We seek out those from whom we can expect acceptance, and we are accepted for a variety of reasons. Pride is an almost universal sentiment among those who show their houses, no less in teeming self-help neighborhoods than within sumptuous nouveaux-riches villas. Thus impressions, though invaluable, cannot be reliably generalized.

People tend to identify with its particular space they inhabit, if not with its broader context. Each visit exposes basic patterns of inhabitation, reinforcing our sense of the familiar. Each visit also brings surprises, reinforcing the feeling that we do not really know how others live. I do remember with particular respect the cleanliness and dignity of the very poor in the most diverse parts of the world.

**People:** Along with places and writings, face-to-face contact with individuals nourished this book. Some I learned from directly—sometimes by sustained exposure to their thinking but more often by thoughts expressed in diverse contexts, examples set by practice or career paths followed, or comments thrown out casually. I cite names of individuals not only to acknowledge a debt but in the hope that others will look into their work and acts as they might look into books or visit places.

In the early days of research, collaboration with Hans van Olphen alerted me to the importance of systemic continuity in design variation. Thijs Bax's reflections on the concepts of structure and levels were crucial. John Carp's insistence on inhabitation as a territorial act opened new ways of thinking, while Henk Reyenga's skills of observation and analysis of urban fabric set a standard. Fokke de Jong bore memorable witness to the building as a product of implicit understandings.

Pioneering architects proved feasible what had been considered impractical by many. Frans van der Werf's building of some seven pathbreaking "supports" projects over several decades changed the tone of the debate in the Netherlands and abroad. In those early days, Nabeel Hamdi and Nick Wilkinson in England succeeded against great odds, as did Bart Wouben in the Netherlands. Theirs, and numerous other implementations of supports principles—perhaps less ambitious but equally tangible—triggered and justified my search for underlying general principles.

This was a time of diverse people coming to similar conclusions independently. Early on,

xix

Georges Maurios in Paris and Ottakar Uhl in Karlsrühe produced projects that demonstrated parallel thinking. So did Katsuo Tatsumi in his Two Step housing projects over several decades in Osaka and Kyoto, in close collaboration with Mitsuo Takada. This reinforced the conviction that general principles were involved.

Lucien Kroll, in his inimitable work, has been an inspiration in many respects since his first projects of the sixties. Later, Jia Sheng Bao and Yun Yu Ma built pioneering projects in China, as did Yositika Utida's Next21 team in Osaka.

Open Building principles touch not just on design but on all aspects of settlement. John Turner, in his lifelong advocacy of tenants' rights as a fundamental issue of control that requires support in economic policy, has inspired many, including myself. Martin Pawley's keen and independent thinking broadened my awareness of the political dimension of the act of building. Age van Randen in Holland and Stephen Kendall in the United States researched the intricacies of technology and production of open-ended systems, as did Utida and Masao Ando in Japan. Joop Kapteyns' characteristically practical and low-key research encompasses systemization, typology, and territory, all from the perspective of change. Karel Dekker and Tempelmans Plat were the first, to my knowledge, to directly explore the economics of Open Building. Much earlier, Dini Vedder, in an inspiring and little-known Ph.D. thesis, explored the economics of incremental and transformational urban development.

Cor Hinnen and a few of his fellow directors of public housing estates first understood and explored the implications of the distinction of levels in estate management. (Early experiments done on that score by the Japan Housing Corporation and Akio Yamada came to my at-

tention only later.) Others provided insights into practical application of Open Building principles: Frans de Vries and Jan van Vonderen in the Netherlands, Zhang Qinnan in Beijing for many years, and Seiji Sawada for over a quarter of a century in Tokyo were undaunted advocates. They continue to contribute to my real-world experience. Robert Oxman pointed toward theoretical contexts too easily ignored by me.

Research into the dynamics and properties of urban fabric has been a constant aspect of my learning over the years at MIT, a common interest jointly explored with many among the faculty. Fernando Domeyko's prior detailed recordings of the uses and transformations of turn-of-the-century fabric in Santiago de Chile and, later, of the historic fabrics of Madrid and Córdoba threw light on the variations of settlement in constant form. They were perhaps most valuable for their unbiased and all-inclusive recording of what was actually there.

Comprehensive studies of actual inhabitation are extremely rare for obvious practical reasons. An example is Toshihito Yokouchi's recording of South Boston interiors in his work with Sandra Howell. Research on Colonia Santa Ursula by Jorge Andrade's team is unique in the long time span it covers and in its detailed record of transformations.

In bringing love of the urban environment of their native countries to bear on the study of general principles of form transformation and projection, numerous students provided me with valuable insights into variations of urban fabric and house typology: Christina Gryboiyanni on Athens, Solly Benjamin on Ladakh, Arjun Nagarkatti on Ahmadabad, Sawsan Bakr on Fatimid Cairo, Ming Chorn Hwang on imperial Beijing, Yi Ping Chang on Taiwanese vernacular, You Xuan Zhu on historic Beijing tissue, John Dale on Fort Point Channel, Thomas Hille on typological transformation in San Francisco, Jorge Andrade on Salinas Vera Cruz, Andres Mignucci on San Juan, Puerto Rico, Wan Abadin on Malaysian vernacular, Doo Ho Sohn on Hawhoe, Korea, and Adnan Khasjugee on Medina all contributed to my learning.

Students also played a key role in my earlier research. A project supported by the Grunsfeld Foundation on the use of levels and type in team design was successful thanks to the particularly gifted team of student participants, listed in the bibliography. A study for the National Science Foundation on concept design games, which illustrated and abstracted elements of environmental structure, gained substantially from the contributions of Mark Gross, particularly but not only in relation to computational manipulation of the games, and of Ellen Saslaw with regard to their philosophical background.

Other students were constant companions over periods of years and remained valuable sources as they went on to teach: Ming Hung Wang's research interests range from traditional façade systems to newly emerging types, to urban tissue and abstract principles of transformation. Jamel Akbar's thinking and writing on patterns of control and the properties of the Muslim urban fabric are impressive in perception, rigor, and range. Stephen Kendall's exploration of the flow of material parts in relation to patterns of control merits close study.

In this general field of inquiry, I produced an early and very different precursor to this book more than a decade ago, privately distributed. Patient reading by students over the years triggered generous comments; their genuine interest provided constant stimulation. Among my colleagues, William Porter's early support for my writing is remembered with gratitude, as is Aaron Fleisher's constant probing. Donald Schön's questions and comments over the years were very important at crucial points. At a later stage, valuable comments were given by Leon Groisser, Ronald Lewcock, and Imre Halasz. Timothy O'Connor at the Harvard-Yenching Library, and Michael Leininger, Omar Khalidi, and the rest of MIT's Rotch Library staff, gave generously of their time and scholarly erudition. Much appreciated encouragement and support were received from Julian Beinart, Tony Grunsfeld, and Stanford Anderson. To Roger Conover, Matthew Abbate, and Ori Kometani of the MIT Press, and to Alice Falk, profound thanks and acknowledgement are also due.

Without Jonathan Teicher's experience, his timely initiatives and cheerful guidance, this book would not have made its way from author's manuscript to print. Each chapter and subchapter have been much improved by his tactful prodding and sensitive application of editorial skills, always revealing true affinity to the subject matter. All remaining shortcomings are mine to account for.

Finally, three guardian angels have protected me over the years.

*Marleen van Hall*
*Piet Sanders*
*Jan Lucas*

To them this book is dedicated.

xxi

The Structure of the Ordinary

## Prologue

For thousands of years, built environments of great richness and complexity arose informally and endured. Knowledge about how to make ordinary environment was ubiquitous, innately manifest in the everyday interactions of builders, patrons, and users. Built environment arose from implicit structures based on common understanding. Environmental knowing-in-action (Schön) was never made explicit, because there was no need for such articulation.

Although master builders had been active for millennia, built environments as such remained unquestioned and taken for granted. In discussing domestic architecture, Vitruvius did not even bother to define the house type to which he referred: an alternative was unthinkable. It is only with Palladio, who, in service to a new class of patron, reinvented the farmhouse villa with a classical front and strict symmetry of plan, that the idea of inventing new typologies took root. But for many generations after Palladio, the domain of professional architecture remained limited. Churches, fortresses, palaces, mansions, and similarly exceptional interventions were designed within an otherwise self-sustaining built environment.

During the modern era, however, professional intervention has extended to encompass domestic as well as institutional buildings, places of production, service, and commerce. Every aspect of the built environment is now routinely reexamined, subjected to alternative solutions. Architectural practice has thus been transformed to a point where it is no longer comparable with that of the past.

What used to remain unquestioned has been taken up as a design problem to be solved:

*0.2* *Amsterdam—View of seventeenth-century canal. Photo KLM Luchtphotographie (page xxii).*

nothing may be taken for granted. Ordinary growth processes that had been innate and self-sustaining, shared throughout society, have been recast as problems requiring professional solution. Built environment, the ubiquitous, stable, ordinary background for architectural innovation, is now itself being reinvented by professionals, bit by bit, time after time.

This radical shift in roles has become irreversible. Called upon to maintain, transform, and expand ordinary built environment at all scales, today's professionals can no longer refuse nor abandon this task. Yet in continuing to rely on design traditions, methods, and tools shaped by the Palladian model, we remain poorly equipped to do our new mission justice. Practices historically developed to create unique and limited acts of monumentality cannot guide us in engaging the commonplace. We need to shake off jaded ambition, among other constraints on our thoughts and actions.

In this new situation, the unspoken ways of ordinary environments must be articulated. We cannot revive the naive past. We dare not promise an unrealizable future. But to make peace with our task of designing the ordinary we must seek more intimate knowledge of it.

Our subject, then, is not architecture, but built environment. It is innately familiar. Anew, we observe what always has been with us—not to discover, much less to invent, but to recognize.

**0.3**  *Rome, 1748—Detail of the* Pianta Grande di Roma *by Giambattista Nolli.*

# Introduction: Control and Form

## 0.1 Transformation and Control

### Change

Built environment, in all of its complexity, is created by people. Yet it is simply far too complex, too large, and too self-evident to be perceived as a single entity, an artifact like a chair, a car, a painting, or even a building.

Moreover, built environments have lives of their own: they grow, renew themselves, and endure for millennia. Conservation may serve to freeze works of art in time, resisting time's effects. But the living environment can persist only through change and adaptation. Thus preservation of Amsterdam's seventeenth-century canal houses sparks ongoing debate about what must be retained and what may be transformed. Façades lining the canals were built over centuries that witnessed profound changes in domestic life, technology, available materials, and style. Restoration, like that of a cathedral built over generations and subsequently modified, similarly means freezing a collage of intervention.

In growing and changing through time, the built environment resembles an organism more than an artifact. Yet, while ever-changing, it does possess qualities that transcend time. Identities of buildings and cities persist for millennia. Despite transformation, they represent values shared with ancestors and passed down to descendants, uniting past and future. Similar continuity exists in public spaces—streets, boulevards, squares, and neighborhoods—and even in details, in the way a doorway or window is crafted, or how a room is laid out.

The antiquity of monuments and public spaces, and the meaning with which they

*0.4* Sounion, Greece—View from the temple of Poseidon (page 4).

are invested, underscores how much else perennially changes. Buildings are demolished; ancient roads are widened; new streets are insinuated into existing urban fabric. Even the fundamental qualities of public space—seemingly so permanent—are gradually altered by the transformation of buildings and streetscapes that define it.

In short, the very durability and transcendence of built environment is possible only because there is continuous change. In this respect, built environment is indeed *organic:* continuous renewal and replacement of individual cells preserves it, giving it the ability to persist.

## Knowing the Built Environment

Change and renewal are the keys to our knowledge of the built environment.

This is not a revolutionary idea: scientists frequently observe transformation to understand the nature and structure of things. However, unlike other symbiotic organic phenomena, the built environment escapes rigorous scrutiny because humans live as an integral part of it. We engage the built environment not to observe from a distance but to act on it, as an object. In judging it and projecting values onto it, we are not accustomed to simply watching it, to learning how it behaves.

We build to endure, to resist time, although we know that ultimately time will win. What previous generations erected for eternity, we demolish. Then, with similar intent, we lay stone upon stone and build again. Permanence is instinctively sought.

But the detached observer recognizes the builder as an agent of change. The builder is an actor who, in striving for permanence, perhaps for immortality, engages the existing field and

transforms what is there. Built environment, like all complex phenomena, artificial and natural, endures by transforming its parts.

## Agents

Thus, the built environment comprises not only physical forms—buildings, streets, and infrastructure—but also the people acting on them. If built environment is an organism, it is so by virtue of human intervention: people imbue it with life and spirit of place. As long as they are actively involved and find a given built environment worth renewing, altering, and expanding, it endures. When they leave off, the environment dies and crumbles, pulled back down to the earth by the ineluctable force of gravity.

The intimate and unceasing interaction between people and the forms they inhabit is a fundamental and fascinating aspect of built environment. We are all players: agents who inhabit the environment, transforming it to our liking and making sure things stay as we choose, within the territory we claim. Few are passive. Office workers arrange flowers, adjust picture frames and books, set down a cup of coffee; students hang posters on the wall. Such humble impulses of inhabitation lead to maintaining and adapting building forms, and ultimately to erecting, demolishing, or replacing buildings and settlements.

To use built form is to exercise some control, and to control is to transform. There is thus no absolute distinction between those who create and those who use. A complex hierarchy of control patterns within a continuity of action emerges: this is a major theme of the study that follows.

For designers and planners, use is typically set a priori—immobilized—to allow optimized problem solving during programming

7

and design. But in reality, use is neither static nor passive. Use marks the beginning and end of each act of transformation, forming part of the cycle of actions by which the built environment lives. To perceive how buildings' intrinsic capacity to adapt and transform represents the key to their survival, the perspective that has given rise to programmatic functionalism must be transcended. We must learn to look afresh at the intricate ongoing symbiosis between people and built matter. There are sticks and stones, and there are people living among them: the two are inseparable, though readily distinguished.

## Control

The key to this way of perceiving the environment is control: the ability to transform some part of that environment. To the extent that we are players—inhabiting office cubicles, fixing up homes, investing in real estate—we exercise control. Control may result in closing a communicating door between two rooms, or in demolishing a neighborhood. Exerting formal control means transforming, and conversely all transformation denotes control. Whenever physical parts are introduced, displaced, or removed from a site, some controlling agent—a person, group of persons, organization or institution—is revealed.

Control thus defines the central operational relationship between humans and all matter that is the stuff of built environment. As dynamic patterns of change echo throughout a built environment, they reveal the structure of control. In light of built environment's organic patterns of growth and change, the transformational "behavior" of its forms, it appears to act very much as a living whole.

8

## 0.2 Three Orders Become Visible

### Suspending Judgment

Our stance vis-à-vis the built environment should parallel that of the botanist observing plants. Unlike florists, botanists do not promote plants based on the shape, color, or fragrance of their flowers. Unlike farmers, they neither choose nor rank what is observed in terms of ease of production, palatability, or marketability. We must similarly resolve not to obscure our understanding of interaction between agent and form in built environments by passing value judgments on what is observed.

The necessity of a disciplined and detached stance, so self-evident in the natural sciences, is by no means self-evident in studies of the built environment. We are fully immersed in the object of our inquiry—in fact, we are part of it—and value judgments color our every observation. As agents—builders, developers, architects, bankers, managers, and inhabitants—we continually ask: *Is it good or bad? Do we want it?* Questions must be asked and answered before anyone acts. Bankers must commit money; developers must decide if they can make a profit; engineers must decide what will stand firm; inhabitants must decide whether to relocate.

With value judgments driving all actions by agents, it is not surprising that almost all literature pertaining to built environment is judgmental, discussing what criteria to use, what to avoid, how to act wisely, how to ensure quality. This book will begin by withholding normative value judgment. To environmental professionals, such discipline does not come easily. In training and in practice, professionals are expected to pass judgment all the time—to advocate what is best, to decide what is to be done.

## Agents Exercise Judgment

An intention to suspend value judgment while observing built environment does not imply that the exercise of such judgment, itself, is not to be considered. Transformations cannot be fully explained without taking into account the fact that agents *do* pass judgment all the time. Indeed, this activity constitutes a singularly essential factor in built environments. For example, certain environmental constants can only be explained as the result of a coordinated preference among actors.

Value judgments are accordingly of keen interest, to the extent that they inform perception of the structure of built environment. But to qualify a judgment as good or bad—in the manner of Kevin Lynch in *Good City Form*—is not relevant here. This inquiry instead explores the nature of urban form per se.

This study also rejects positivism. In observing built environment in a nonjudgmental fashion, we find that forms and formal transformations cannot be explained by inevitability. Given continuous judgments by agents, observed form must be assumed rather to reflect their active selection and rejection of alternatives.

## Three Orders Become Visible

But personal judgment is by no means the only major mechanism that structures built environment. Three other forces are revealed in distinct but interrelated "Orders," which underlie the wide variety of forms that we observe and inform our interpretations.

The first is the physical order. In scrutinizing built form undergoing transformation, we observe a hierarchy of unique qualities.

Built environment is composed of distinct levels of intervention, which largely govern what agents do. Interaction among agents may, in turn, affect and alter the hierarchy of levels itself.

The second is the territorial order. Here, agents are witnessed in control not of form but of space; they decide what goes in and what does not. Territorial control is equally pervasive and similarly structured in all built environment. It is hierarchical, too, but the hierarchy it imposes need not precisely parallel that of form: the two interpret and define one another.

And last, as the parable of the Tower of Babel long ago taught, built environment assumes common understanding among agents. To a large extent, such understanding is about judgment. It creates the recurring themes and variations that we see in patterns, types, and systems. These reveal a third and cultural order based on consensus among agents.

When the three orders are referred to as "Form," "Place," and "Understanding," each term implies a very particular meaning. The Order of Form engages the built environment as part of all physical matter. The Order of Place, encompassing control of space, reflects territorial behavior observable among all living creatures and thereby connects environment to the biological realm.

It is only with the third order that we find ourselves within a purely human organization. It is characteristic of people that they reflect and weigh alternatives before they act. People must choose; therefore, they must deliberate and achieve consensus for any act concerning more than one person. The Order of Understanding is primarily social.

I

Form, The Physical Order

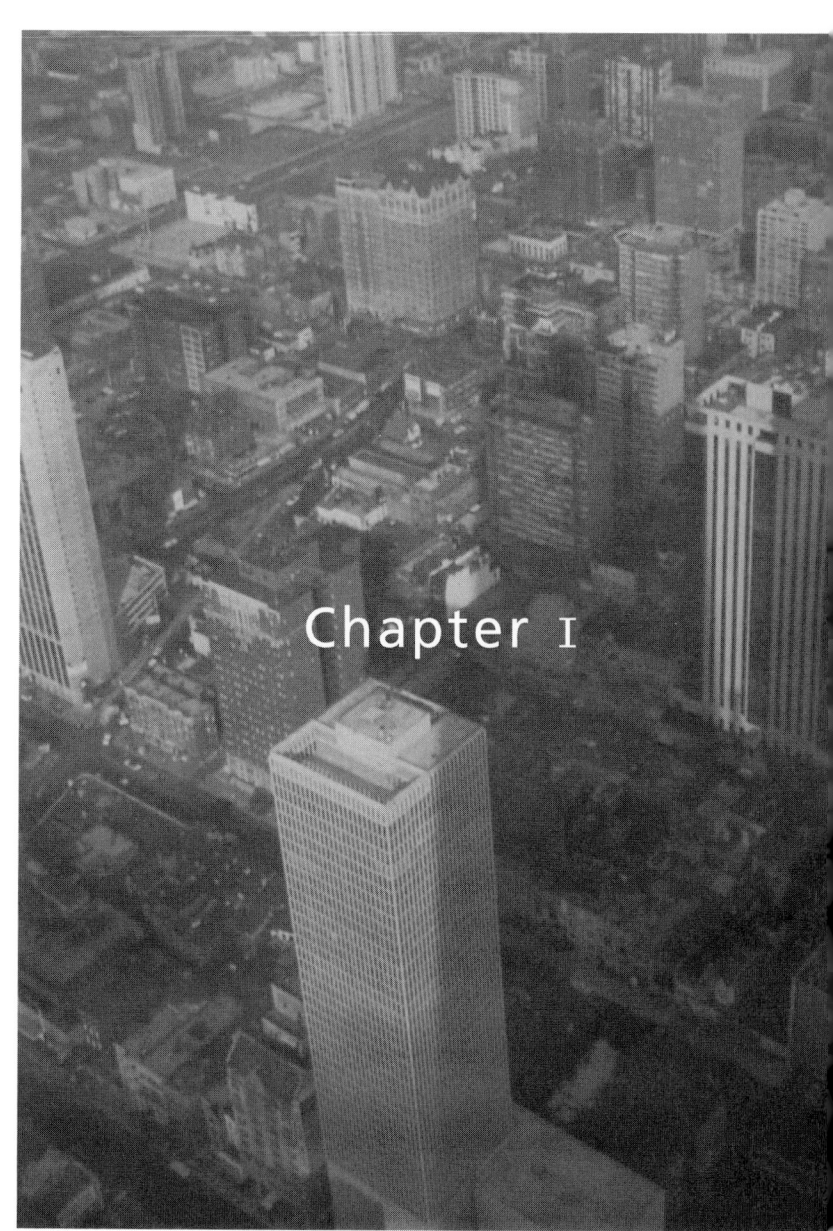

Chapter I

# The Physical Structure of Built Environment

## I.I  Live Configurations

### Perceiving Configurations

The physical organization of a built environment may be described in many ways, depending on one's particular scale and focus of concern. Typically, descriptions will name and distinguish parts, then group these parts into more complex configurations.

For example, an architect may describe a house as a composition of spaces. But a builder may prefer to describe it as an organization of material parts. A painter may describe it as a combination of planes distinguished by their colors. In describing the same house, a poet may name parts whose properties evoke reference to things in the past or at other places. Or she may allude to feelings, drawing unexpected analogies that give it new meaning. Finally, inhabitants tend to think in terms of rooms and places: not mere spatial entities, but combinations of many types of things—furniture, artwork, views—that jointly make an environment identifiable.

Human beings exhibit a universal tendency to conceptualize in terms of elements combined and grouped in various ways. Any such grouping may be called a *configuration*. Descriptions of form tend to differ in the choice of parts we elect to see, and in the way we group them, rather than in the fundamental conception of what constitutes a configuration.

A particular configuration, thus defined by its parts, may be named. It, in turn, may constitute a part combined with yet other parts,

*Cairo—View from Hassan Fathy's house (page 13).*

*__1.1__  Chicago—View from the John Hancock Building (page 14).*

making a more complex configuration. In this way, we continuously reinterpret the world we inhabit, shifting from one perspective to another in a dialogue with the forms around us, as well as with others who are inhabiting them.

## Control Defined

To understand environmental structure, elements and configurations must be designated in ways that relate to the actions of agents. Because transformation results from agent action, it highlights parts and configurations under agent control. That control, in turn, defines the units of transformation.

Consider a room in a retirement home, inhabited by an elderly lady. All of the furniture—as well as plants, pictures, photographs, figurines, and other mementos of a long life—has been arranged to form a configuration reflecting her preferences. She is free to rearrange the furnishings however she pleases. Her right to do so is fundamental and indisputable.

Therefore, these disparate objects share a common attribute: their placement relative to one another—the very fact that they are in the room at all—depends on the inhabitant's action. She has the ability to move things around and determine their relative position. She can also discard items, give them to grandchildren or friends, or add others she receives. These parts within the dwelling are under her control.

*1.2*  *Cairo—Interior furnished in King Farouk style.*

Together, they constitute a configuration defined by exercise of that control.

## Live Configurations

Configurations actively under unified control of a single agent—like the things in the above example—we will call *live configurations*. Any grouping of parts entirely under control of a single agent, such that their distribution in space has been determined or accepted by that agent and can be changed by that agent, constitutes a live configuration. Thus defined, a live configuration "behaves" like a single self-organizing entity.

Conversely, any group of elements not under such active unified control is not a live configuration. Thus, though individual row house façades may form a continuous wall, we have good reason to assume that this configuration is not "live": each dwelling is presumably under control of a different agent. However, where the street network is under the unified control of the municipality (which, in turn, may represent the collective of citizens in the houses), the streets, as distinct from the houses along them, will jointly constitute a live configuration.

Static form proves unreliable for determining if configurations are live: behind a row of preserved historical façades, a new hotel or office building may arise under control of a single agent. Thus, the observed variety of expression is a vestige of former control patterns. Or we may find that the street network itself is actually not under control of a single power, as in historic towns throughout the Middle East, where streets were often closed by gates controlled by residents. Ultimately it is not forms but their transformations that reveal whether a configuration is live or not. These transformations subsequently lead to new forms, which express existing distribution of control.

In what follows, we are primarily concerned with the built environment as composed of live configurations. Therefore, unless context or explicit statement confirms otherwise, wherever the term *configuration* is used, the reader may assume that a live configuration is meant.

Though the terminology is new, the existence and workings of live configurations are not: that one is free to arrange the things in one's own room at will is so self-evident that it is taken for granted. Typically, no one else will rearrange the furniture in the room, or move the objects displayed in it.

We are expert at recognizing who controls what in the built environment, almost instinctively. However, in this study, we are not interested in the specific *identities* of agents in control but in configurations that link people and built form: those configurations that can be identified as live. Observing configurations and the way they behave reveals a great deal about the way built environment is structured.

Suppose an office worker, having independently occupied a room, is now joined by a colleague. He agrees to admit her with her own desk, computer, and books. Soon each occupies part of the room and each has a private book shelf above the desk, within arm's length.

This scenario presents a profound transformation. The furniture and books reveal two live configurations instead of one. They resemble one another, having similar parts. The relationship between the parts is similar, too: both desks place computer and bookshelves in easy reach. Yet any visitor familiar with office arrangements recognizes two distinct configurations. If uncertain, she may wait and watch to find out which parts are under each colleague's control.

## Control vs. Ownership

Control does not imply ownership. Office furniture may be owned by the employer, although the books may be the employee's. Perhaps the computer on the desk is leased. Nevertheless, for the configuration composed of desk, books, and computer as a whole, that makes no difference. Each item is under the employee's control; and this alone will explain its presence and its transformations in the environment.

Of course, control of a borrowed chair is limited: one may not shatter it, for instance. But it may be shifted, offered to a visitor, or replaced at will. In general, an object that is not owned by the agent in control may undergo somewhat different transformation than would occur if it were owned.

If all observed office furniture is, for example, a particular Herman Miller system, an observer may readily conclude that one company owns it all. Nevertheless, distinct live configurations of furniture and equipment will still be found.

## Control Games

This way of seeing things is certainly not unfamiliar. Human beings play control games every day and have a good grasp of control patterns in operation. We also know how to glean information about agents in control, and about the environment itself, based on observations. The metaphor of game playing is apt: in board games, for instance, we frequently control parts and manipulate their configurations, following certain stated principles—the rules of the game.[1]

## Learning from Observation

While observing play, we learn about both a game's rules and its players.

In chronicling a chess game, for instance, it is customary to refer to the configurations observed on the board as *Black* and *White*. Watching the moves play by play, we learn about unknown players. If we see no daring moves, if fairly safe and advantageous opportunities are not seized, we judge White to be extremely cautious—indeed, somewhat timid. At the same time, perhaps we observe moves by the opponent that we do not fully understand. Occasionally brilliant, they nonetheless sometimes lead to losses: Black is reckless.

An observer ignorant of chess and unable to communicate with any other bystander might eventually learn the rules of the game exclusively through observing play. But whenever the game is explained by another observer, the discussion is about live configurations: *There are two opponents, Black and White, and six kinds of pieces. Pieces of each kind may move only in specified ways.*

One does not explain the game of chess by elaborating on the behavior of particular players, commenting on the timidity of the one and the brashness of the other. Nor does one learn the rules of the game by engaging the player immersed in the game: *I plan to push pawns on the left-hand part of the field, to shield my queen, to threaten her bishops. Or worse yet, He beat me with some dirty tricks, but this time,*

*I'm going to show who is the master.* This would not much help an observer to learn the rules of the game.

In the environmental game, we must watch the game played, observe the live configurations, and deduce the rules. For reasons similar to those outlined above, we may be wise *not* to ask agents acting in the built environment what they are doing, much less why.

## I.2 Levels

### Two-Level Organization

In addition to playing pieces, chess includes the board on which they move. The board provides a context for the two configurations controlled by opponents—a stable, unchanging background for the movement of pieces.

Like chess, the furniture arrangement game needs a stable, unchanging higher-level form to play in. The building provides context, space within which furniture may be deployed. Live configurations of furniture can be rearranged: existing pieces can be modified or removed, and others can be introduced.

The chess board is a configuration of sixty-four checkered squares. By analogy, the building, composed of walls and floors, is itself a configuration of parts. We play both games by making configurations on a lower level, within the stable context provided by a configuration of a higher level. Both are examples of two-level organization.

The analogy can be pushed too far. Buildings are found in all manner of sizes and forms, with all sorts of room configurations. Chess has only one fixed and uniform higher-level configuration: a board composed of sixty-four squares. Moreover, the rules governing placement and distribution of furniture within rooms are not uniform.

Even given distinct patterns within a particular culture, the rules of the "environmental game" played on the level of furniture arrangement are far more fluid and implicit than the rules of a board game. Nonetheless, the analogy may help the observer appreciate levels manifested in the built environment.

## Multilevel Built Environment

Patterns of transformation reveal environmental structure. Long-term observation confirms that within built environment, change universally occurs within clearly defined *levels*. These levels will parallel a given environment's hierarchy of control.

Levels clarify intuitive understanding: for example, it is easy to visualize how streets (a configuration on one level) jointly define city blocks. Within those blocks (on a lower level) buildings are built. It seems natural that within buildings, partitions can be reconfigured to rearrange individual rooms, within which, in turn, furniture is arranged under the control of different parties. Street network, building, partitioning, and furniture are different kinds of configurations, each allowing control and change on its respective level.

The concept of levels is of prime importance because it provides a way to discuss environmental organization in concrete ways, presenting a real and observable structure within which transformation occurs predictably.[2]

## The Domain of Control: Context, or Consequence?

By definition, the level represents a domain of control. Actors on each given level will have different perspectives. The same entity is at times perceived to be on a level higher or lower than, or the same as, the observer's own level of operation.

The building within which one arranges one's furniture is not perceived in its entirety. From within, we experience only the walls, ceiling, and floor of our room, parts of the total configuration. But to construct an entire building, we must perceive and arrange a complete configuration of parts. And when we control the street network, then the same building constitutes a single part of a larger configuration of many buildings, a configuration that, as a whole, is not "live." While the "building level" remains the same, perception of it will vary. Thus, in ascending levels, it is perceived as broad context or background, then as the specific level of intervention in question, then as a configuration residing within a larger intervention.

From each perspective, the building will be described quite differently. The listener, the observer, and the player all tacitly understand the level implied. Although levels are rarely explicitly spelled out, there is little ambiguity concerning them—either in general conversation or in professional practice.

## Configurations Represent Agents

Thus far, the concept of levels has been demonstrated in analogy with games, but without identifying players. Although levels are defined by physical parts, we equate them with the agents in control. Indeed the same words— *street, building, furniture*—may denote players as well as parts, much as *Black* and *White* in chess mean both the configurations on the board and the players in control of them. Agents operate on different levels by virtue of what they control.

Agents can have quite varied social identities: they may be individuals, organizations, or institutions. Yet they are to some extent interchangeable. As long as the role is played, the game remains the same. This suggests that the form possesses a certain autonomy.

23

On the other hand, there is some reciprocal influence between culture and levels. Societies develop different environmental games, and levels do shift or transform in response to a culture and its technology. But in all cases, the players are eventually defined by the game played.

## Profession and Level

Each level connects to a professional domain of intervention, which in turn defines both a way of acting and the expertise needed to manipulate and arrange particular parts. Intervention is inherently organized to recognize the levels found in built environment. Professional agents—urban designers, architects, interior designers, and furniture designers—each focus on certain levels. This division of professional expertise confirms and reinforces the hierarchical organization of the physical form: the game creates the professional player.

## I.3 Built Environments Seek Equilibrium

Built environment and chess may be comparable as multilevel organizations whose configurations are controlled by different parties. But the analogy can lead to serious confusion, absent explicit understanding of fundamental differences between the basic purpose of board games and the purpose of built environment.

Chess, like many other board games, begins in perfect balance. Before the start of play, there is no configurational advantage to either Black or White. White moves first, upsetting the balance. The resulting imbalance is intended to remain, increasing until the game ends in one player totally dominating the other. Board games abstract warfare or more general conditions of competition. The goal is to win: that is, to be in control of the whole situation. Opponents must be annihilated.

By contrast, within a stable long-term environment, a single party simply cannot control all environmental levels at all times. Rather, on every level, each party controls his or her own pieces. The built environment is a complex game, played by far more players on many levels over an extended period. Its objective is not for any of the parties to win and control all, but rather to allow a large number of inhabitants and other active agents to coexist in peace and mutual well-being. We build to live together.

Successful environments offer equilibrium. As will be observed below, they are structured to avoid situations of imbalance, to ensure stability, while allowing for continuous transformation.

Board games start with a complex situation in perfect equilibrium and end in a starkly reduced situation of total imbalance: there remains one solitary player, a victor who controls the field. The environmental game starts with a simple and unbalanced situation and seeks, through gradual transformation, to arrive at an increasingly complex equilibrium between many players.

## User Participation and Equilibrium

Where the poor must fight for even the most fundamental right to inhabit, the built environment may appear to be a battleground as well. Such struggles sometimes result in actual conflict, with real blood flowing. Activists for participation by the disenfranchised—or those settlers or authorities actually on the front lines of pitched battles—may have difficulty conceiving of built environment as harmonious or balanced.

*Barriadas* and *favelas* throughout the developing world daily witness a mass attempt by the disenfranchised to force entry into the game, to become players with control over their own configurations on their appropriate level. Such struggles must not be minimized. The lot of those who are entirely left out of the game is real and hard enough: not to be a player at all is intolerable.

And even among those who may play, there are indeed those who gain and those who lose all. Achieving equilibrium does not require that all parties participate with equal grace or opportunity, at the start or at any other point. The environmental game is not all sweetness and light, nor is it intrinsically fair. Some players exploit advantage unfairly or play hard. Nonetheless, they "bend the rules" in a context in which deals must be struck, agreements reached, and promises honored. Ultimately, something must be built.

This is very different from war, whose end is a field swept clean of all but one player.

## A Range of Environmental Games

The environmental game of balance and stability is played in many variations. The history of urban development provides striking evidence of human beings continually creating new environmental games. Vestigial artifacts record the ways in which indigenous peoples throughout the Americas developed shelter. The more fragmentary records of African and Australian settlements provide other ranges of examples. While less complex in form or technology use than their industrialized counterparts, "primitive" settlements were frequently no less sophisticated, often developing over many millennia.

Recorded evidence represents only a fraction of human settlement that has appeared on earth thus far. Nonetheless, the variety of known forms is astonishing. Recent centuries, with the advent of new technologies and new forms of communication, have spawned yet new ways of settlement—both high-rise and low-rise, formal and informal, exhaustively documented and poorly recorded—never before seen.

Nonetheless, somewhat as all board games have certain features in common, all environmental games do share a common structure that makes them, in a very specific way, variations and transformations of one another. That structure is the subject of this book.

## Environmental Structure Is Autonomous

*This building offers plenty of room for paintings and large furniture.*

*These villas turn their backs to the street.*

*That new development invades the woodland.*

Such common statements strike us as perfectly natural. We indicate agents by personifying the configurations they control, much as we speak of chess players by referring to Black or White. Even complex, variable distributions of control over a multilevel form, as discussed below, can be studied without actually knowing the identity of the agents in control: it is the physical properties of the particular forms in play that reveal how agents distribute control.

Therefore, built environment may be described solely in terms of live configurations operating on different levels. In doing so, we describe it as dynamic form controlled by people, fully taking into account that built environment is the product of people acting.

To learn about the game, we need not know who, in particular, is acting. But to play, we must know the identities of the other players.

## Agents Assume a Role

While on stage, the performer remains the character played. Similarly, within built environment, people play the role of the live configurations they control. Agent becomes configuration, seeing the world from that perspective.

# I.4    The Identity of Agents

Of the abundant roles that society determines for people to play, many are determined by the built forms with which we live. The form is the role played. When people gain or lose long-term control, behavioral change commonly results. When renters buy multifamily houses, they become landlords and come to view the world differently.

## Agent Identity and Specific Play

Each player brings private interests to the field. Why, in a given neighborhood, are some gardens well kept by owners and others less so? Social conditions of play may explain variation in form. There is, for instance, a marked difference between absentee landlord and owner-occupant landlord, a difference often recognized in law. Generally, the latter is considered beneficial to environmental quality, the former less so. All other factors remaining equal, we cannot explain the vastly differing condition of two equivalent properties without knowing about their agents.

Some players have more resources than others; some are willing to spend more than others; some play more skillfully than others. In all cases, the way the game is played decisively expresses player identity. The notion of live configurations controlled by anonymous actors, revealing the structure and "behavior" of built environment, thus constitutes a clearly limited, albeit extremely useful, generalization.

To understand why a certain environment thrives and another similar environment does not, demographics and economics should be studied, but the individual identities of actors must be known too. Similarly, a specific built environment may uniquely develop, prosper, or decline because of the way its inhabitants act as agents, independent of prevailing trends and conditions. Settlements with virtually identical physical locations, sizes, and demographics may develop into vastly different communities, as a result of their distinct historical development or of the differing social origins of their founders.

## Consensus and Negotiation

In all games, personal qualities determine the quality of play. But in any particular built environment, the significance of the player's actual identity goes further still. The quality of the environment, and of the play within it, will depend not only on players' individual qualifications but also on their socioeconomic environment. Built form reflects the broader field of social interactions within which it occurs.

29

Moreover, play is not fully described in terms of live configurations, because pursuing the purpose of the environmental game—achieving and maintaining dynamic equilibrium—also depends on how agents are constituted. On the level of the room or the home, an agent may be a particular person; on higher levels, it is invariably a corporation, organization, or institution. Agents are social bodies and their composition determines to a significant extent the way the game is played.

Agents in control must communicate, negotiate, bargain, and cooperate. Such direct interactions are necessary for built environment to remain in stasis, and they have their own conventions. Although agents may contest portions of a built environment, it exists to be shared as a whole. Hence, reaching formal consensus is an important aspect of the environmental game.

The degree to which a built environment embodies, by virtue of its form, common values and qualities is explored in the Order of Understanding (part III). There, too, we will adhere to the constraints imposed here, setting aside those interactions among agents that are not mediated by form. The goal is not to observe how agents interact, but to understand the structure and behavior of the form that is the cause and the goal of their interactions.

## Levels Reveal Dominance and Dependence

Levels manifest an asymmetrical relationship between live configurations. For example, in a network of streets with houses strung along them, the houses within any city block can obviously change without any reorganization of the street network. The reverse, however, is not the case. Realignment in the street network requires serious readjustment—frequently in the form of demolition—in the distribution of houses.

The arrangement of furniture evinces a similarly asymmetrical relationship. Arranging and rearranging furniture occurs in the normal usage of rooms. If, on the other hand, rooms are rearranged, it is certain that their furniture will be disturbed. In general terms:

*The higher-level configuration* dominates *the lower level; and the latter is* dependent *on the former.*

We are intuitively familiar with the environmental condition of dominance and dependence, although it is generally too self-evident a phenomenon to be explicitly recognized. Because the concept is of fundamental importance in understanding built environment as a living, dynamic entity, a more precise formulation is in order:

*Observe two live configurations* A *and* B. *If transformation of* A *causes* B *to adjust its distribution of parts, while transformation of* B *leaves* A *undisturbed, we say that* A dominates B *and that* B *is dependent on* A.[3]

When we examine live configurations, this operational definition allows us to determine if a

## I.5 Dominance and Dependence

situation of dominance exists, by observing what happens as transformations take place.

## Dominance Imposed by Form

Levels can thus be defined in terms of dominance. In all previous examples, two live configurations were related in terms of dominance/dependence, as a direct result of their physical properties.

It is quite uncommon to find a furniture configuration dominating a building configuration, or a configuration of buildings dominating a street network. They seem to exhibit an inherent dominance/dependence relation as a formal imperative. This is also evident in chess: a situation in which the pieces dominate the board, forcing it to adjust with every move, is difficult to imagine.

At those points in the environmental hierarchy where dominance inherently occurs as a result of the form of interrelated configurations, levels emerge.

The game as set by the form must be carefully distinguished from specific plays within it. One party can always influence another into exercising control in a certain manner. Thus, a tenant whose control is limited to furniture may convince the landlord who controls the walls to adjust them to accommodate a desired furniture arrangement. This neither alters nor negates the general formal condition: walls cannot freely move without disturbing furniture, but furniture can be rearranged without disturbing the walls. We do not therefore conclude that now furniture somehow dominates building walls. Rather, the relationship between players has allowed the lower-level player to influence the acts of the higher-level player.

## Dominance Imposed by Behavior

Consider a woman walking her dog. The dog has no leash. It bounces around in apparent freedom, darting up and down the street, pausing at lampposts, hydrants, and shrubs. The woman pursues a steady course and, ultimately, the dog follows wherever she goes. This dominance is not intrinsic: it results from the woman actively and continuously dominating the dog. The dog is trained to follow her commands and signals, or else simply to respond to her presence.

We assume by habit, and as a result of frequent observation of similar situations, that the person will dominate the dog. The dominance/dependence assumption is then verified by observing spatial transformations—the movements of the two bodies—within their physical context. Nothing in the physical setting mandates dominance between woman and dog. There is no imperative of form involved: parallel experience tells us not to expect this relation between humans and cats.

In physical configurations there are also cases in which asymmetrical relations are not dictated by the forms. In chess, no physical property of Black or White predisposes one to dominate. Yet as the game unfolds, a situation may well occur in which the black king is hounded into submission by white pieces.

Examples of dominance without a form imperative are rare, however, in built environment. As we will observe later, it abhors the instability inherent in such situations.

## Horizontal Relations are Unstable

In some circumstances, a dog will decide not to follow his mistress, choosing to ignore her commands. The dog's rebellion illustrates that while dominance can and does occur between two configurations operating on the same physical level, such dominance, when unsupported by form, is vulnerable and inherently unstable. Eventually, the owner may end up desperately chasing after the dog.

This instability is even more evident in chess. White may move freely for most of the match. But under siege, each time Black produces check or otherwise threatens checkmate, White's king must adjust. Suddenly, the tide may turn, placing Black on the defensive. Dominance, which is observable only if we understand the rules, can—and does—shift from White to Black within a single move. Chess, being a game of war, has been designed to exploit this instability.

## Avoiding Horizontal Relations

Direct "horizontal" relationships, such as may be found in board games and contests, are volatile, unpredictable, and restless. They do not work for an environmental organization intended to sustain itself for generations. In seeking stability, built environment therefore avoids open and direct horizontal relations between live configurations. In fact, such avoidance constitutes the single most important principle in the generation of built environment.

Yet on any given level, some configurations predictably find themselves in a dynamic horizontal relation. Within a single block, we expect to find a number of buildings, most fre-

quently under the control of different parties. Within a single room, as we have seen, we may find multiple live configurations of office furniture. Why don't we then see the kind of continuous conflict we find on the chess board?

There appear to be two ways in which the built environment keeps live configurations apart. The first is formal: separation by virtue of the shape and organization of higher-level forms. For instance, each room in a house may contain only one agent's belongings (a single lower-level configuration). In that case, partitioning (higher-level form) functionally prevents interaction between configurations (lower-level forms).

But the shape of the higher-level form is not always sufficient. In shared space, elaborate social forms—including civility, politeness, and deference—go a long way to prevent live configurations from facing off like Black and White on a chess board. In the case of abutting building lots on a block, the horizontal relationship is constrained by territorial bounds. Territory and its markers subdivide space, allowing similar configurations to coexist on the same level: good fences make good neighbors. The operative concept of territory will be examined in the Order of Place (part II).

In general, to avoid horizontal relations among live configurations, a hierarchy of levels acts to establish stability by dominance among environmental forms. But it is, by itself, insufficient.

## I.6   Control Distribution

### Vertical and Horizontal Distribution

Given two levels, different distributions of control can take place: *horizontal* control occurs on a single level, whereas *vertical* control involves distribution over a number of levels.

In horizontal distribution, a single agent may control one or more live configurations on a given level. In controlling furniture in different rooms or different buildings on a block, multiple control is horizontally distributed. As a landlord, an agent controls a building, but not the furniture under control of the tenant. The agent operates on one level only.

But when parents or housemates own and inhabit both a house and its master suite, control is vertically distributed. (At the same time, other members of the household may have their own rooms with their own furniture.) There still remain two live configurations: a lower configuration (furniture) and an upper configuration (building). The owner, exercising control on two levels, must play two roles. On the furniture level, owner control may well be limited to one configuration out of many within the building under his control. In all such variations of control distribution, no matter how players play the game, control is still exercised level by level.

Although the form retains a certain autonomy, it may also be subject to change and variation. When the client grants a single architect vertical control, furniture may be replaced by building-level elements: built-in seats, beds, and storage. The overall content of the furniture level—and of the tenant's domain of control—is consequently reduced. Moreover, within a given culture, somewhat different games may be played simultaneously. Once isolated instances modifying the rules begin to occur in a consistent pattern, the game at large may be changed. As we will see in more detail later, entire levels can—indeed do—appear or disappear.

## Control Distribution and the Condominium

Yet we quickly discern situations where control distribution does not precisely follow levels. A number of attached or freestanding single-family residences, together with the land on which they stand, may constitute a condominium. The condominium trust will then specify the extent of control granted to individual owners. This control does not coincide with the forms at hand: buildings or parts of buildings, though owned by specific individuals, are not fully under their control. Nor are garden fences and driveways. Exterior changes involving façades or trim may fall under the control of the condominium association. Between the demising walls, the owner may do as she pleases.

None of this changes the actual constitution of levels. Roads, house lots, buildings, and interiors all observe their customary hierarchy of dominance, which must be obeyed when transformations take place. But within these normal constraints, transformation will betray a peculiar control pattern. When all façades, for instance, are repainted or remodeled at the same time, the underlying distribution of control is revealed.

A freestanding condominium residence is no longer a single live configuration. It is actually split in two: one live configuration under the control of the condominium trust, the other under the control of the owner-occupant.

## Control vs. Ownership

Ownership is not necessarily congruent with control. Other, less form-driven situations in which control and use are not the same are also observed.

In restaurants, there are typically two levels under the control of one agent. The restaurateur controls the restaurant's space and furniture, but patrons also use tables and chairs. They shift chairs when seated, push back and excuse themselves from the table, then return. They may even bring in another chair to accommodate someone joining their table. Use inevitably entails a certain amount of control, and all this is considered reasonable and normal, depending on the particulars of the play.

But it is ultimately the manager who controls furniture and its distribution. When spontaneous furniture rearrangement oversteps a boundary, a waiter may be dispatched, rushing over to "help." Equilibrium is reestablished, and all parties again cooperate to maintain it.

No matter who arrives, restaurant patrons are certainly not expected to start rearranging the tables. We are, in fact, very good at understanding ways of distributing control over otherwise constant levels of form.

## Form and Control Distribution

For any given combination of levels, patterns of horizontal and vertical control distribution may vary greatly. They will also change over time, while the same formal organization across two or more levels persists. Form remains accordingly somewhat autonomous with respect to control.[3]

When one agent controls the higher level and a part of the lower level, unified control does not result in a single live configuration. The agent continues to play two roles. However, if an agent in control of a configuration on one level (e.g., furniture) acquires control of another configuration on the same level, these two live configurations may merge into one. This is the case when one assumes ownership and control of a former partner's furniture. Nonetheless, if the initial configurations are in different locations—one may, for instance, control furniture in two different rooms or two different buildings—they consequently remain, of physical necessity, distinct.

As has already been noted on the furniture level, live configurations initially under the control of a solitary agent may come to be controlled by two or more. When the configuration in question is a single building, distribution of control can mean that agents physically split control of the building, as one can divide responsibility for arranging furniture. Controlling agents may then transform each part exactly as they please.

But clear and simple subdivision is not always possible. When a building is divided into top and bottom halves, the lower agent dominates the higher one because of the constraints of gravity: one may expand or rebuild penthouse structures without disturbing other inhabitants' configurations, but not basement foundation walls.

Levels may help where gravity does not. If each agent can independently rearrange partitioning and equipment internally, the building then becomes a two-level organization. Building and conveyance systems proper make up the higher level, and individual infill of partitions and equipment becomes the lower level, each agent having his or her own live configuration. For the shared building structure, separate tenants find themselves jointly constituting a single agent in control of a single configuration, which will demand unified action when they repair foundations, roof, and so forth.

In all of these cases, form shapes play. Regardless of how control is distributed, the distinction between levels remains. On any single level as well, the form itself determines to what extent live configurations can be organized. In horizontal distribution, live configurations can, to a certain extent, group and regroup depending on control distribution. But the ultimate disposition of configurations will be constrained by *location* (live configurations in different places cannot become one) and by *gravity,* when the need to maintain the configuration's structural integrity simply may not allow certain forms of separation (as when a two-story building is divided between two agents).

Segregation by location and coherence necessitated by gravity both contribute their own form determinants to the game at hand. They are explored in more depth later. At this point, it is sufficient to note the considerable extent to which the form actually determines the game played.

Chapter 2

# Recognizing Levels

## 2.1  Levels and Intervention

### Change Reverberates Downward

The city block is a stable urban structure, typically remaining constant for centuries. Within its periphery, over time, many buildings are completely replaced or transformed.

Change on the building level assumes many forms. When the building remains in place, its volume may change. In tight urban settings, expansion may happen in two directions: upward, by adding floors, or horizontally, into the backyard. Less frequently, volumes are subtracted. When building volume remains constant, parts may change. Old doorways are filled in and new ones cut into old masonry. It is not surprising to find original stairwells closed off, and others framed in elsewhere. Façades are altered for less utilitarian purposes, updated to reflect new tastes and trends.

While building shells may remain unchanged, their interiors—products of intervention on a yet lower level—are modified frequently. The restoration of vintage houses frequently reveals several ceilings hung one under the other, many layers of paint and wallpaper, and perhaps old parquetry, tiles, or other materials under current floor cover. Simply applying another layer to cover the original surfaces is easier than selectively demolishing beforehand.

Levels ensure that while change reverberates downward, it is contained upward. The city block provides continuity. It is the stable backdrop against which buildings transform. The building's form, in turn, remains constant during interior renovation and repartitioning. Lower-level configurations transform more

*2.1* *Amsterdam, 1625—Seventeenth-century extension of the city, showing the Jordaan Quarter under construction. Detail from map by Balthazar Florisz (page 40).*

easily—and therefore with greater frequency—than higher-level configurations. The lower the level, the higher the frequency of change; conversely, the higher the level, the more severe the reverberations of any change, and the less often it will occur. This asymmetry guarantees a measure of stability for the whole.

## Gradual Higher-Level Change

Change of buildings and interiors is ubiquitous. But higher-level forms change as well. As urban streets widen to accommodate increasing traffic, front yards may be absorbed, until house façades abut the sidewalk. Within urban fabrics like that of nineteenth-century Amsterdam, no front yards were available to widen the streets. There, canals were consequently filled in to widen vehicular routes.

Where annexation of surplus space is impossible, laws may stipulate that, as buildings are replaced, façades must be set back to add to the street, the higher-level structure. In places like Santiago de Chile, this slow, barely perceptible process results in seemingly erratic setbacks along an otherwise straight street wall, identifying buildings that postdate the decision to eventually widen the street.

## Higher-Level Intervention

When gradual change proves too slow, active intervention may take over. This became widespread during the nineteenth century, with the introduction of new infrastructures in age-old urban environments. It was the century in which Baron Haussmann introduced the Parisian boulevard, in which railroads, bridges, and stations proliferated to service growing cities. It was also the time when the subway systems of

Paris, London, Boston, New York, and Chicago were carved into the urban fabric. In the United States, elevated tramways came to occupy urban space with miles of steel structure.

Following the Second World War, another wave of infrastructure building—notably highway linkages to accommodate car traffic—transformed cities worldwide, excising extensive areas of healthy urban tissue. This reverberation downward was an inevitable result: to carve out roadways, lower-level urban fabric—houses and streets—simply had to give way.

## Reversed Priorities

Urban growth had traditionally begun at the bottom level, with higher-level form often lagging behind. Stepping-stones frequently crossed the unpaved streets of ancient Roman towns, despite the sophistication of the houses. Sixteenth- and seventeenth-century European prints and paintings bear witness to prosperous new buildings lining unpaved streets. Similarly, Amsterdam's canals were initially lined with wooden quays and spanned by wooden bridges. These were replaced with brickwork only long after the proud traders' houses were built.

After the Second World War, priorities reversed. In postwar new towns in Europe and elsewhere, investment emphasized wide and fully equipped road networks, sewage systems, and other, higher-level structures, in anticipation of projected populations which often failed to appear. The dwellings they serve neither adequately anticipated future needs nor facilitated eventual transformation in response.

In contrast, traditional priorities remain observable in third world bottom-up processes. There, even low-income citizens tend to build ambitious houses—often on relatively large lots—with projected square footages far ex-

43

ceeding comparable allotted public housing space. For a decade or more, all resources go into completing the dwelling. Makeshift power lines and other infrastructures are eventually formalized under political pressure exerted by a growing constituency. Finally, a public sewage system relieves on-site waste management. In short, higher-level structures emerge gradually, fueled by successful lower-level development.

New towns and informal developments are driven by different distributions of control across various levels of form.[1] Theories of environmental growth explaining their differences must include the relative weight of control on different levels, as well as the self-interest of the parties exercising this control.

## Level Distinction and Form

In many historic environments, we find a tight fabric wrought in a single material. In medieval Dutch towns, streets, buildings, and quays are all of brick.

Traditional Mediterranean and Middle Eastern hill towns are even more homogeneous. Individual houses are frequently not discernible from the street. Rooms, courtyards, and street widths are of a similar scale, all reflecting human-size activities and interventions. It is as easy to divert a street by connecting a few courtyards as to build a house or vault a room over an existing alley.[2] Nevertheless, levels remain distinct and unambiguous. Houses cluster rooms tightly around courtyards, following a principle of containment. Streets form a continuous infrastructure—part network, part branching of dead ends.[3]

Despite the similarity of constituent spatial dimensions, and despite exchanges taking place over time, levels remain as distinct in an environment under scrutiny as they do when we look at a map or a leaf. Form, more than size of parts, material expression, or even intensity of control, distinguishes level.

## Forms Establish the Game

Constructing or transforming a street is technically less complex than renovating a single house. Streets may harbor water and sewage lines, cables, and many other infrastructures, but they involve fewer subsystems and less elaborate technical and trade coordination. Nonetheless, transformation of higher-level form is exceedingly difficult. The issue is not technical complexity but rather political relations between agents on different levels, relations based on form. Higher-level decisions are accordingly more elaborate than lower-level decisions.

Level dominance is frequently a relationship of one dominating many. When the party in control of higher-level form has been chosen or appointed to represent many lower-level actors, change is necessarily dependent on consensus: it is likely to be slow and elaborate, when not tightly restricted in scope. When the higher-level agent's actions remain autonomous, neither including nor responding to lower-level concerns, exercise of control inevitably becomes coercive. Between the extremes of brute force and complete consensus, a host of variations is observable, within which the ingrained inertial resistance of levels always acts to stabilize the environment.

The environmental game established by the interaction of forms in a relation of dominance and dependence can be played in many ways. We cannot say the forms are freely chosen. Nor can we say they are beyond human influence.

Or can we?

**2.2**   *Tunis Medina—Urban fabric with dead-end streets, each serving a cluster of dwellings. Being gated made the streets a combination of many live configurations, rather than a single configuration. Base map courtesy of the Association Sauvegarde de la Medina, Tunis.*

## 2.2    Levels Revealed by Use

### A Century and a Half of Inhabitation

In the fifth century B.C., as Macedonian power continued to grow, the classical Greek city of Olynthus was founded in Thessalonika to bolster Athenian hegemony. Like so many transplanted colonial city forms, Olynthus was laid out and constructed within a short time.

Archaeological excavations conducted in the 1930s revealed vestiges of rows of courtyard dwellings in long, roughly east-west urban blocks. Evidence suggests that the blocks were built as a single project by a single agent. Units uniformly repeat key overall plan dimensions, occupying a square about sixteen by sixteen meters. Each house orients around a courtyard located to the south, regardless of its position within the block.

Important plan variations do appear, but we also observe an unmistakable regularity and rhythm. Façade and party walls do not vary. In addition, walls located north of the courtyard, parallel to the street, exhibit remarkable regularity. D. M. Robinson suggests that these walls carried a second floor.[4] They were accordingly difficult to change throughout the 150-year life of the town.

Inhabitants would instead alter room sizes by shifting non-load-bearing perpendicular partitions, and indeed these are the walls that are placed differently in units. This also explains the greater irregularity of the remaining one-story buildings around the courtyard: although they still had to hold up a roof, they could be changed more easily in their entirety, because they did not carry another floor above.

### Higher-Level Form Emerging

Occupants changed those parts requiring minimal effort or investment, following the technical and social path of least resistance. Excavations show the forces they responded to:

1.  *Gravity.* The sheer difficulty of transforming load-bearing masonry structure makes it relatively permanent, although lintels permit fenestration, framing in new doors, or infilling existing ones.

2.  *Territory.* The façade wall between house and street is under the control of the dweller. However, it cannot move into the public street, and to move inside would expose private territory to the outside, rendering it useless.

3.  *Social agreement.* Common party walls are only changeable when such change is desired by both parties at the same time, which makes frequent changes highly unlikely.

These three constraints—gravity, territory, and social agreement—create a higher-level form of constant walls within which individual interpretation takes place. This common structure revealed itself over time, as other parts were shifted, removed, or added. The level distinction was not planned; it emerged from technical, territorial, and social conditions, in response to inhabitant preferences.

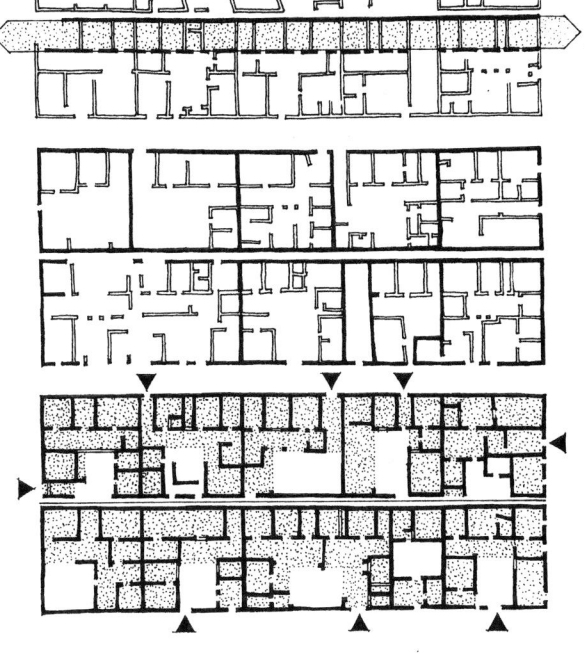

*2.3*  *Olynthus, destroyed 348 B.C.:—Urban residential blocks. An interpretation of the courtyards and entrances is superimposed on the lowest block shown. All houses face south: therefore some are entered from the courtyard side and others are not. (The narrow space between walls in the middle of the blocks is not for circulation: it is a sewer.) Territorial boundaries are emphasized in the block in the middle. The two-story-high virtual higher-level infrastructure that runs continuously across the houses is indicated in the upper block. After Robinson.*

Bounded by the structure of more permanent form, inhabitation manifests itself in the exercise of control. Whatever can be successfully manipulated becomes, by dint of action, a lower-level organization.

## Shift of Control

Residential building in historic towns typically occurred piecemeal, as citizens built individual houses. Although subject to implicit rules, styles, typology, and other conventions, the house was created under the control of a single party. Thus houses in historic towns are not uniform; they are variations on a vernacular theme.

Olynthus had no time for this organic process. It exemplifies the large project in which a single party, in full control of the unified whole, designs and builds a large number of dwellings. For a single agent exercising vertical control, it is most efficient, hence predictable, to standardize, repeating uniformly and simplifying design and construction. In this case, the reiterated house form was a familiar type.

Evidence suggests that control within Greek colonies shifted to inhabitants in their respective houses subsequent to completion of an entire block, perhaps immediately after it was finished. At Olynthus, the shift in control was reflected in the distinction of permanent and variable parts discussed above. As social behavior is thematic and variable by nature, individual citizens exercised control differently in modifying houses.

## Control and Form

Three generic kinds of constraints distinct from the forces of gravity, territory, and social agreement also governed transformation of individual houses in the case of Olynthus. Each of the three is significantly different:

1. *Control distribution.* The distinction between load-bearing wall and infill is determined by gravity and construction, resulting in a true level distinction. Control distribution, however, does not follow it. The owner of an Olynthian house, being in control on both levels, manipulated load-bearing elements—for example, the one-story roof supporting walls lining the courtyard—as well as infill.

2. *Type of control.* Party walls under joint control of citizens on both sides constitute a dominant form as well, but not for technical reasons. Because they are subject to mutual agreement, they are unlikely to move much. Here, dominance results from the kind of control exercised.

3. *Universal preference.* The façade walls are controlled by individual inhabitants. Outward expansion is constrained by territorial boundaries. But nothing constrains withdrawal. Consequently, the permanence of all such walls is a matter not of dominance but of preferences clearly shared by all inhabitants.

Interaction between form and territorial structure will be examined in part II; forms reflecting shared preferences are the subject of part III.

## 2.3    The Urban Façade

### Unified Control on Two Levels

Longtime familiarity brings an innate sense of which parts of the environment belong to what level. At the same time, we are accustomed to a certain amount of freedom: some elements may be found on more than one level. Table and seating may be built in. A place for hanging clothes can be part of the building, or it can be a piece of furniture. The designer in control of both levels has a margin of freedom in deciding on what level to respond to a given function.

In the act of inhabitation, too, control can tie lower-level elements to a higher-level configuration. Children are not always permitted to move around beds or wardrobes located in their rooms. These lower-level elements then become virtual parts of the higher-level form. We have already noted that in restaurants or hotel rooms, control of both building and furniture levels is unified. Therefore, the conditions are favorable for integrated design. Furniture may remain physically distinct or be built in. In either case, it is part of a single live configuration.

### Upward or Downward Attachment

Vertical co-option as described above works best in an upward direction. Whereas lower-level elements easily become part of a higher-level configuration, the reverse proves exceedingly difficult. Nonetheless, as documented by Jerzy Wojtowicz, owners of Hong Kong tenement apartments commonly break through the façade of their unit to extend out three or four feet. The cantilevered floor then supports a new enclosure. The façade, previously part of the building level, now is locally integrated with the infill level of the apartment, on a par with partitioning, kitchen, and bathroom equipment.[5]

## Place Vendôme

In 1686 Louis XIV decided to build a public
square. It was to be enclosed on three sides by
a uniform façade, designed by Jules Hardouin
Mansart. The fourth side remained open to the
rue Saint-Honoré. Aristocrats and affluent
commoners were expected to erect their own
houses behind it. The street wall, normally
perceived as part of the individual building, thus became part of the urban design, on
a par with the roads and squares. The idea is
powerful: the façade always contributes to the
communal urban space, while remaining the
product of building level intervention. The shift
entailed in transforming it into the product of
an urban level intervention subtly tips the balance the other way.

Yet Louis XIV's scheme failed.[6] A decade
later, the urban façade, still freestanding, was
demolished. Mansart was then asked to rede-
sign the square. This time, it was to be orthogonal and fully enclosed. Individual owners would
build their own buildings behind the integrally
erected façade. That process produced the Place
Vendôme as we know it.

## Similar Examples

The successful Vendôme scheme had its prece-
dents. Earlier, Henri IV had the Place Royale
(now Place des Vosges) built in a similar way.
Citizens were invited to build houses on con-

**2.4**  *Hong Kong—Apartment building façades altered
and extended by individual owners. Courtesy of Jerzy
Wojtowicz.*

dition that a predesigned façade forming an arcade around the square was simultaneously erected.[7] The more piecemeal nature of this approach is reflected in minor differences still visible among the individual elevations.

Of course, the Georgian façades of the circuses and squares of Bath and London present similar upward movement, in which building elements become urban infrastructure. There, the design of houses and façades tends to be more integrated, and house plans are consequently more uniform. But over time, the façades have remained unchanged despite adaptation and replacement of the houses, demonstrating the actual distinction of levels.

A less deliberate example of the same phenomenon is found in the block-long urban

**2.5**  *Paris, Place Louis-le-Grand, begun in 1685—In the etching by Pierre Aveline, façades without buildings behind them are visible.*

52

façades of many of Amsterdam School apartment buildings dating from the 1920s and 1930s. A significant percentage of these were built by private developers, at significantly lower cost than those constructed directly by public housing authorities.

The private developers designed their own plans, dispensing with architects except for façade development (which required municipal approval). Unhappy with the submissions, the authorities created a short list of architects of renown, among whom developers had to choose. Some preeminent architects (H. P. Berlage, K. P. C. de Bazel, P. L. Kramer, M. de Klerk) participated on principle, stating that "a bad plan with a bad façade was worse than a bad plan with a good façade."[8] As a result, mediocre, uniform, repetitious plans of no distinction were screened with exuberantly detailed and sculpted façades, maintaining the appearance of a consistently high level of design to mark Amsterdam's new extension.

Thus tradition was reversed. In prior examples, façade design had imposed the formal discipline of a repetitive order to screen variation among individual buildings. In Amsterdam, designers strove to suggest freedom of form and movement with façades, masking the uniformity of mass-produced dwellings.

Chapter 3

# Hierarchies of Enclosure

## Enclosure Implies Domination

One configuration is frequently enclosed by another: furniture is enclosed by partition walls, city blocks by a circumference of roads. In such cases, enclosed configurations can transform independently within the space enclosed. But transformation of the form that encloses will require adjustment of whatever is enclosed.

Thus, the agent in control of the enclosure predictably dominates whatever lies within. This provides perhaps the first and most instinctive way of recognizing form on different levels. Though we will discuss other form families as well, forms of enclosure remain foremost in our consciousness of environment.

## 3.1   Forms of Enclosure

## A Variety of Enclosure Forms

Enclosure comes in many forms, from the walled compound accessed through a gate, to the roof held aloft by columns. The former delineates the exact boundaries of enclosed space; the latter provides a reading of the space bounded by the roof's projection. Chinese architecture traditionally combines both—hence its elemental power.

The Beijing courtyard house comprises an arrangement of pavilions entirely enclosed within its walls. Pavilion space is clearly defined by roof, columns, and platform. Walls beneath the roof are partitions only: neither replacing columns nor carrying any roof load, they serve only to delineate or subdivide those spaces al-

*3.1*   *Delft, 1574—Detail of city map by Georg Braun and Frans Hogenberg, published in* Civitas orbis terrarum *(page 54).*

ready defined. In this way, the traditional Chinese compound uses the wall as an enclosure form twice: on a level higher than the pavilions, to enclose them; on a level lower than the pavilions, to subdivide the space under their roofs.

Wall, roof, and columns, individually and in combination, make almost all architecture. We read the space they delineate, and we sense place within the volume they indicate. The built environment, as a composition of enclosure forms, indicates volumes. Indeed, space defined by forms of enclosure may be most powerful when the form leaves part of that volume undefined. The walled compound open to the sky, the roof held aloft without walls, or even a group of freestanding pillars—each is a configuration that may give us a reading of space more evocative than the fully enclosed room or building. Space traced within a larger area provides a hierarchical depth and context not offered by fully segregated space.

## Space Undefined by Enclosure

Enclosures are not the only forms that claim space. The isolated dolmen erected in Neolithic times still dominates the space around it. Approaching the upright stone, at a certain point we seem to cross a boundary. The anthropomorphic presence of the stone lends it power. It is as though we were encountering an individual who occupies space by force of personality. Solitary tree, cenotaph, and bell tower convey a similar spatial presence. But monumentality implies singularity. Its spatial

**3.2**  *Delos, ca. 1st century* B.C.*—Courtyard of private house in classical Greece.*

claim diminishes as forms multiply, as when skyscrapers crowd cheek by jowl across a skyline, or tight rows of stone slabs stand erect in a graveyard.

## Control of Form: Making Space

In observing space in this way, we perceive material objects, which in turn make space. We are at present concerned with the control of form by transformation of physical objects. Forms of enclosure are controlled by transforming the walls, roofs, or columns: physical space is a result. Part II will consider the control of space proper, observing how such control manifests itself. This latter mode of control constitutes a hierarchy of its own, interacting with, but distinct from, the hierarchy of form.

## Inhabitation

Upon entering an empty room we ask: "Where might I place a chair and sit?" "Where can I place a work table?" Assessing an enclosure's capacity for inhabitation almost inevitably follows reading it. We ask ourselves what could be done in the space observed. This question relates not only to bodily movement within the space but also to those objects brought to intensify or sustain inhabitation. In essence, we assess what lower-level configurations the space may contain.

This way of seeing space recognizes that space and material configurations are inseparable. In observing space, we read material forms indicating its boundaries. In assessing spatial capacity for inhabitation, we imagine objects placed within. Inhabitation inherently situates spatial understanding firmly within the order of form, as one way to understand the conjunction of forms on different levels. This is not the only way space can be understood, but it is arguably the most universal way. Requiring no particular abstraction, it directly links form with control, as well as agents with configurations they can transform.

## Dwelling and Level

Inhabitation is an act of settlement, occupying space within built form. What we call a *dwelling* is that part of the built environment defined by the act of settlement. While *room, house,* and *apartment* indicate particular forms, these become dwellings when actually inhabited.

If the dwelling, as physical entity, is a unit of control, at what levels is control exercised? The answer can vary greatly, with many possible combinations. This is illustrated in figure 3.3, where five levels of form relate to eight modes of dwelling, each occupying a different combination of levels.

## A Variety of Dwelling Modes

Of the five levels in the chart, four have previously been addressed. Together, they constitute a hierarchy of enclosure, in which each lower level is enclosed by the configuration of the higher level. This level distinction, though generic, is sufficient to classify variation in all forms of inhabitation known from current and historical evidence.

The road network commonly found in urban and suburban environments is itself the lower level of a hierarchy of circulation networks, which includes major urban arteries and those of metropolitan, regional, or even continental scope. These larger networks, although very much part of environmental structure, do not directly relate to the act of inhabitation and have been omitted from the chart.

Partitioning like that within the traditional Chinese house is frequently found in historic and vernacular structures, as well as in contemporary office buildings. Proposing hierarchically distinct building and partitioning lev-

## 3.2  A Classification of Dwelling Modes

| | A | B | C | D | E | F | G | H | J |
|---|---|---|---|---|---|---|---|---|---|
| **5 Road network** | | | | | | | | | ▓ |
| **4 Building** | ▓ | ▓ | | ▓ | ▓ | | | | ▓ |
| **3 Partitioning** | | ▓ | ▓ | | ▓ | ▓ | | | |
| **2 Furniture** | | | | ▓ | ▓ | ▓ | ▓ | | |
| **1 Body and utensils** | ▓ | ▓ | ▓ | ▓ | ▓ | ▓ | ▓ | ▓ | ▓ |

**3.3**  *Nine modes of dwelling:*

*Column A.* Although the domed Nubian mud brick house is vaulted with sophistication, it exhibits neither partitioning nor furniture. Niches within the building mass accommodate sitting and sleeping; utensils are also present, of course. The wood-and-straw dome of Burundi is similarly inhabited without furniture. Such dwellings operate on only two levels.

*Column B.* The traditional Japanese house is a building internally subdivided by screens: the partitioning level is self-evident. But no furniture is found within. Including the invariably present first level, this form manifests three levels of control.

*Column C.* Opinions vary as to whether the tent used by nomadic tribes belongs in level 3 or 4. Here, the configuration is placed among the elements of partitioning: it appears to elicit that kind of control. This dwelling also exhibits only two levels of control.

*Column D.* Whenever all walls and floors constitute a solitary system, as is the case in some masonry and small balloon-frame house types, the partition level technically does not exist. The furniture level is now present as well.

*Column E.* The culture of the integral furniture level is epitomized in the freestanding urban or suburban single-family dwelling. When partitioning is used to subdivide interior space, we find levels 1 through 4 combined. That it encompasses all four levels may well be an ingredient of the universal appeal of this form of house.

*Column F.* The condominium has at most three levels of control. Partitions can typically be moved during renovation, and are therefore included. Yet the actual building is clearly beyond control of owner-occupant. This leaves three included levels.

*Column G.* The rented apartment offers only two levels of control. Exceptions notwithstanding, few tenants are willing or allowed to renovate what is not their property. Even when the partition level is technically separated from the building proper, the furniture level is where tenants operate.

*Column H.* The hotel room is the ultimate case of minimal control, for occupants do not even control furniture. Only one level is acted upon by inhabitation: tenants only control the things they bring.

*Column J.* The private estate exists at the other end of the scale, encompassing five levels of control. As a contemporary dwelling for a single family, this represents an extreme case. But in feudal society, the manor or castle housed extended family and retainers, or even one's entire clan. The farm, a small society encompassing all levels shown, may also be placed in this category.

els recognizes a common pattern within overall building organization, to be examined in greater depth below.

The lowest possible level includes utensils and other furnishings brought to inhabit space. These are on a par with the human body itself: as final objects in the enclosure chain, they neither enclose nor support but are supported and enclosed. Such objects find a place on shelves, tables, and cupboards, while the body rests in chairs and beds.[1]

The levels on which the classification of figure 3.3 rests do not constitute a complete physical model of the built environment. We have already noted the exclusion of some higher-level forms. Technical systems—like sewer lines, power cables, and systems for water supply—also belong to the sum of environmental forms. While they may sometimes significantly influence organization of the whole, they remain similarly excluded. For the present, we are focusing on enclosure forms because they relate most directly to our experience of the built environment as a place of inhabitation.

## Forms Carry Multiple Meanings

Forms encountered in real life can be understood in more than one way; forms of enclosure may figure in other ways as well. Thus, perimeter walls may also carry roofs, and they can therefore be portrayed as forms in a gravity hierarchy as much as in a hierarchy of enclosure. Road configurations, already discussed as forms of enclosure one level above the building, will later be discussed as network forms.

The ability of form to carry multiple meanings and to serve more than one purpose is, of course, a good thing. Multiplicity is what built environment is all about. But we can only describe by reduction—by partial interpretation for the sake of a better understanding of a whole that, by itself, will always escape full description.

The words that denote forms have multiple meanings as well. The same word may indicate several forms. Consequently, a name designating a specific form can never carry the singular, unambiguous meaning of which models are ideally built. In normal speech, it is possible to call upon several meanings at the same time, or to alternate between meanings without difficulty. One's *room,* for instance, clearly designates not only space and the enclosure forming it, but also the objects—furniture, books, pictures on the walls—within it. Were these objects removed or rearranged, the inhabitant might well declare upon reentering, "This is not my room any more!"

In ongoing discourse with people with whom we share considerable knowledge, and in circumstances requiring little explanation, multiple meanings present no problem. On the contrary, they enrich understanding among participants. But in a model, we can use only a

## 3.3 A Hierarchy of Enclosure Forms

single meaning. As we will soon see, different meanings of the word *room* will call for different models.

## Nominal Classes, Configurations, and Spaces

Figure 3.4 models a hierarchy of enclosure, including the five levels posited earlier. But now our terminology is more precise, and we have three columns in which three aspects of the same levels are named. Because parts can be classified and distinguished in many ways, we need a specific name for those which jointly represent a level. The first column, *nominal classes*, lists the classes of parts that define a level. The second column lists the *configurations* formed by these parts, which we see on their respective levels. Finally, the third column names the *spaces* on each level formed by the configurations in the second column.

*Road* typically denotes the actual material surface on which we walk and ride. For defining the material parts that constitute forms of enclosure, this term is preferable to *street*, which also has powerful spatial connotations, referring to public space between buildings or to social space of inhabitants living along the way. To name the configuration of roads *local network* once again restricts a term that usually includes much more than just a road network. The multiple readings of *block*—as space, as material form, and as social unit—have already been discussed. In what follows, it will signify a space only.

As remarked earlier, non-load-bearing partitioning has been given its own level. Distinguishing partitioning from the rest of the building presents another vocabulary problem.

65

| | A. Nominal Classes | B. Configuration | C. Space Within |
|---|---|---|---|
| 6 | Major arteries | City structure | Neighborhood |
| 5 | Roads | District | Block |
| 4 | Building elements | Building | "Built space" |
| 3 | Partitioning | Floor plan | "Room" |
| 2 | Furniture | Interior arrangement | "Place" |
| 1 | Body and utensils | | |

**3.4**  *Identifying levels—Levels can be identified as a class of physical parts, as configurations of such parts, or as the kind of space resulting from the placement of configurations.*

Whereas the term *building* normally includes such partitioning, here the term is simply used to describe a configuration of building elements, excluding partitions. Denoting the configuration of partitioning elements with the term *floor plan* represents a severe restriction of the normal use of this word.

At the level where the nominal class of parts is composed of furniture, *interior arrangement* may perhaps better convey the configurations resulting from outfitting a room than *interior decoration*. The term *place* has many connotations; here, it denotes space articulated by furniture. One inhabits space offered by a furniture configuration together with the utensils and belongings stored in and about the furniture as parts of the lowest level.

Figure 3.4 names only those parts and configurations that relate to, or resemble, forms of enclosure. Such forms most readily present built environment as habitable form. But on all levels, we can easily think of additional parts to include in constructing models for more specific purposes. For example, local roads work together with squares, canals, and parking places to form the total configuration on a particular level of environmental form. Likewise, tramways, subways, railroads, and boulevards are included in the term *major arteries* in the same way that curtains, lamps, floor coverings, and paintings are included in the term *furniture*. At the partitioning level, kitchen and bathroom equipment and cabinetry together complete floor plans within the space of the building.

The multiplicity of parts and subsystems operating on a given level is intuitively consistent with experience. Moreover, closer scrutiny of such diverse systems on a given level may reveal that they subsume included hierarchies of their own.

## Levels Combine to Form "Wholes"

The simplified chart presents a reductive model of the order of enclosure. As a theoretical skeleton or armature, it indicates recognizable and familiar levels, as well as hierarchy. But in referring to a particular "space," we generally allude to more than volume. Typically, we do not distinguish between parts and configurations; normal word usage is more holistic. It is therefore useful to construct a model in which we connect the parts, illustrating the relationship between levels and the unities we ultimately use and recognize.

Column B of figure 3.5 denotes common environmental unities. We find that a "room," holistically speaking, is a combination of two (material) levels: partitioning and the furniture within it. In the same way, a "block" represents a combination of buildings within a road network. Recognizable spaces within the building result from the additional introduction of partitioning.

Thus, what we perceive as a "whole" is, in fact, a conjunction of levels. This is consistent with the idea of inhabitation as action and control: to inhabit, we must first have a space to move into; we next add the parts and configurations we bring. The combination makes up environment as we know it. The configuration on the higher level is the one that we, as inhabitants, cannot transform by ourselves. The lower-level configuration is the one that we control. Thus the whole names the context within which we exercise control, as well as the parts we control. It is therefore pointless to ask whether the words of the right-hand column denote spaces or configurations. They do both; and in structuring meaning, we may refer to one or the other, or to both.

Finally, *dwelling* does not figure among the wholes. Dwelling as a complex holistic notion is not tied to any single level, nor is it always identified with the same levels. Ultimately, dwelling denotes action more than form.

| Nominal Classes | "Wholes" (Types) |
|---|---|
| 6  Major arteries | Neighborhood |
| 5  Roads | |
| | Block |
| 4  Building elements | |
| | "Built space" |
| 3  Partitioning | |
| | "Room" |
| 2  Furniture | |
| | "Place" |
| 1  Body and utensils | |

*3.5* *Wholes—As experienced in daily life, wholes combine two levels.*

Chapter 4

# Changes in Enclosure Hierarchy

## 4.1 Emergence of a Level

### Function Accommodated on Different Levels

Since dwellings encompass varying combinations of levels (see chapter 3.2), it may reasonably be expected that specific functions like sleeping, eating, bathing, and cooking can also be individually accommodated on different levels. Historical evidence bears this out.

For instance, the sleeping alcove traditionally present in northern European farmhouses was a built-in bed closed with curtains or shutters. It could hold a couple, and sometimes contained a cradle at the foot of the bed. The sleeping alcove gave protection against cold and drafts in houses that were only partially heated by stoves or open fires during waking hours—at night, they might not be heated at all. In contrast to the bed that eventually replaced it, the alcove accommodated sleeping on the level of the building.

While sleeping shifted downward from building to furniture level, storage traveled the other way. Medieval paintings show us the Virgin Mary sitting on or near a chest: a means of storage commonly doubled as furniture. From the sixteenth century on, cabinets with doors and drawers and decorated entablatures found a place in affluent homes throughout Europe. Storage is now also served by the North American walk-in closet with sliding or folding doors, operating on the level of building, or by systematized storage walls, on the level of partitioning.

*4.1* *Osaka, 1994—Next21 experimental building for Osaka Gas Co. The independently designed base building constitutes a three-dimensional urban design within which houses by a variety of architects were subsequently designed and built. Overall concept and base building (support structure) design by Y. Utida, K. Tatsumi, S. Fukao, M. Takase, and S. Chikazumi of Shu-ko-sha architects (page 68).*

Seating is easily equated with chairs and sofas. But it can be served on the building level by inglenooks, by built-in dining niches, or by deep window recesses, as found in medieval and Renaissance castles. In restaurants, we often find banquettes built into niches, or built along a wall and combined with movable tables and chairs in arrangements designed by interior decorators on the infill level.

The Korean vernacular kitchen featured an earthen floor a few feet lower than the rest of the house. A cooking stove was built into the edge of the raised house floor. Smoke was drawn under the raised floor to a chimney on the other side of the building, thus heating the floor of the entire building (see figure 5.10). But in the Indonesian house of bamboo, wood, and thatching, the cooking stove is found not on the building level but in an appliance, a portable earthenware brazier that holds burning charcoal.

Most acts of inhabitation can be served on varying levels. Dining table illumination can be performed by built-in task lighting on the building or infill level; or it can be accomplished on the furniture level, by means of plug-in fixtures.

Until Benjamin Franklin invented a dependable cast-iron stove for domestic use, fireplace and chimney formed a solid core in the New England timber frame house. That chimney core also might contain a cistern for hot water, later to be replaced by the hot-water boiler. In the historic Dutch canal house, the open fireplace was integrated into masonry walls until the eighteenth century. Eventually, the cast-iron stove became the standard domestic source for heat. In all of these cases, functions first provided on the building level were subsequently relegated to manufactured household appliances.

## Utilities and Levels

During the last half century, the kitchen has gradually become an independent configuration, migrating away from the building level. The modern kitchen is a system manufactured and sold like other durable goods. Kitchen systems connect to the building for power, gas, water, and wastewater disposal, just as the cast-iron stove connected to the chimney. Although utilities hookups for fluids distinguish kitchens from mere furniture, they are no longer part of the building level. Clearly, they are becoming increasingly independent and flexible.

Modern infrastructure development introduced lines of supply and waste disposal. Water was no longer fetched from a private or communal well, but was piped in. Fluid wastes were no longer disposed of in pits dug in private yards, but were removed by sewage lines. Such conduits became incorporated into the building level. Utility services, including meters and hookups, became part of that level as well.

Human wastes in preindustrial urban Europe were gathered in privies and chamber pots, deposited in barrels, and regularly collected for fertilizer.[1] With the invention of the water closet—a manufactured product connected to a sewage system—toilet equipment became integrated into building design.

Well into the nineteenth century, the Western urban bourgeoisie washed with pitchers and basins. Subsequently, wash basins were manufactured to connect to mass-produced supply and drainage lines were built into walls and floors. This brought the lavatory up to the building level.

The first industrial bathtub stood on graceful cast-iron feet: a piece of furniture. It replaced the simple tub, a household appliance elegantly portrayed in figure studies by Degas. Supply and drainage lines eventually connected the tub to the building, as it became a tiled-in part of that level. At present, like the modern kitchen, bathrooms are increasingly developed as coherent systems, by means of which a preferred configuration for a specific inhabitation can be independently composed.

## The Emerging Infill Level

Interior designers and architects frequently custom design commercial and office tenant space, specifying a variety of partitioning systems, raised floors accommodating cabling, ceiling systems integrating acoustic tiles and light fixtures, and so on. Specialized "fit-out" contractors install systems, parts, and other amenities for proper occupation, creating and articulating interior space. They operate on a level of intervention that, while incorporating the age-old partitioning level, is far more comprehensive, combining an increasing number of technical systems. Operating between the building level and the furniture level, it has been labeled *infill*.

Shopping malls distinguish clearly between building and infill as well. Tenants rent empty space to be fitted out to their specifications by specialized contractors. When franchises of large chains adapt standardized details, fit-out may be completed almost overnight.

In places like southern Florida, high-rise condominiums serving well-to-do clients are now beginning to adopt similar "Open Building" principles, as these clients are sold prime unfinished "vertical" real estate. Specialized contractors and designers work on the infill

level to create or remodel individual dwellings. In contrast with commercial enterprises, however, these expensive residential operations employ little systematization, relying mostly on labor-intensive customized installation.

For practical, cultural, and managerial reasons, the mass-market residential infill level has been slow to emerge or to encourage more systematized fit-out. For some years municipalities, housing corporations, and developers in Europe—particularly in the Netherlands—have been experimenting with clearly separating residential infill from the building shell. Gradually, proprietary infill systems for residential use are being introduced into the market. In Japan, advanced residential infill research, development, and experimental projects are moving forward with substantial support from government, manufacturers, and the housing industry.[2]

## Forces behind the Emerging Level

Together, such occurrences signal the gradual but unmistakable emergence of a new level throughout contemporary environmental structure. The infill level has been called into being by fundamental forces beyond the control of any single party or interest.

The inexorable pull of industrialization and off-site production is one cause. Suppliers who were traditionally content to react to on-site contracting needs now act as entrepreneurs; their innovative off-site production and systematization of products is triggering far-reaching changes in on-site procedure. In advanced infill system installations, a solitary small crew executes fit-out work that would previously have been distributed among a number of trades and subcontractors: plumbers, electricians, environmental systems specialists, and so forth. Thus, fit-out of a single office, dwelling, or shop amounts to discrete infill intervention. It is by nature independent of similar interventions elsewhere in the same building. As such, it is no longer subject to overall contractor coordination on the building level.[3]

Growing consumer culture is another source of change. As technical development creates distinct new markets, consumerism drives technical innovation. Not so long ago, the notion that the user/client might choose partitioning or ceiling systems, kitchens, or bathrooms by visiting showrooms similar to those maintained by car dealers was unthinkable. In Japan, this already is done on a mass-market scale for the individual home; in other countries, for a more exclusive market. New generations of sophisticated infill systems are significantly increasing application of this approach to apartment dwelling.

Infill systems development restores a lost balance. Historically, individual offices, dwellings, or shops were accommodated by the small-town building in a rough unity of use and form. They enjoyed a degree of formal autonomy that the contemporary big building then usurped. The infill level reintroduces formal independence within the large office building, apartment building, or shopping mall, restoring control distribution to the actual level of inhabitation. In regaining finer-grained environmental organization, the large building becomes a neighborhood structure replacing the small-town street.

Architectural and urban expression of this new reality is inchoate and often confused. Its implications thus far have escaped clear articulation. Although urban concerns are integrally connected with changes within the large building, urbanism has traditionally tended to stop at the front door. Architecture, in turn, traditionally models the building as the product of a single intervention, although in reality the large building reflects dispersal of smaller-scale internal control, as a continuation of the urban fabric.

## Utility Lines: Moving to Infill

Detached appliances for cooking, washing, viewing, computing, storing, refrigerating, and the like are attractive to both user and manufacturer because of their autonomy as products and replaceability as consumer goods. But such rapidly multiplying appliances need power. Many must connect to water lines and drainage to function. Refrigerators, computers, copiers, and bathroom and kitchen equipment are all somehow bound by umbilical cords to the building level. As a result, the overriding technical constraint has increasingly become the need to access utility lines, pipes, conduits, and cables. The emancipation of the appliance is thus now being followed by a gradual but unmistakable movement of the utility lines serving them, away from the building level and into the infill level.

Once incorporated into infill, conduit design, manufacture, and installation become increasingly sophisticated. Power circuitry for entire offices can be installed by means of click-on cable extensions. Simple push-fit drainage pipe connections have been available in Europe for decades. Formerly embedded in concrete floors and walls, these same systems are now installed on the infill level in dedicated raised-floor systems and chases. Flexible hoses for hot- and cold-water supply serving kitchens, bathrooms, and heating systems are likewise migrating from building to infill level.

73

This trend releases the large building from the increasingly unmanageable complexity of conduits, cables, and pipes serving every outlet in every room. It returns the building to the relative simplicity of preindustrial construction.

As a general principle, in both physical and social organization increasing complexity eventually leads to deeper hierarchy. Newly developed levels facilitate what has become unwieldy. As they emerge, control patterns will adjust accordingly.

## The Integrated Building Reexamined

The long-term trend toward greater technical complexity and larger size of buildings continues. Buildings are increasingly intricate multilevel environmental entities. Yet the traditional architectural view of the building as a singular design object, a one-time intervention best controlled by a single party, has continued unabated and has even intensified.

In the early twentieth century, Frank Lloyd Wright and Charles Rennie Mackintosh sought to unify the designer's control of all building levels, extending traditional architectural practice into interior decoration and furniture. Against the clearly emerging trend toward incorporating independent, industrially produced furniture and appliances on an autonomous infill level, they routinely insisted on custom-designed and -fabricated freestanding or built-in furniture, cabinetry, and appliances. Perhaps even more than modernists like Ludwig Mies van der Rohe or Walter Gropius, they thereby set standards for absolutely integrated design as a central tenet of modern architectural practice. Those standards still routinely prevail in schools of design.

The issue goes beyond style. It is fundamentally about control: the ideal, and the goal, is total vertical design control. The large office project appeals to architects because it can encompass all disciplines on all levels to make possible such comprehensive design control.

The real estate industry, effectively recognizing the infill level as autonomous in modern office buildings and shopping malls, has reorganized itself accordingly. Architectural clients—owners, managers, and renters—implicitly recognize levels, and the range of the design task and the architectural scope of services are set accordingly. The architect must then pursue coherence and integration at the appropriate level. Clearly, many decisions about control distribution are simply beyond the scope of the designer. Nonetheless, architectural design ideology steadfastly favors fully vertically integrated design.

With ongoing industrialization and systematization, building design is increasingly a matter of selecting and combining systems. The range of system components and rules about how they combine are predetermined. Partitioning systems, sanitary and kitchen equipment and cabinetry, and furniture and lighting systems result from long-range product development and marketing, far beyond the reach of any single intervention, or any designer's desire for innovation. To a great extent, such systems now set the terms of the design game.

Technical and economic realities have thus rendered obsolete vertically integrated design and the unified architectural control from which it springs. Once environmental levels have been widely recognized, their potential for a new architectural articulation will become clear. But because design ideology and practice lag significantly behind the trend, recent archi-

74

tectural history yields few clues as to that potential.[4]

## Rietveld's Experiment

Gerrit Rietveld's Schröder house, however, displays an intuitive understanding of the issue. In that house, applied understanding goes beyond symbolic representation: the building, partitioning, and furniture levels are understood and explored in their own right. The result enhances the levels themselves.

The Schröder house was, by all standards, a custom house under unified design control. Rietveld could easily and justifiably have followed the same impulses that led Mackintosh

**4.2** *Utrecht—Plan of second floor of Gerrit Rietveld's Schröder house (1924), highlighting three levels: furniture, partitioning, and building. After Rietveld.*

75

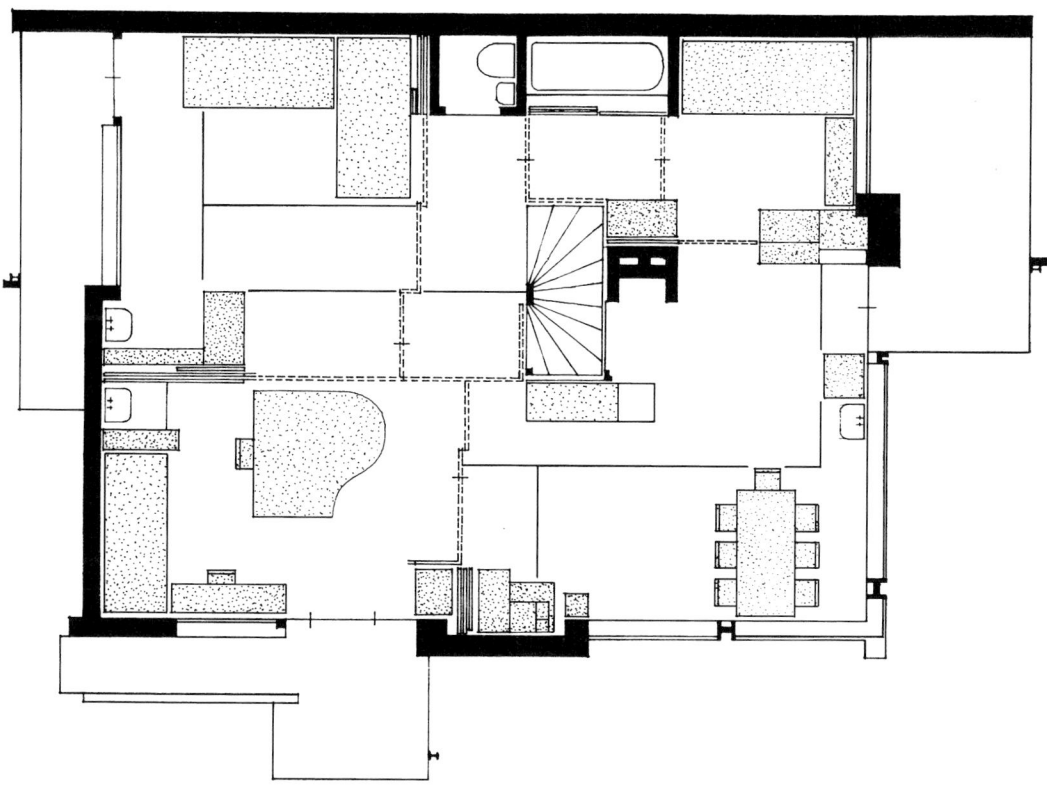

and Wright to build in seating, lighting, and cabinetry. On first impression, we sense no clear level distinction at all in the Schröder house. But closer inspection reveals that there is no built-in furniture. Beds, chairs, and tables remain independent repositionable items. There is also a distinct partitioning system of sliding and folding panels.

With unerring instinct, Rietveld articulated all three levels of residential form. Nonetheless, the details, materials, and color scheme of the partitioning are similar to those of the fenestration and custom furniture. The result is a rich coherence. Dimensions are carefully chosen to coordinate levels. The bed fits perfectly into a corner provided by building and partitioning. A chair fits next to the stairwell banister as if recognizing kinship. A table under a windowsill makes for such good fit that we might assume it is built in.

Enshrined as an architectural icon of modernism because of its minimalist forms and primary colors consistently applied at all scales, Rietveld's Schröder house seems to advocate "integrated design." But its strict recognition of level structure points toward a future beyond modernist design ideology. At the same time, combined with Rietveld's craft approach, this icon of a new era easily fits into the Netherlands' best tradition of a timeless vernacular. There, in a prior era, canals, bridges, façades, stoops, and garden walls, existing on different levels controlled by different agents, had been rendered with similar stylistic coherence in the same materials.[5]

On the other hand, Rietveld's skillful articulation of three levels doubtless reinforced the case for total vertical control in design. His house does not address how similar coherence might be achieved when control is dispersed among multiple agents operating on their distinct levels.

## Next21

Next21, an Open Building project in Osaka, squarely addresses this issue in residential design. The building results from a principled distinction, not only between the physical levels but also between the agents involved. The team led by Yositika Utida and Kazuo Tatsumi designed a building as a multistory three-level neighborhood. A network of public space extends from street to roof garden.

The technical coordination of utilities and rules for the interface between dwelling and public space were carefully devised. Individual architects subsequently designed individual dwellings within the base building on behalf of individual clients. Within the constraints of a predetermined three-dimensional volume, individual articulation of dwelling space occurred. A preselected façade system allowed this articulation to extend to the dwelling exterior.[6]

The achievement of architectural coherence between two levels under the control of different agents has been negotiated successfully for ages between urban design and architecture and between architecture and interior design. Surely, were it not for contemporary architecture's remarkable persistence in promoting and insisting upon unified vertical control, Open Building projects would hardly be worthy of note. But except for Next21 and one or two modest attempts elsewhere, articulation of the separation of vertical control—but now in three-dimensional space—remains to be explored.

## 4.2  With and without the Furniture Level

### A Furniture Level of Control

Although familiar to the ruling class of ancient Egypt, furniture remained sparse, a luxury item, throughout history. Pieter de Hooch's almost empty Dutch interiors portray furniture as a yet scarce commodity during an age of prosperity. A contemporary etching of women clustered around a sculpted hearth in Rembrandt's house shows a starkly bare room. Chairs might be available for the elderly, but people often sat on three-legged stools, low benches, or the floor. Sleeping occurred in built-in bedsteads.

Vermeer's interiors of the same era feature those who wrote letters, balanced accounts, studied mathematics, and played the harpsichord. These are not average citizens; and his studiously arranged scenes, with their conspicuous show of furniture, may paint an idealized world rather than reality.

Despite increasing industrialization during the nineteenth century, the working-class majority continued to make do with a few chairs, a table, and simple beds. By contrast, bourgeois interiors in nineteenth-century photographs overflow with furniture, rugs, and lamps; objects whose primary function was now to demonstrate the affluence of inhabitants.

Furniture emerged only gradually as a level, and then not universally. But by now, in the affluent "developed" world, the fully furnished house has become the standard. The furniture level has become as self-evident, available, and necessary as the building level. Access to furniture is universal, regardless of income.[7]

In rented dwellings, furniture, including appliances and a television set, becomes the most readily controllable environmental realm. On this fully established level, manufacturing reaches the dweller directly without any need for specialized intervention.

## Integrating Furniture into Japan

In the recent history of furniture, we can also witness the introduction of this level, full-blown and elaborate, into an environment that for centuries had no use for it.

From the Japanese islands down to Malaysia and the Indonesian archipelago, with the important exception of China, the wood frame house with matted floor, devoid of furniture, remained the norm. Furniture had been known to the Japanese for centuries through the West and China. But exposure did not lead to adoption. This suggests that agent preference can affect the structure of environmental levels.

The gradual advance of the furniture level in Western culture has been interpreted as a token of growing sophistication. But the traditional Japanese house—although devoid of furniture—may still be rated the most sophisticated domestic environment ever created. Japan's sudden adoption of the furniture level, after centuries of doing without, marked a profound change in the fundamental quality of its culture.

Furniture in today's Japan has to do with "modern" behavior. But at home—be it apartment or villa—a "tatami room" is frequently found. In the traditional restaurant or inn, space without furniture is consistently maintained.

The contemporary "tatami home" virtually devoid of furniture is now often a symbol of wealth and class for the select few. But in poor rural areas, as well as in very low-class apartments (those with just a room or two), traditional tatami rooms entered via a lowered

**4.3** *Rembrandt (?),* The Women at the Fireplace at Rembrandt's House *(ca. 1654). Reprinted with permission of the Royal Museum of Fine Arts, Copenhagen.*

earth or concrete floor for cooking and bathing are still found.

## Preference vs. Necessity

The selective use of furniture in present-day Japan, and the long history of refusal preceding it, do not necessarily prove that its adoption is purely a matter of preference. Modern equipment may well require it. At home, a table makes it possible to work at the computer; couches and easy chairs serve for watching television; tables and chairs match modern kitchen cabinets. In the office, furniture holds computers, printers, and xerox machines; cabinets and tables store and handle ever-growing stacks of paper. Within international business culture, furniture is essential in creating identity. Desktops serve to display evidence of individual identity, utensils, and tokens of prestige and achievement. Conference room furniture sets the tone for corporate personae and establishes protocol and hierarchy in meetings.

A utilitarian rationale for the presence of furniture has its limits. Could we have modern equipment without it? A furniture-less house that nevertheless held all the machines and equipment we need to communicate and process paper, food, and drink would suggest an alternative culture, but surely a possible one. Could this imply that beyond a point, furniture is not forced upon us by the growing amount of equipment we need to live and work? that the adoption of the furniture level is ultimately evidence of universal culture and preference?

Consideration of the nature of levels suggests another possibility. As we have observed, a given function can be addressed on different levels. For instance, in the traditional Japanese house, the kitchen stove and work surfaces are built-ins that form part of an earth and stone area distinct from the wood frame tatami rooms. Storage spaces are built in and closed with sliding doors. To allow people to sit on the floor, the latter-day low table offers a floor recess for the feet. It is immovable—part of the architecture, not furniture.

In a similar way, modern buildings devoid of furniture could no doubt incorporate and accommodate the equipment we need to use. The post-furniture dwelling might be a true "machine for living," in which walls, ceilings, and floors would transform, ejecting and receiving all kinds of equipment as required. In short, the furniture-level functions would be taken care of by the partitioning or by the architecture of the building.

That hypothetical approach helps us better understand the furniture level. It liberates equipment for daily use from the building and infill levels. It introduces a lower level that is readily manipulated, instantly revised. Consequently, we need not rebuild a house or an office to exercise control over equipment. Furniture serves functional requirements and the need to express issues of power, prestige, and taste in a far more fluid way. It provides a level of control requiring no long-term commitment, eminently suited to the fast-paced transformational rhythm of the individual and the small group.

The furniture level thus supports the intensive interaction we now expect to have with our immediate environment. Moreover, furniture offers a design level closely tied to less durable goods. It offers manufacturing a new domain in which consumers can take the initiative. Quick market response on this level increases the frequency of cycles of transformation that come with a culture of equipment. Neither the building nor infill level could easily accommodate the furniture level's continuous changes.

## 4.3  Disappearance of a Level

### A Historical Perspective

The disappearance of a level in the hierarchy of enclosure can be seen in the sequence of extensions of Amsterdam. Figure 4.4 portrays transformation of the city's tissue over time. H. P. Berlage's design of Amsterdam South represented the last time that urban space functioned as positive space to organize the position and height of buildings.

### Berlage's Extension

Berlage's urban spaces connect well in scale with the extant fabric. His scheme has approximately the same building height and the same strong, horizontal spatial structure we find along the major historic canals, although it no longer significantly integrates water into the cityscape. The architecture is original and lively, with the keen sense for materials and detailing that rightly earned the "Amsterdam School" an international following.

But on closer inspection, the urban fabric of the Berlage plan reveals a much coarser structure than the historic city's. The living cell of Amsterdam is a canal house approximately twenty feet wide and four or five stories high. The living cell of Berlage's extension is a horizontal building the length of an urban block. Dexterous and sensitive design of the extensive Amsterdam School façades notwithstanding, the units behind them already display the repetitive uniformity so characteristic of later mass housing.

### Control Distribution in Design

This coarsening of the tissue went hand in hand with increasingly centralized design and

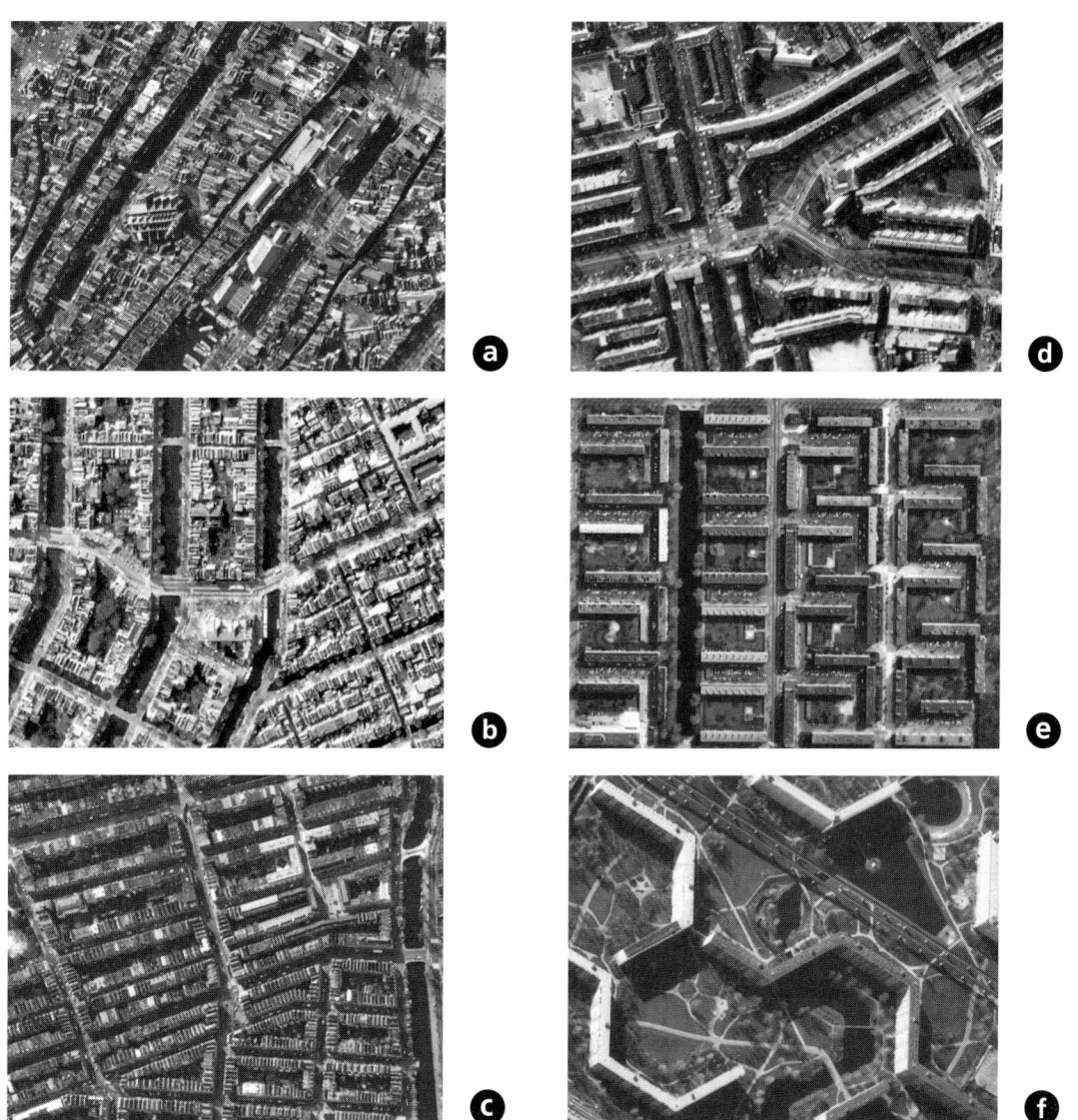

**4.4** Amsterdam—Transformation of urban fabric over time. Selected images from KLM aerial photograph, reprinted by permission.

(a) The medieval core of the city. The axis was originally formed by the Amstel River (now partially filled). Successive extensions were made by digging canals parallel to the river.

(b) The seventeenth-century "Third Extension." Rich traders built their houses along the three major concentric canals around the old city. Small traders and artisans built along the narrower canals to the right of the photograph (Jordaan Quarter), following existing ditches in the original farmland.

(c) Nineteenth century working-class tenements. The four-story townhouses hold a family on each floor.

(d) Berlage's Amsterdam South extension with its famous Amsterdam School architecture. Apartment buildings the size of a block define the urban space of streets and squares.

(e) The van Eesteren post–World War II extension. Note the freestanding blocks and early high-rise buildings.

(f) The Bijlmermeer extension of the 1960s and 1970s. Megablocks on pilotis are set in uninterrupted public green space.

building. In any two-level form, it is possible for a single agent to control both levels. Thus in the Berlage plan, while architectural expression at two levels was varied, Berlage and his colleagues maintained control of both. They designed street and building together as a homogeneous and integrated form, giving both remarkable expression.

This two-level integration was achieved by ingenious means. In many cases, actual street profiles and silhouettes of street walls were conceived first. Individual architects were then required to conform to them. Peer groups oversaw their colleagues' designs. Particular attention was paid to those points where the work of two architects met. In other cases, as already discussed (see chapter 2.3), façades became virtually independent creations, enacted on the urban level rather than the building level.

In Amsterdam South, urban space was paramount. Architecture had to serve it, even to the point of separating façade design from building design as a whole. The intention of all involved was to ensure that the quality of public space as executed would live up to the intent of the Berlage plan. Its success can still be witnessed in those neighborhoods today.

However, an important precedent had been set. In integrating the design of block-long buildings and urban space, the distinction between levels blurred, becoming decreasingly operative. As long as Berlage's plan was adhered to, the result was beneficial. But without it, in subsequent extensions, the building took over. As building size increased, typology weakened. Under the pressure of new programmatic uses for a new class of clients, the building itself became the dominant design problem. Urban design became a matter of arranging buildings. The space of streets was abandoned.

The modernist city was born.

## Freestanding Buildings

In postwar Amsterdam, the large building as sculptural object has come into its own. Standing free in space, observable from all sides, it is no longer governed by predetermined, clearly articulated urban space. The street level has disappeared from enclosure hierarchy.

To be sure, there remain roads to accommodate traffic. In fact, they have come to claim an increasing part of the urban field. But as spatial entities, roads no longer play a figurative role. They now form an autonomous system in the hierarchy of nets and infrastructures, still useful but no longer part of the enclosure hierarchy. Space is now free flowing and passive, and building forms no longer derive from it. On the contrary, urban space occurs as a by-product of building.

## Loss of a Higher-Level Form

Higher-level form functions to organize lower-level forms, universally imposing a common relation of dominance. Hence higher-level form is what elements on the lower level have in common. When it disappears, only horizontal relations at the same level count. The urban field thus becomes a composition of buildings in free space. The relationship between building forms now absorbs all attention: formal stability is sought through balanced composition of independent shapes.

The loss of the structuring power of a higher-level system of urban space ultimately meant the loss of a domain of intervention for the urban designer. Berlage was among the last of the truly urban designers. Cornelis van Eesteren, who oversaw Amsterdam's plans in the 1950s, and his followers in the 1960s and beyond, could no longer shape space.

Their Hobson's choice was either to determine the spatial composition of buildings or to cede that authority, as well. The first option placed urban designers in direct conflict with architects, who wanted to exercise their newly won freedom on the building level. The alternative redefined the urbanist's role: by mediating between architects, he or she might still attempt to achieve a harmonious and well-planned city.

Individual inclination notwithstanding, having lost an autonomous level of operation, the urban designer had to share the building level with the architect. The distinction between the two modes of intervention, between architecture and urban design, has been blurred ever since.

Chapter 5

The Act of Building

## 5.1  Assembly Hierarchies

In discussing relationships among forms under the control of agents, we have not yet taken into consideration how form is built. Like design, the act of building also represents an exercise of control over form. Operative while the building takes shape, it is ultimately temporary. Once building is completed, inhabitation takes over. Eventually that inhabitation will trigger additional transformation of form. The act of building then resumes.

Part/whole hierarchy reflects the way complex artifacts are assembled, from the builder's perspective: parts are combined to form wholes. Such wholes in turn can be parts in larger wholes, and so on: bricks make walls, walls make buildings.

The same configuration can usually be broken down in alternative ways. One way to begin to break down a building into parts is to define three subsystems: foundation, walls, and roof add up to a whole building.

This breakdown also reveals dominance hierarchy. By nature, walls depend on a foundation: while moving the foundation requires that walls adjust, walls—and the doors and windows within them—may be transformed without adjusting the foundation. This dependence results directly from gravity. During construction, the parties in control are sequenced accordingly: the higher-level foundation is built first, the walls are subsequently framed.

The two ways of seeing are illustrated in figure 5.2. Note that the dominance hierarchy (5.2b) does not have the item *building*, while in part/whole representation (5.2a), *building* is the sum of its constituent parts.

**5.1**  *Giza—Great Pyramid of Cheops (page 86).*

## Assembly Hierarchy

Usually, several part/whole hierarchies are observable in the same form, depending on point of view. This is illustrated in figure 5.3.

Of primary interest are those part/whole hierarchies which coincide with control during construction, wherein identified parts distinguish individual subcontractors responsible for them. These *assembly hierarchies* reveal dependence and dominance in play during the process of construction. Such diagramming methods are equally applicable to other environmental levels.

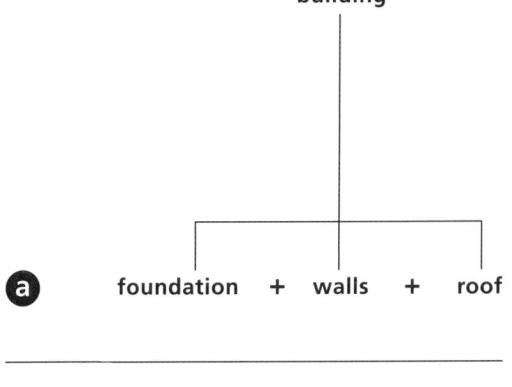

*5.2*   *Two ways to represent a building*

*(a) Building as a part/whole hierarchy.*

*(b) The dominance hierarchy of the three constituent parts. (Arrows point from dominant forms toward dependent forms.)*

*This simplified diagram includes intermediate levels neither for the full range of infill discussed in chapter 4.1 nor for basic partitioning. It may well represent a very simple one-story building.*

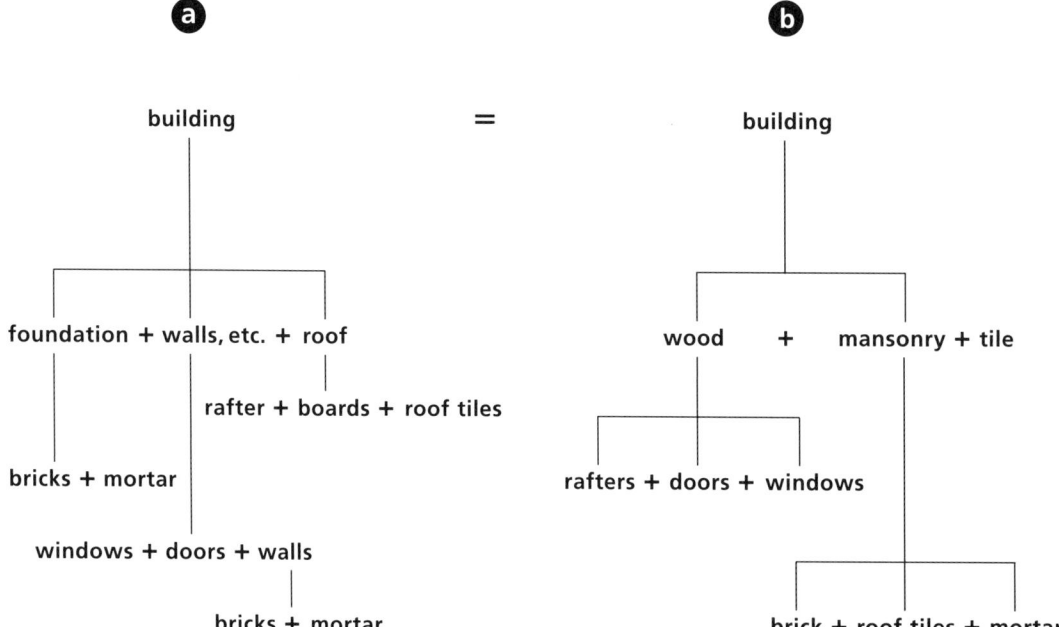

**5.3**  *Alternative part/whole hierarchies for a given form—The same building modeled in two different ways.*

*Diagram (a) continues the earlier breakdown of figure 5.2—i.e., the roof may further be composed of rafters and roof tiles, etc.*

*Diagram (b) proceeds from a primary distinction between lumber and masonry.*

*Note that the same basic parts occur in both diagrams.*

### An Environment of Assemblies

The building diagrammed in figure 5.4a represents one level in the environment. Following the enclosure hierarchy of chapter 3.2, but without partitioning, figure 5.4b adds the higher level of the street network and the dependent levels of furniture and utensils. Each environmental level has its own assembly diagram.

Once more, a comparison with chess may be made: the manufacturing processes that make the board and the pieces resemble the assembly chains leading independently to build-

## 5.2  Dominance Hierarchy and Assembly Hierarchy

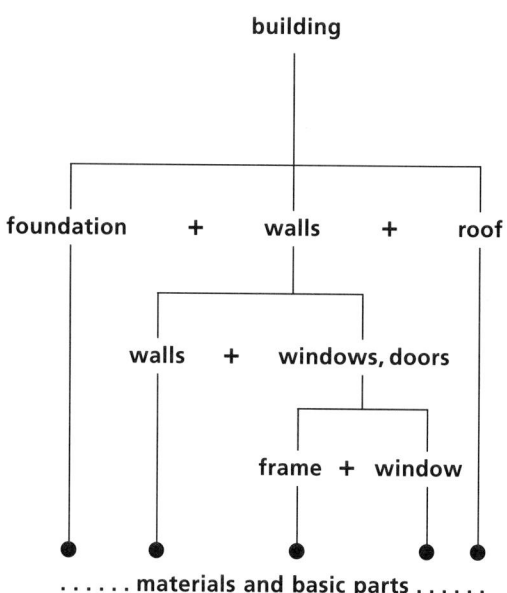

ing and furniture. Once pieces are placed on the board, we have not just another assembly but an environment in which agents play.

*5.4*  *Environmental levels of enclosure and their assembly diagrams:*

*(a) Assembly diagram of a (possible) building. This represents a single level in the enclosure hierarchy.*

*(b) Four levels are shown in the enclosure hierarchy. Each level has its own assembly diagram. Arrows between levels indicate direction, from the dominant to the dependent.*

93

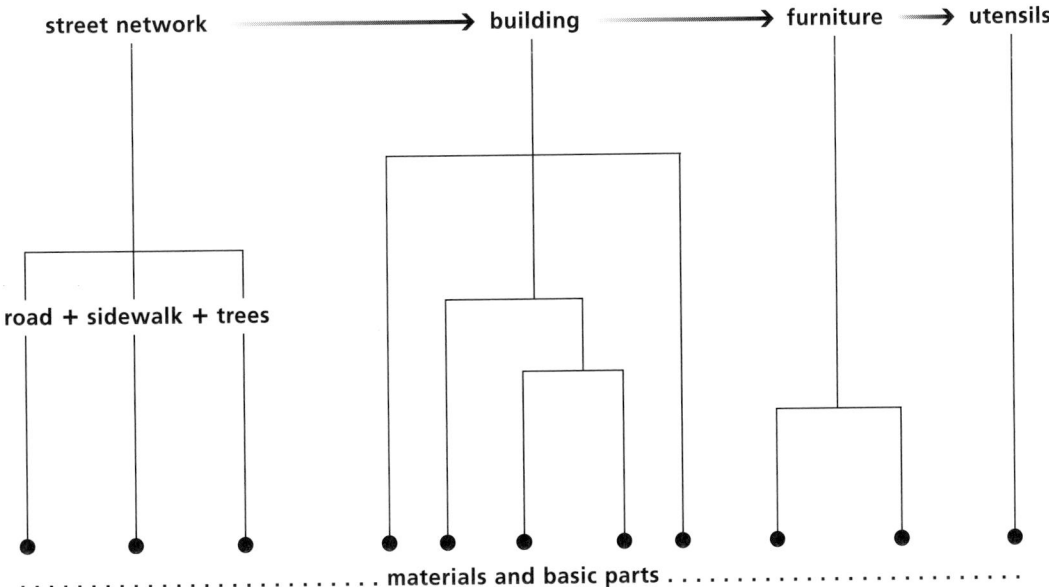

Also, more along the environmental levels suggested in chapter 3.2, figure 5.4c adds the level of partitioning.

Finally the diagram is extended to include infill as discussed in chapter 4.1, giving figure 5.4d.

Again, these illustrative examples do not advocate any particular environment; they are intended solely to clarify environmental structure in general.

## Basic Parts and Materials

Although each environmental level has a distinct and unmistakable identity, they may originate from the same basic materials: brick both forms building walls and paves sidewalks. Hardwood is used for rough sawn timbers, flooring, trim, and furniture. The bottom of the assembly hierarchy contains basic and universal materials used for many different assemblies: masonry, timber, straw, clay and ceramic tile, gypsum, sand, cement, steel, glass, plastic, and so on. From such humble materials, environmental forms rise like varied plants from common soil.

Each form finds completion in its own assembly chain. Once completed, they function in the environmental game, each operating on its appropriate level in the enclosure hierarchy, each offering an opportunity for control and transformation.

94

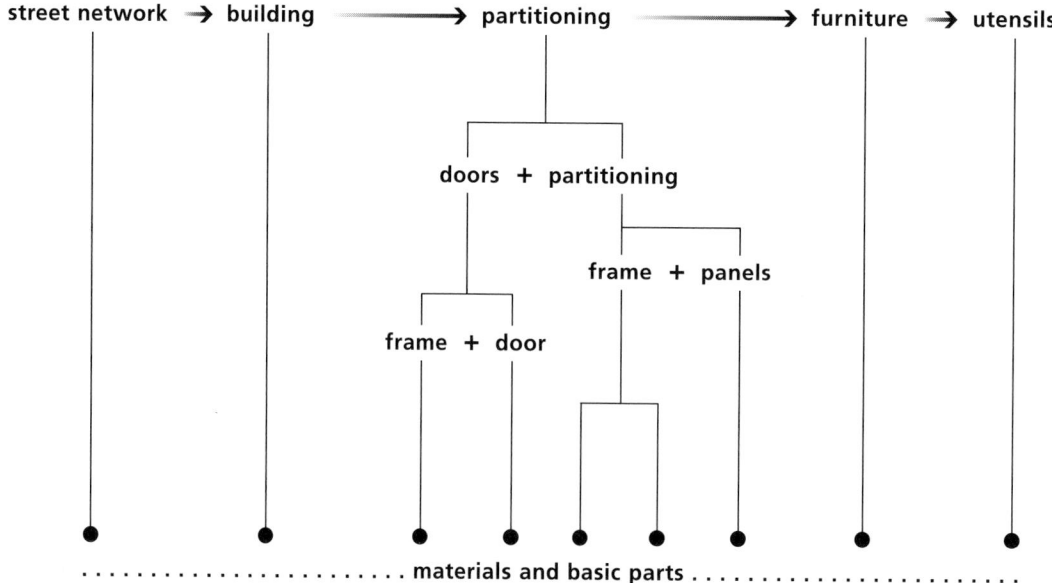

c

**5.4** *continued*

*(c) The levels already diagrammed in (a) and (b) are now represented by a single line. A partitioning level has been added, illustrating one possible assembly diagram.*

*(d) The contemporary building in its full complexity is shown with added assembly diagram for equipment. Together with partitioning, this makes up the infill level.*

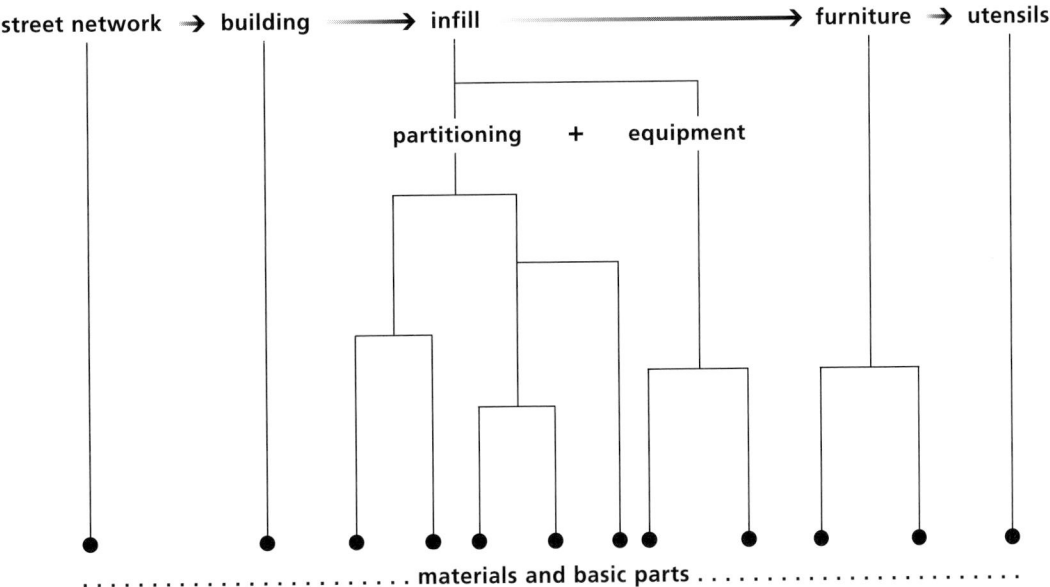

d

## 5.3 Inside the Assembly Chain

### Gravity and Enclosure

Forms of enclosure thus appear at the end of assembly chains. They represent objects of permanent control, the environmental pieces with which we play. As long as they persist, dominance relations remain at work, albeit with possible variation in control distribution over time.

Within the assembly diagrams, we find the structure of the building process itself. There, control patterns are temporary. The subcontractor who builds the roof remains in control of it during construction. After completion, gravity continues to hold the building together but does not necessarily shape the level structure on which the environmental game is played. The given subcontractor exits upon completion, and until such time as the controlling agent of the final form—the building as a whole—decides to act upon the roof again, it is no longer a unit of control.

Thus within assembly chains, relations of dependence and dominance also occur between constituent parts. But that internal game is operative only during construction.

### Gravity's Role in the Assembly Chain

Foundation, walls, and roof clearly represent a chain of dominance, for the simple reason that gravity demands it: the foundation must be in place before the wall can be raised. Yet not all sequences of work depicted in the diagram represent this dominance. Gravity does not dictate the assembly sequence road–sidewalk–trees within the street network. Forming and pouring concrete road before sidewalks may seem logical, but this nonetheless reflects deliberate production sequencing rather than gravity. Although gravity plays a crucial role in the assembly diagram's sequence of building acts, it does not determine everything.

## Up and Up Again from Basics

The assembly diagram in figure 5.5 relates to the process of construction. Because foundations must be constructed before walls are erected, we work upward in the assembly chain until the foundation is done. We then descend again, to ascend once more as walls are completed. The assembly chain climbs (then descends) successive peaks from left to right, as the building moves to completion. With each peak, we leave another part completed, then again start assembling basic parts and materials.

## The Emergence of New Levels

The diagram also more critically illustrates what was earlier asserted: the way in which form is arranged, not the use of certain parts, determines a level.

At some point, the building chain becomes too unwieldy. For example, *equipment* joins the infill chain only after having been part of the base building chain. As discussed in chapter 4.1, sometime after the recognition that equipment has its own frequency of change, it eventually becomes part of another level. Therefore, the sequence of diagrams in figures 5.4b, 5.4c, and 5.4d recapitulates the history of built

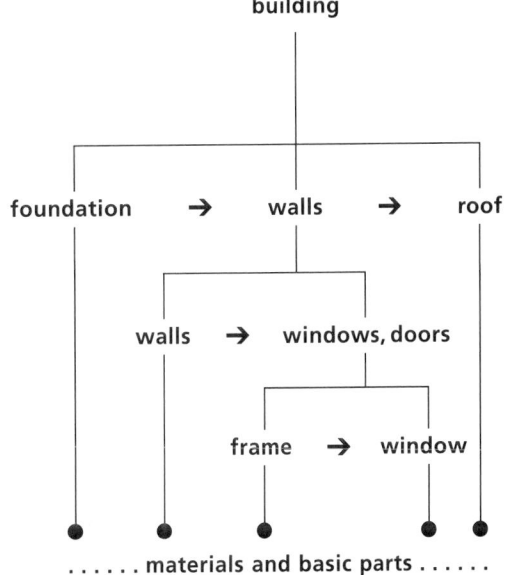

**5.5** *Diagram of the building process—Implied dominance/dependence relations, shown by assembly hierarchy and arrows.*

form: the relatively recent levels of partitioning and infill represent the emancipation of parts that originated in the building chain and subsequently were extracted to facilitate construction and enrich the game of inhabitation.

## Imperatives of Form

Dominance by gravity is indisputable; gravity must be obeyed. When we violate its imperative, things fall down. Such dominance constitutes a *form imperative:* that is, it is inherent in form itself.

The dominance of enclosure that we read in form constitutes another aspect of dominance. But compared with gravity, enclosure seems less imperative formally. It may well be far more conceptual. Although we quickly agree that furniture depends on partitioning because the latter encloses the former, perhaps our agreement is based on experience: we know and anticipate that this is how partitioning and furniture interrelate. Technically, the forms do not preclude other possibilities; in many circumstances, partitioning can follow furniture.

It is hard to determine where form imperative leaves off and habit and consensus begin. "Knowing" that partitioning dominates furniture, and much else in the enclosure hierarchy, may be a matter of custom and convention, an agreed-upon way to work with things because this way suits us best in living with complex form. What is truly conventional is not noticed. Therefore we tend to perceive all such dominance as inherent in the form.

## 5.4 Traditions of Two Stage Building

### An Architectural Quality

We previously examined how separation of partitioning from building reflects ways of building: the assembly chain is clear, as is the role of gravity. But the technical distinction is only the beginning. Kept in play over time within a society, and molded by experience of inhabitation and construction, the technical combination acquires a particular architectural quality not found anywhere else in exactly the same way. Only then does it become a true level distinction. Several examples follow.

The primary structure of the classical Chinese pavilion—a massive roof supported by unanchored, solid wood columns standing on a stone platform—recalls a table standing on the floor. Clear space defined by the building structure is subdivided and enclosed by a secondary system, usually of masonry walls. Their mass belies their freedom: they neither carry building loads nor provide stability. The whole is then complemented by partitioning and façade paneling in wood. These forms are distributed in space and detailed to create a sophisticated architecture, of which a rational way of building forms only a modest part.

Virtually all wood frame structures offer their own variation on the two-level theme. The large thatched roof of the traditional Japanese house harbors a more dispersed post-and-beam structure than the Chinese model, and it is fitted out with screens and partitioning. Because of its slender posts, architectural expression is largely determined by the screens in the shadow of the large roof. The more modest Malaysian house exhibits its own version of the same principle: its woven bamboo screen walls admit the tropical breeze and render the post-and-beam structure more visible.

In vernacular masonry houses on the island of Skyros, we find a beautiful example of "two step" building.[1] The house's envelope is of heavy masonry with a wood-framed and slated roof. Within, a wooden mezzanine floor creates two low-ceilinged spaces: above, a sleeping loft reached by narrow wooden stairs; below, a space enclosed by a wooden screen with a door. It is like a small house within a larger one. This composition mirrors the small Byzantine churches throughout the Greek islands; in them, a simple masonry volume with a timber roof is erected, within which we find an elaborate wood screen. Only the priest may penetrate behind its two doors.

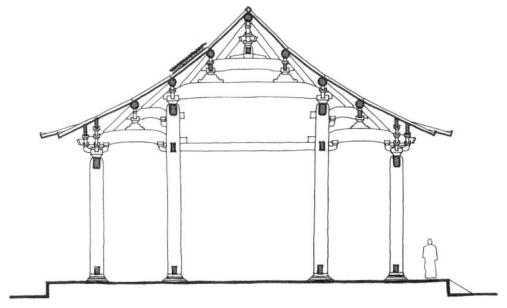

**5.6** *Chinese timber frame construction—Section after Liang Ssu-ch'eng.*

**5.7** *Skyros, Greece—House with* boulmes *timber infill mezzanine, with rooms beneath, set within the masonry building. After Arnaoutoglou.*

101

## A Two Step Process

The two-level building structure in traditional domestic architecture did not necessarily develop in response to need for flexibility. It simply made sense as a way of making a house. In almost all cultures, the first purpose in making a building is to enclose a single volume. The shell typically anticipates functional and conventional distribution of space. But the design, detailing, layout, and execution of internal subdivisions remains a secondary process.

Two step building makes sense in harsh climates, where shelter is essential and the concerns of domestic life are secondary. But it also reflects a technological distinction, for what is necessary to provide basic shelter is not necessarily sufficient for comfort. Two step building therefore ultimately reflects fundamental priorities: basic decisions regarding shelter leave open secondary decisions addressing more detailed accommodations.

Symmetrical brick houses with wooden roofs borne on internal posts are still built by villagers in central China, continuing the rural tradition of the peasant house. Over a considerable period of time, the occupant collects the brick, timber, and tiles needed to make the shell. The building is then erected in a few days with the help of neighbors. Interior rooms are later partitioned with thin brick and plaster walls to a height of about eight feet, below an unfinished attic for storage.

The combined use of masonry and timber does not always coincide with a level distinction. In traditional European architecture, a distinction must be drawn between characteristic northern wood frame building and the load-bearing masonry structures of middle and southern Europe. The Dutch canal house represents a hybrid. Originally a wood frame house, it became, in time, a combination timber frame and brick-and-masonry structure—first by the introduction of brick party walls for fire protection, and subsequently by the introduction of brick and stone cladding for durability and prestige. Nonetheless, floors and roof still bear directly onto interior post-and-beam framing. Within this composite structure of the building level proper, we find wood-framed partitioning on a secondary level whenever primary space in the building is subdivided.[2]

## Within a Single Material

The rationale for two step building need not involve the use of different materials. Its signal advantage is to make possible the rapid erection of the overall volume. The freestanding wood frame house still accounts for the majority of Japanese domestic construction. Traditionally, the carpenter would hew frame and roof parts on site. Now they are precut in automated mills and shipped to the site for assembly. Raising is still done in a single day, at the end of which the frame is ready to be roofed and closed in. Once closed, a lengthy process of interior fit-out begins.

A similar approach is found in the widespread North American tradition of barn raising typified in nineteenth-century New England. Following the cutting and preparation of the barn frame's many parts, the structure is erected over a weekend with the participation of neighbors and relatives. First, individual bents are assembled flat on the ground. They are then sequentially raised and connected to those already standing. Finally, roofing and sheathing are applied.[3]

The quick sequencing of this raising operation ensures that the structure will maintain sufficient stability to resist gusting wind. It must also occur quickly because the volunteer manpower needed for erection is available for a short time only. Once raised, the shell provides a sheltered place to complete the building at a more leisurely pace. A similar process typified seventeenth- and eighteenth-century post-and-beam house building throughout the American colonies, and continues throughout Amish and other similar communities.

## Units of Enclosure

The unit form of enclosure—be it bay, vault, or pavilion—is not a room; indeed, it may contain a number of rooms. Conversely, a large room may straddle more than one unit of enclosure. The building's architecture is a combination of such units, with the resulting volume to be subsequently subdivided by inhabitation. The house as a composite of rooms is an abstraction. The act of building effects enclosure first. Traditionally, house form was seldom conceived as a combination of rooms, the sum—or wrapper—of which became the building proper.

A prime example is again found in the Chinese "house," an arrangement of individual pavilions distributed according to strict rules of symmetry, by which courtyards are made. The act of enclosure is the building of a single pavilion. The house is a combination of pavilions, each of which may be subdivided internally.

Informal house building in Latin America demonstrates how courtyard houses emerge in a sequence of separate building acts. Usually, a wall is first built around the territory. The house then grows incrementally, bit by bit, as the means become available.

Mediterranean hill towns juxtapose roofed volumes—the picturesque white or pastel cubicles that combine to make a whole town—that are neither houses nor rooms. Just as their windows do not indicate the number or size of rooms, the actual dwellings may encompass more or less than one such volume. Acts of building visibly combine to form a discrete entity, the domestic subdivision of which remains invisible.

Even in the New England tradition, the house comprises more than a single volume. Eventually a smaller and subsidiary one is built in the back and later yet another one, while outbuildings begin to dot the landscape. The process was sufficiently common to find expression in an old New England children's refrain: "Big house, little house, back house, barn."[4]

Thus the contrapuntal relation between the act of building and the act of inhabitation can be found in a rich variety of expression the world over. What is found in vernacular building is repeated in the contemporary large building: it is first structured of bays, and only subsequently subdivided. Discrete acts of building, such as the repeated adding of volume in a familiar technology, cumulatively determine typology and provide a vocabulary for architectural articulation. Functional distribution of the rooms inside comes second, providing the purpose but not the means of such articulation.

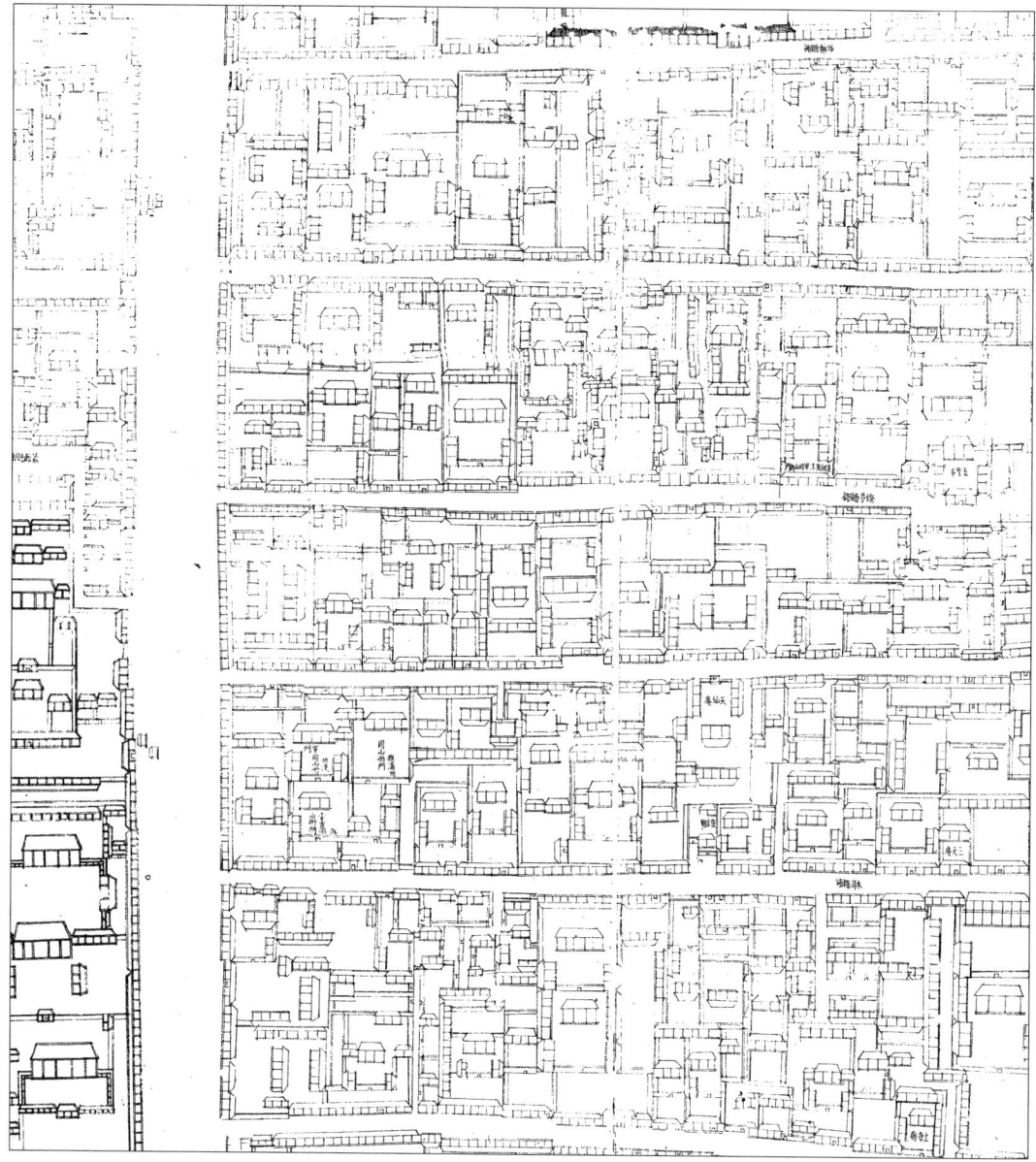

**5.8** *Beijing, ca. 1750—Classical houses: walled compounds with pavilions within. Detail from the* Complete Map of the Capital City *during the Qianlong era. Reproduced courtesy of the Harvard-Yenching Library.*

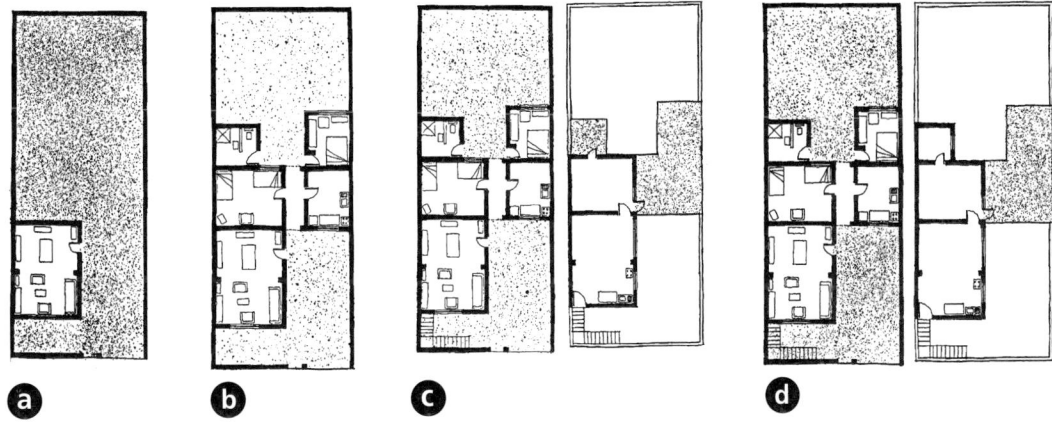

**5.9** *Colonia Santa Ursula, Mexico City, 1952–1974—*
*House growing over time in fixed enclosure. Courtesy of*
*Jorge Andrade, Rodolfo Santa Maria, and Alfonso Govela.*

## 5.5  Gravity Recognized

Stones seldom leave the earth in Japanese traditional houses. Rather, they protrude to support a post or to provide an intermediary step between earth and wooden floor. The house's timber parts—posts, screens, and eaves—drift above the earth, in apparent weightlessness.

In the historic village of Hawhoe, Korea, the "Master's Pavilion" likewise hovers, now above a heavy stone platform several feet high. Stone and timber relate, but hardly touch.[5] We may again compare this with the traditional Chinese house (figure 5.6), in which the platform acquires far more autonomy, relating to the roof more than to the intermediate volume. In both cases, a timber frame structure takes over at the first floor.

In the Swiss mountain chalet, the point of transition is raised. There, the entire first floor may be heavy masonry, supporting several floors of timber frame structure.

Many vernacular building types combine the ways of mason and carpenter. Dialogue between the two takes many forms and constitutes one of the fundamental architectural relationships defining form. The precise point of transition, the instant of heavier structure giving way to lighter, can occur just above the foundation, just under the roof, or anywhere between. In all such cases the relation between two subsystems translates directly into a sequence of action by tradespeople, a dominance relation easily understood.

The relation is not necessarily vertical. Nineteenth-century American warehouses with heavy timber floor framing and interior columns frequently have solid masonry perimeter walls for fire protection. There, the carpenter, who assumes control of overall coordination once the foundation is in place, works in tan-

**5.10** *Hawhoe, Korea—Section of the Master's Pavilion,
a traditional house, illustrating earthen platform on which
a stone floor on masonry walls is raised. After Sohn.*

**5.11** *Hawhoe, Korea—Traditional farmhouse.*

dem with the bricklayer. In Boston's Back Bay, houses combine masonry party walls with wood frame structure and façades of brick veneer.[6]

Similar and more intricate combinations of the two materials can be found in vernacular architectures as well. In such cases, mason and carpenter may alternate several times as work proceeds. The architecture is eventually determined by subsystems whose pattern of dominance and dependence becomes intricate. But it is ultimately governed by gravity.

## The Classical Orders

Three distinct subsystems clearly expressed in the homogeneous marble of the Greek temple witness earlier distinctions in material and trade specialization. A raised platform is followed by anthropomorphically shaped columns, then sheltered beneath the horizontal volume of the pediment with its sculpted roof. The Greek temple may vestigially recall a wood frame structure on a stone platform, or a timber roof on masonry columns and walls, but its final form articulates three sets of component parts that can be expressed in any material. The sequence of separate acts producing distinct subsystems is still there, but the material that caused it has been abstracted away. The technical principle throughout is simple stacking—pure gravity. But each marble block, once placed, becomes visually weightless. What was born from gravity eventually transcends it.[7]

The classical order has been emulated in masonry, plaster, wood, and cast iron. The properties of the materials actually used have become secondary. The juxtaposition of base, frame, and roof has become a universal expression following general principles, its abstract

order expressing a tripartite recognition of gravity that is accepted even where its classical provenance is forgotten.

## Frameworks

The ordering effects of gravity are most easily recognized in the frame, which represents a function rather than any particular shape.

Flesh and organs combine into a single individual by means of an animal's skeleton. They create a living and movable entity loosely connected to the earth's surface. The rooted tree trunk carries branches, the latter in turn loaded with leaves and fruit. Similarly, a steel or concrete armature holds a building together. The chassis on which are fastened a vehicle's body, wheels, and engine; the rigid shell of the latter-day car and the airplane fuselage; the board on which transistors and chips are fastened, to be connected by wires, thereby enabling them to communicate: all are examples of *frameworks*.

Frameworks are singular entities created solely to organize support, resisting gravity's pull. They distribute lower-level parts in three-dimensional space, after which lower-level configurations connect and relate among themselves as required.

Strictly speaking, the framework is not a principle of form but of arrangement. It is recognized more by its function of holding things in their proper place and relation than by any particular configuration or shape. Gravity always requires a technical response. The need to array parts functionally keeps us reinventing the framework, creating new shapes for it.

Chips and capacitors connect by wires, which transmit electric impulses. Animals' organs connect to allow nourishment to flow through the digestive system. Automotive parts are likewise related functionally within the power train to produce movement. Building frames support envelope panels, which are then joined to create a continuous membrane.

The framework does not seek spatial identity. It has only a single purpose: positioning related things in space.

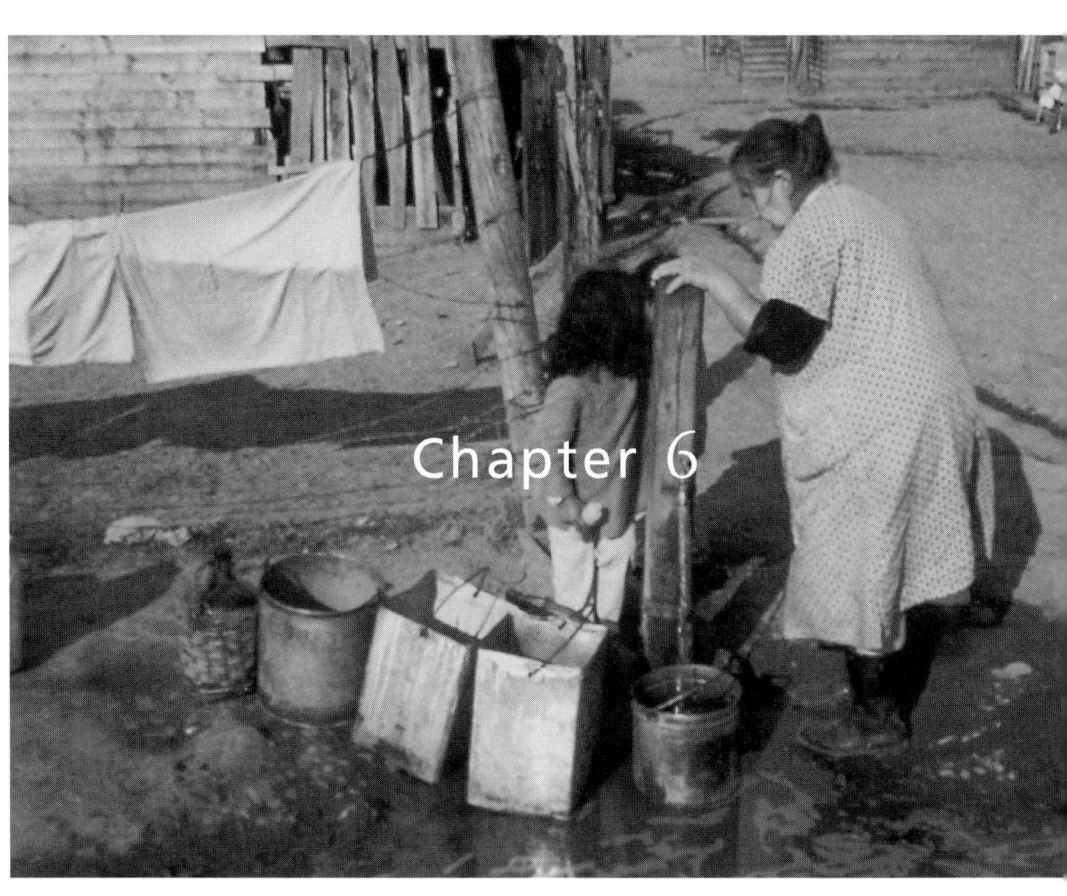

Chapter 6

Other Forms at Play

## 6.1   Supply Forms

### Invisible Forms

From large reservoirs in the hills, water flows through pipes that branch and proliferate, ultimately reaching the bathrooms, kitchens, gardens, and workplaces of hundreds of millions of individuals in metropolitan regions throughout the industrialized nations. Widespread supply systems similarly reach water taps in informal and illegal settlements throughout the rest of the world.

The ubiquity of supply systems is new in the history of environmental form. Even distribution of fresh water was historically achieved at or near the source. Human or animal labor was then needed to transport it home.

Throughout extensive self-help neighborhoods ringing Latin American cities, inhabitants frequently dig wells and latrines in their own yards, as did their ancestors. Eventually, under pressure of numbers, municipal sewage systems, water, and electricity are extended to them. In Egypt, cheap electricity courtesy of the Aswan Dam is ubiquitous, powering even the unfinished houses and drills and saws of squatters. Similar stories can be told in other parts of the world. Today, to inhabit is to connect to the numerous supply systems of the contemporary urban fabric. As hallmarks of contemporary environment, they exist on a par with shelter and may indeed precede it; for instance, mobile homes and yachts move from hookup to hookup of preinstalled infrastructure.

In contemplating and deliberating the qualities of buildings and urban spaces as the malleable building blocks of modern city fabric,

*6.1*  *Santiago de Chile—Campiamento Che Guevara.*
*Squatter settlement communal water tap (page 110).*

we typically do not recognize the vast, proliferating undergrowth of pipe, cable, and channels. Though it has become essential that supply services be extended to wherever we are, we routinely accept their extremely haphazard burial within walls, ceilings, floors, streets, and fields.

It is only the equipment that supply lines serve—sink, range, Jacuzzi, and outlets for power, telephone, and television—that we register in everyday life, consider in our design decisions. Supply forms themselves are like gravity: ubiquitous but unseen. Like gravity, they also shape building and designing to a significant, albeit unrecognized, extent.

Supply system distribution in large buildings represents a major component in equipment and installation costs, as well as a major portion of time spent in design and coordination. In equipment-intensive buildings like hospitals and laboratories, supply service installations far exceed the cost of the enclosure forms, the "architecture" proper.

Within high-density urban areas, necessary supply forms have entered the public imagination. By the nineteenth century, the Parisian sewage system became a mythical domain populated by fantastic creatures, just as legendary alligators in the New York sewer system are a staple of twentieth-century ethnographic collections of urban American folk tales.

Supply systems gave rise to an architecture of large-scale infrastructure long before the modern city. Aqueducts traversing the Roman countryside fed a distribution system terminating at the city's fountains. (Water did not reach

**6.2** *Village near Suzhou, China—Stone wellhead. Grooves in the stone have been worn by ropes over centuries of use.*

individual houses, except for the gardens and courtyards of the privileged.) Today, the most visible high-level forms of supply are the high-voltage power lines strung from towers marching unrelievedly across the landscape and the telephone and cable lines strung from telephone poles, paralleling the street.

The penetration of multiple supply systems into lower levels of environmental fabric, to workstation and bedroom, is a modern phenomenon.

## Tree Forms

Supply forms often assume the shape of branching structures. Water is distributed from one place to many, as a tree's trunk distributes nutrients to its leaves. The sewage system collects from a multitude of points to a single main, mirroring tributaries feeding a river.

There are variations. Combined tree forms can be found: large hot-water central heating systems often have a distribution line to feed radiators and a collector line to return water to the source. Electric cables are strung in tree-like distribution to bring power to all outlets, but each cable is technically a loop. By and large, though, supply forms do branch in tree-like structures.

The tree form is a prime example of a dominance hierarchy. Branches may be transformed without disturbing the trunk, and the leaves and twigs may be rearranged without forcing transformation of the branch: thus the trunk dominates the branches, which in turn dominate the twigs. Connection from many points to a single point implies a hierarchy in which each node in the structure constitutes a junction between two possible control levels:

between the municipality, for instance, in control of the main and the home owner in control of a branch.

## Flow

A tree form may distribute or collect, depending on the direction of flow. In both cases, the party in control of the trunk dominates the one in control of the branch, dominance implicit in the form notwithstanding.

Flow nevertheless is an independent variable. The agent who distributes water can close the main. The agent who collects wastewater can do so, too. Dominance by flow is not effected through actual transformation of the system of conduits; instead, it constitutes part of a game of use. It is one step removed from controlling the conduit as a form. Clearly, anticipated control and intended uses of supply forms dictate decisions about their layout and interactions.

Flow and form as distinct variables are illustrated by the system of irrigation found in the medieval Persian city of Yazd. Mulberry trees for breeding silkworms were irrigated using gravity-fed water lines, originating in collector channels buried in the sloping ground of surrounding hills. Many conduits converged toward the fields near the town. Thus, a field at the center or trunk of the form depends on water flow from its branches. In terms of flow, dominance rests with whoever controls the branches. In terms of form, the reverse remains true: branches can be shifted without forcing relocation of the field they feed, but relocation of the field would require readjustment of the branches.

## Gravity, Enclosure Forms, and Supply Forms

Roman aqueducts and high-voltage power lines are independent forms, built from the ground up. But within cities and buildings, supply forms tend to be held up or contained by forms of enclosure and frameworks; thus, their largely invisible existence affects the production of environmental form.

An axonometric drawing illustrating conduits present within an average Dutch townhouse gives a vivid impression of the hidden arteries in the spatial fabric (figure 6.4). Ten or more independent supply forms must be accommodated. Each may be distributed throughout the volume of the house.[1]

This explains why minor residential remodeling readily becomes a major operation. It may involve many subcontractors dealing with as many utilities as there are systems of pipe and cable beneath the surfaces of wall, ceiling, and floor. It also explains why interior fit-out of a modest dwelling takes so much longer than erection of the shell. The critical issue is certainly not installing partition walls, appliances, storage systems, or finish trim. Rather, it is coordinating supply and drainage systems and other equipment installations, many of which subsequently require full or partial concealment. Together with appliances, these costs generally far exceed all other interior work.

The general contractor choreographs the moves of many agents installing systems to achieve environmental control and water, electrical, and communications flow. It takes several iterations of alternating actors to finish a partition wall. To cite the North American example: after framing, electricians, plumbers, information and security system installers, and

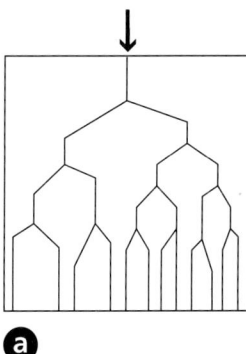

**a**

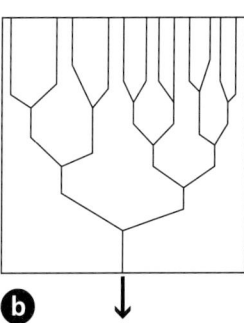

**b**

*6.3* Diagram of the tree form—Whether flow proceeds toward a higher or lower level, dominance relations of the form (as distinct from control of the flow) remain the same.

(a) Flow toward the lower level: distribution to many points.

(b) Flow toward the higher level: collection at a single point.

115

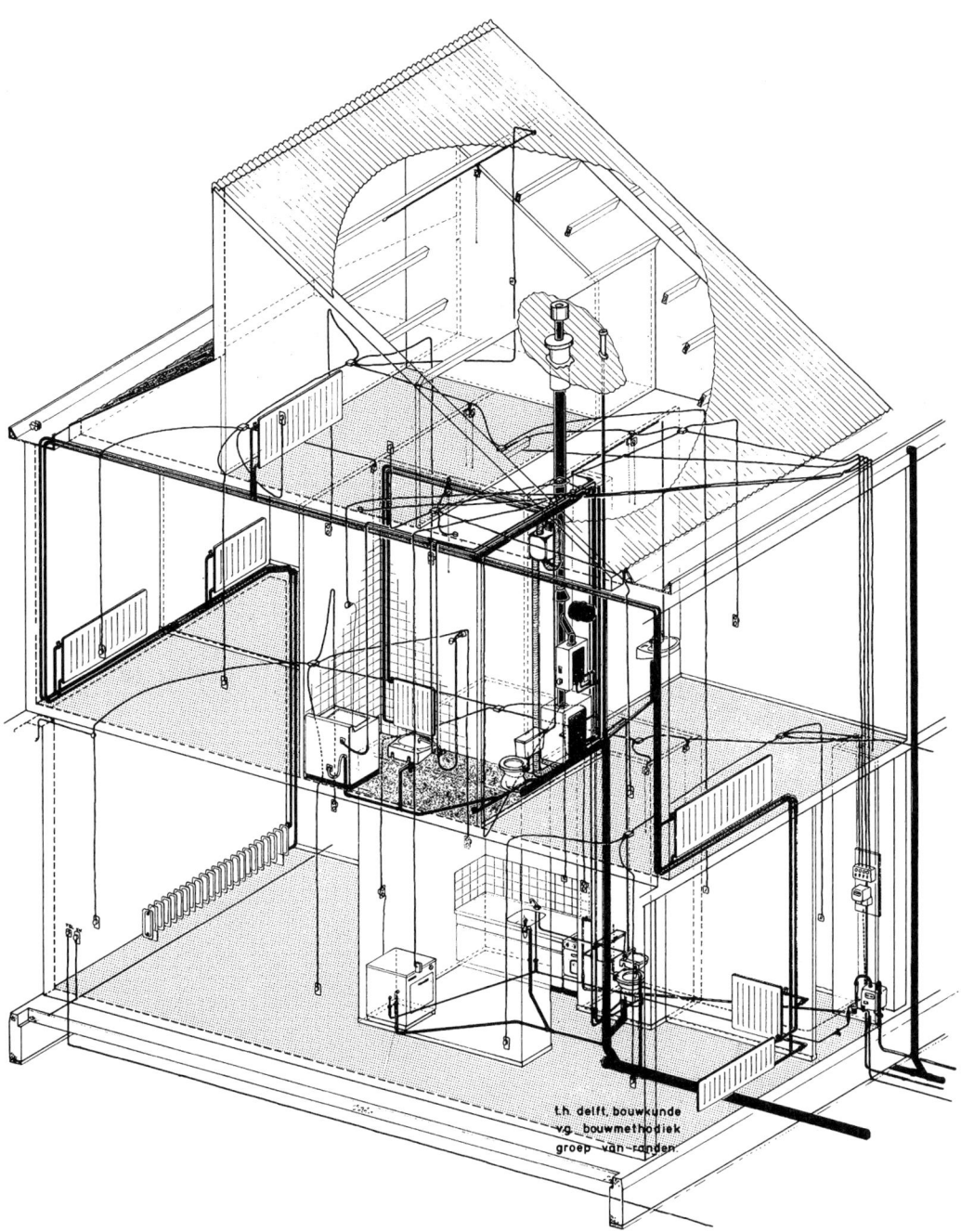

**6.4** *Netherlands—Typical contemporary townhouse, showing the distribution of conduits embedded in the building's walls and floors. Illustration by Age van Randen, reprinted courtesy of OBOM Research Group.*

environmental systems installers rough in their systems. Each independent subcontractor's work may be followed in each phase by an independent scheduled inspection, by trade. As the wall is closed in with sheets of gypsum board, holes for outlets and connections must be repaired or covered. Tradespeople then return to connect outlets, hardwire or plumb-in fixtures and appliances, and so forth.

Coordination between environmental and supply forms remains reasonably clear and ordered at the scale of the urban block. But within the building, order degenerates as supply forms branch and interfaces multiply rapidly. Visible clarity in the enclosure hierarchy is then belied by the haphazardness of hidden supply forms. At lower levels of environmental form, supply systems are hopelessly entangled within walls, floors, and ceiling assemblies, crossing or penetrating major structures and one another, attached to the building frame and almost any other surface of enclosure.

To avoid such entanglement leading to open conflict, conventions of deployment, familiar to all actors, have been established by trial and error over time. This does not necessarily render the process efficient. And as soon as the building form departs from a familiar typology, the problems of distribution, entanglement, and coordination escalate.

The level structure of forms of enclosure is rendered considerably more rigid by the need to distribute multiple supply forms within it. Better articulation of the infill level, which mediates the large building's response to the flow of life within it, does not require improved or more flexible partitioning systems or equipment: it depends almost solely on finding better ways to distribute supply lines. Related issues crucially affect initial building and response to use over time. The most critical issues for

improving the building process regard the installation of supply systems. Rigorous adoption of universal principles for disentangling these complexities is sorely needed. The resultant gains in speed, efficiency, and flexible response to use would be considerable.

There is a clear chain of causality. Environmental levels are in transition. For architectural articulation to evolve with the changing environment, in ways that go beyond questions of shapes, surfaces, and styles, will depend on how the infill level emerges. This emergence, in turn, is closely dependent on a new topological, systemic, and logistic understanding of the host of supply forms already distributed in the contemporary building.

Most important in that understanding will be determining how to synchronize the supply form's own dominant hierarchy with that of the enclosure hierarchy as it travels through the latter, ultimately reaching down to the smallest room in the dwelling.

## 6.2 Nets, Grids, and Webs

### Net Forms

Branching, the quintessential formal characteristic of supply forms, exists fundamentally to support unidirectional flow. Supply forms are intended to channel flow toward predetermined destinations. The net seems a more natural form for accommodating traffic that freely filters through the environment, selecting paths and destinations en route.

Recurring nodes or crossings, each one allowing directional choice, epitomize net form. In combination, they allow a looping movement. Orthogonal grids represent one common way to make a net form, but the four-way node can be found in concentric nets as well, or in any twisted, skewed, or bent version of these. The concentric version is typical of towns with radial roads leading out to the countryside, subsequently connected by lateral ring roads as they grow over time.

The three-way node is also very much in evidence in nets that grow organically over time. It is the fork in the road, asking us at a certain point to bear either left or right. Frequently unplanned, it can be found in metropolitan areas like Boston and London that, over time, incorporate surrounding villages and settlements and the roads that led to them. It is the bane of visitors used to the orderly grid of the planned town.

The net form is ubiquitous for roads, creating multiple linkages and inherent possibilities for passage within a built field. Through redundancy, nets create the potential for traveling at will between many disparate points. Latter-day suburbs attempt to relieve the rigidity of net grid forms by means of winding suburban roads and cul-de-sacs; typical Middle Eastern urban fabric is characterized by the presence of dead-end streets; Tokyo's residential quarters historically branched into nested structures of T-junctions. All these constitute net forms, albeit of an irregular or organic kind. Dead-end streets, including cul-de-sacs, constitute lower-level loose ends attached to a net. But topologically, they remain net forms all the same.

## Enclosure and Net

The road system, although a net form by itself, is a form of enclosure in its relation to the buildings in the block. It is a spatial container of lots and buildings, defined at the neighborhood scale by three or four nodes and their connecting roads. Larger-scale nets, such as highways, encompass entire continents. However, at a scale beyond the urban block, nets no longer act as, or in close interrelation with, enclosure forms, as noted above (see chapter 4.3).

## Hierarchy

In large metropolitan areas, combinations of grids of different modules and orientations are stitched together to make a single net. These grids reflect distinct interventions. They may result from distinct stages of growth of a single urban entity or from discrete municipalities merging. Distinctions visible in the larger net form therefore may or may not coincide with jurisdictional boundaries. Moreover, control distribution over time may shift away from initial boundaries.

Control distribution over large networks is basically distribution on a single level of form. Neighboring parties—countries, states, municipalities—share the larger net form, as roads cross borders. Such control distribution

on one level over the net form is largely territorially determined, as discussed in part II.

Back alleys behind houses that form a block are easily read as a lower level included within a larger grid block. The two-level form is recognized by the difference in size between alley and street. Alleys can be individually displaced within the block or otherwise transformed without disturbing the larger net. The morphology of net forms thus presents a nesting hierarchy as well. A single alley may become part of a second net when crossed by another in the middle of a block.

Hierarchy can also result from the growth of cities. This results from annexation (by encircling what coexists, adding ring roads and major arteries to existing nets); from transformation (as neighborhood streets are widened); or from intensification (as streets are upgraded into collectors or arterials, higher-level nets come into being). Through infill, incorporation, enhancement of existing parts, or deliberate design from the beginning, we obtain the familiar hierarchy of roads: back lane, residential street, neighborhood road, collector road, and so on.

## The Pedestrian Net

In Pompeii, streets must have teemed with the combined traffic of pushed or drawn carts, litters, pack animals, equestrians, and pedestrians. Nonetheless, the scale of streets is on a par with courtyards and rooms: all are human-size spaces. The same dimensions are found in all documented historic towns. Urban fabric was human-scale environment; the human body and its pace provided the measure of things. Horse, cart, and coach were made to fit in the given scale, with occasional minor adjustments.[2] Even when building at a monumental

119

**6.5** *Amsterdam, 1890—The Geldersekade, showing predominantly pedestrian use of the urban street. Photo by Jacob Olie.*

scale, the human body remained the measure of things: the main north-south arteries of ancient Beijing, for instance, were measured in number of soldiers marching abreast. So were the ramparts of Xi'an in the Ming Dynasty.[3]

The size of rooms, the width of streets, the length of blocks: environmental scale was historically derived from the human body. But on the North American continent, from the be-ginning of the movement westward, the horse-drawn vehicle became the measure of things environmental.

As every western movie buff has observed, the width of the street had to allow horse and carriage to turn around, while leaving undisturbed hitching space on both sides. That dimension subsequently suited the motor vehicle very well. Urban fabric has shifted into a "secondary scale," in which vehicular traffic determines the measure of things while maintaining marginalized pedestrian circulation. Thus the urban net remains part of the enclosure hierarchy, but it is no longer dimensionally defined by the human body.

Urban fabric has great capacity to absorb change. Just as size of buildings can change dramatically within a given road network, so the mix of pedestrian and vehicular traffic can, too. In photographs of late nineteenth-century Amsterdam, carts and coaches still weave their way among pedestrians walking in the middle of the street. There are no sidewalks, and transition zones occupied by stoops are marked as private property (see chapter 9, note 2). By the end of the century, the urban sidewalk has been introduced in an attempt to mediate between pedestrians and increasingly numerous vehicles. At all densities this prefigures contemporary residential streetscapes, in which through traffic is with difficulty further restrained by means of signage, legislation, police enforcement, speed bumps, and traffic barriers.

As speed increases and the number of vehicles burgeons, the net form occupies ever-widening swaths of real estate. At a certain point it acquires a formal expression of its own. With cloverleafs, elevated junctions, high-speed merges, and crossings to expedite vehicular flow, it no longer partakes of traditional environmental fabric. In abandoning the hierarchy of enclosure, it eventually joins with rivers, ridges, valleys, and coastlines to become part of the landscape while maintaining its own presence as artifact.[4]

This creates a "tertiary scale," in which the enclosure hierarchy no longer includes the road network. Buildings and traffic thus enter into a new relation.[5] External pedestrian circulation is inevitably reduced and ultimately displaced. The intense interaction on the pedestrian scale between private and public built space, historically so characteristic of the town, turns inward. It is now sheltered within the large building.

The pedestrian realm moves into the shopping mall, the office tower, the institutional complex or residential apartment complex. Atria, escalators, and corridors begin to articulate hierarchy in an exclusively pedestrian three-dimensional net form. These buildings possess the volume of a neighborhood; and what seems, on the outside, a coarsening of the city fabric becomes, inside, a lively and fine-grained intensification.

Widespread manifestation of this trend is not much more than half a century old. We may be witnessing the emergence of a shift in environmental structure, still inchoate and not yet digested by our collective understanding. Intensive relations between form and use, familiar to us from the historic pedestrian fabric, may be reinterpreted in the large building. The result may ultimately create richer hierarchy within city form.

121

II

Place, The Territorial Order

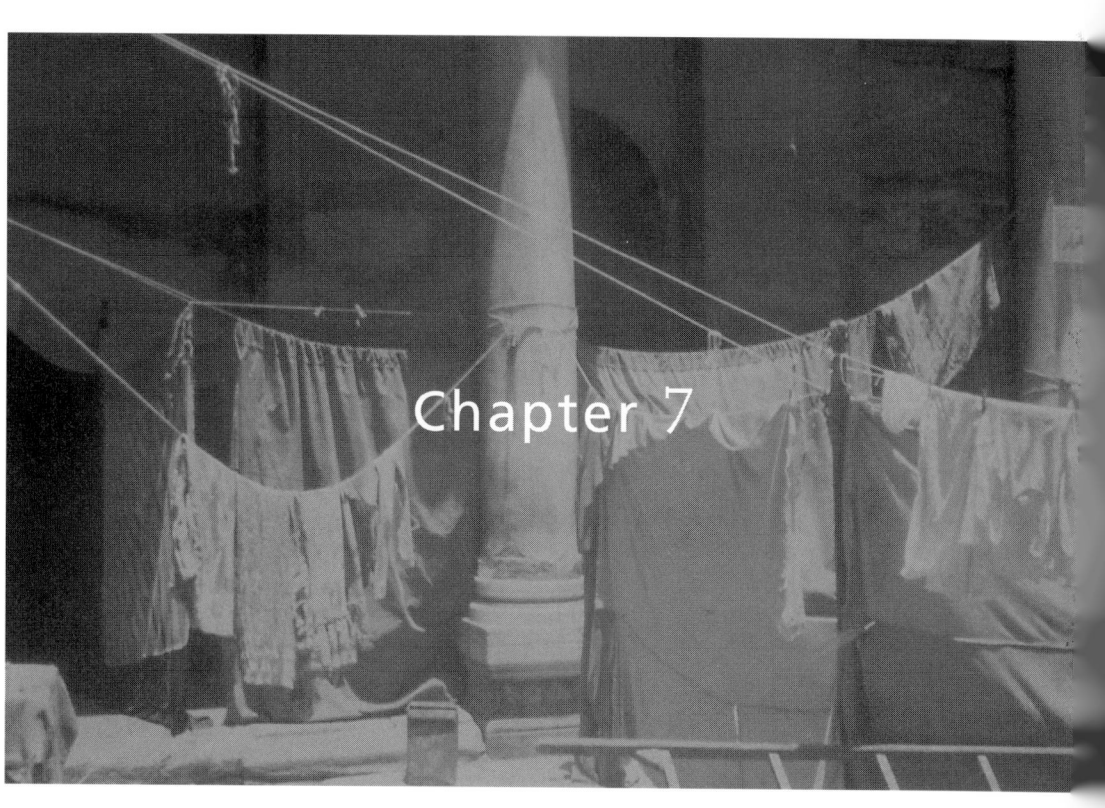

Chapter 7

Territory

## 7.1  Control of Space

### Territorial Space Defined

What does it mean to *control* space?

Control of form is a matter of transformation of form. But control of space cannot simply imply transformation of space: to transform space requires acting on the material parts that make that space. This in turn means transforming a material configuration—that is, controlling form. Yet control of space is clearly distinct from control of form.

Control of space denotes the ability to defend that space against unwanted intrusion. Space under control is territorial, and distinguishing such territory is fundamental to inhabiting the earth. Territorial control is the ability to close a space, to restrict entry. It is perhaps the most instinctive way by which humans have learned to understand built environment (and also, much earlier, natural landscape).

The very act of inhabitation—of occupying a space and selecting what comes in and what stays out—is fundamentally territorial. In what follows, the built environment is observed as a territorial organization, as space under the control of agents. We will find a distinct hierarchical structure related to the hierarchies of form.

### Control of Space and of Physical Parts

Previously, in observing live configurations and the levels defined by them, we examined the behavior of configurations under agents' control,

*Great Wall of China, near Beijing (page 123).*

*7.1   Cairo, 1978—Homeless shelter in a mosque (page 124).*

rather than studying agents directly. In observing the control of space, we will similarly attempt to limit our observation to material parts that represent agents acting on them. Territory will thus be recognized as space into which only certain items may enter. The ability to move material things across borders is the ultimate test of territorial control.

The act of strolling down a neighbor's walk and ringing his doorbell falls within normal social conventions, and thus it does not constitute a territorial violation. Sitting down uninvited on the curb bordering a neighbor's suburban lawn represents at most a minor territorial incursion. The neighbor will most likely treat you as a guest, albeit an uninvited one. But place your garbage can on his lawn, and he will express displeasure.

Human *behavior* can surely reveal cases of territorial infringement. But in a study of built environment it is appropriate, once more, to focus first on the location and the movement of inanimate material parts in order to learn about territorial structure.

Again, we will not inquire into the preferences and motivations of individual inhabitants. Rather, in focusing on how the organization of parts in the environment is governed by territorial rules, we will seek to determine how, based on the movement of parts, territorial boundaries can be deduced. In short, we are interested in the overlapping relationship between physical form and territorial control.

127

## Controlling Space and Form

In the environmental game, players control spaces in addition to configurations of form. Rules determine how parts are admitted or excluded from territorial space. Generally speaking, to exercise control of a configuration, one had better be in control of its space as well. But there are exceptions and variations. Under certain conditions, it is possible to control a configuration in someone else's territory or to have one's territory within another agent's configuration.

### Form Replaces Action

Territory is defined by acts of occupation. Form, as such, does not yet come into play. A corresponding space formed by physical parts is not required for territorial space to exist. All that is needed is an agent exercising spatial control.

Purely territorial control without any indication of a spatial form can be observed on the beach in summer. Individuals or groups occupy part of a planar surface. Unseen boundaries are observed despite the absence of walls or property stakes. Children and pets are retrieved on violating such boundaries. When a ball lands within a neighboring domain, it is recovered with due apology.

As Edward T. Hall and others have demonstrated, personal space is a universal phenomenon, although the particular dimensions of such space are culturally determined.[1] Reasonable proximity in one culture is intrusion in another. Personal space, as described by Hall, has strong territorial connotations.

Territory likewise represents the inhabiting and controlling agent's spatial extension of self. But territory cannot be maintained merely by gestures and body language. Artifacts may serve to represent the bounds of control exercised. We tend to mark our territory by tokens. Such indications are usually read easily by others, without error: we all understand territorial meaning in the positioning of objects. Even on the beach, we see the beginnings of demarcation of turf: chairs, towels, beach bags, and other belongings are placed strategically to claim space.

The most basic territorial demarcations are not walls, fences, or other forms of enclosure, but the simple stone or stake that may mark the turn of a boundary line or where a path crosses that boundary. There still remain,

## 7.2 Territory and Control

for example, stones placed by the wayside during colonial times throughout Massachusetts, which indicate the crossing over municipal borders. Today, stamped metal highway signs signal the name of the jurisdiction being entered.

Early settlers in the American West "staked out" their claims with sticks driven in the ground at the corners. Such signs, like marking the corners of one's territory on the beach, symbolically replaced action. A token was placed in preference to patrolling the invisible border. The boundary was then read by means of its markers. Physical acts of control were only needed when, whether intentionally or by mistake, markers were unheeded.

Forms may not convey consistent territorial meaning. A fenced pen, for instance, is there to keep animals in, not to keep trespassers out: the territorial boundary lies elsewhere. Walls and gates likewise divide space, and may or may not mark territory. Consequently, one is never sure whether the untested marker—and its intent—is territorial. If so, is it backed by real enforcing power?

Forms that seem to indicate territory are constantly tested. When no response follows a boundary incursion, it becomes evident that a marker is just a stone: of historical value perhaps, but indicating no "live" territory. Boundaries may then be crossed at will.

Only the marked boundary backed up by real control is taken seriously.

## Sheltering Form vs. Territorial Claim

Varied customs and laws deal with erecting and maintaining the common boundary between neighbors. Fences, walls, or plantings usually mark property bounds. These forms sometimes fall within the territory of the party who erects them; at other times they are shared forms straddling a boundary.

Landscaping in the North American suburb represents an anomaly, carefully designed to avoid explicit boundary marks. The lawn is open and unprotected—although often subtly marked—to convey a sense of affluence and freedom, an image of the house standing free in the prairie, unbounded. Yet each boundary is known and vigorously defended by the neighbors who share it. The lawn is regularly mown, retracing the presumed property line on a continuous lawn surface—a horticultural act confirming the territorial claim. Rear side-yard fences frequently appear as well.

Space read into form and territorial control of space are quite distinct. The heavy front door, though clearly a boundary form, is not necessarily a territorial marker in the suburban house. The enclosure formed by the house shell, with its front porch and entry, is not the territorial boundary. The territorial boundary, as determined by the transfer of surveyed land on which the house is built, exists somewhere at the periphery of the lawn.

In a similar way, territory historically ranged far beyond the turrets and gates of a town's walls. It included the pale of settlement around the town, a realm within untamed nature that was frequently cultivated by the citizens, but at other times just remained an uncultivated claim. The municipal boundary was marked with a stone at the wayside and otherwise established by legal deed and by custom.

In time of war, however, open land would be abandoned. At the first sign of attack, the territorial line withdrew behind the fortification walls.[2] Once danger or siege had passed, the territory would again expand. Individual claim

129

was again laid to customary boundaries, either by the act of cultivation or by other assertions of control.

Throughout the territorial boundary shifts, actual physical forms remained constant.

## Shifts in Territorial Claim

Temporary occupation of sidewalk space is common; for commercial uses, it is universal. Sidewalk occupation varies from placing discreet signs to indicate restaurant entrances, to actually displaying wares in front of a shop window, to creating sidewalk cafés.

*Hole-in-the-wall* may literally describe shops in many ancient cities, as it has since before the time of the Roman *taberna* and Middle Eastern souk (see figures 15.2 and 8.4). Upon opening, the shop door is unlocked. The shopkeeper then extracts wares and places them on the sidewalk. A cloth may span overhead to provide shade, further expanding the sidewalk claim by an act of occupation.

Such practices are not restricted to exotic climes. Sidewalks are habitually used by Manhattan's greengrocers, as well as by any variety of shops lining Canal Street. In all cases, unmarked exterior boundary lines extend the assumed property lines within the party walls between shops. The territory withdraws back behind a modest storefront by sundown, when the shop closes up and all its wares are stored for the night. When the shopkeeper leaves for home, so too does the power to sustain a wider territory.

Thus built form may suggest territory, but it is the ongoing act of occupation that fixes the actual extent of the claim. In playing the territorial game, the more permanent form is not

ignored: it is subjected to interpretation, spatially and temporally.

In the examples cited above, street wall and sidewalk curb form a *margin,* a zone within which the boundary may move. The actual territorial boundary is indicated not by the building but by lower-level configurations and parts. The shop, for instance, leaves part of the sidewalk free for passage and positions its boundary somewhere between building and road as determined by custom, practical use, and occasional negotiation.

In the corridors of elegant apartments as well, inhabitants may place potted plants, door mats, and umbrella stands in front of their entries. Their claim, paralleling the shopkeeper's, is understood and respected as an identification of territory. In both cases, the margin created softens and articulates the razor-thin line of demarcation offered by the architecture.

In these ways, we act out shifting spatial claims in relation to stable form. Territorial boundaries are established by acts. Such acts usually seek stable forms to relate to, if not always to abide by.

## 7.3    Inhabitation and Territory

### Architectural Form Interpreted by Inhabitation

The features of every form, natural and built, offer potential territorial boundaries. Rivers and mountain ranges are natural invitations for boundary lines. But as any map reveals, they are not the ultimate determinants of boundaries: neighbors adopt borders along geographical features only when they serve the prevailing balance of power. Architectural and urban space function in much the same way, offering an articulated context on which inhabitants impose territorial interpretations.

Built form plays a dual role relative to territory. On one hand, humans express territory explicitly—building walls, making gates, and placing marker stones. On the other hand, we draw implicitly understood territorial boundaries as custom and inhabitation dictate, within the artificial landscape of the built environment. Often, as in the shopkeeper's claim of sidewalk space marked by the placement of wares, territorial boundaries are drawn by setting lower-level objects in relation to architectural form. Territory interprets architecture, but by no means in strict obeisance to it.

### Space and Function

We are so conditioned to label every room by function, in conversations and floor plans alike, that it has become difficult to understand that people instinctively settle built space. Yet inhabitation remains fundamentally territorial, not functional.

Ancient palaces offered progressions of halls of great character, yet devoid of any formal indication responding to specific use. Users passed through space after space in succession, as corridors were unknown or rarely used. Within an architecture that offered varied spaces of power and dignity, people settled into daily life, creating places to sit, to eat, to sleep. The Gothic Venetian palace, the English manor, and many vernacular house types similarly offer clearly articulated architecture, and spatial organization firmly established by the enclosing forms, without strictly defining a specific program for any given uses.

The early-seventeenth-century Dutch canal house (figure 17.2) exhibited a range of rooms. Their spaces were large by current standards, differing in characteristic shape, height, character of light, and so on: the architecture is not neutral. The entry hall has a very high ceiling. It is lit by tall windows, with a mezzanine-like space behind. Upstairs, ceiling heights vary again.

In contrast to dramatic sectional differences between rooms, the plans remain rather generic. We cannot read functions in room size or location. For instance, the oversize space that accommodates a kitchen may also contain a sleeping alcove, a built-in bed closed off by curtains. The sleeping alcove is an added configuration with a dedicated function, in the manner of fireplace and window. Neither the alcove nor the hall in which it was built constitutes what we now call a bedroom.

Historically, spaces in vernacular house types rarely assumed function names: *mezzanine, hall, attic, cellar, stoop,* and *porch* do not describe functions. Actions and functions in the building were linked not to specific rooms or spaces as much as to specific attributes or configurations present: fireplace, type of window,

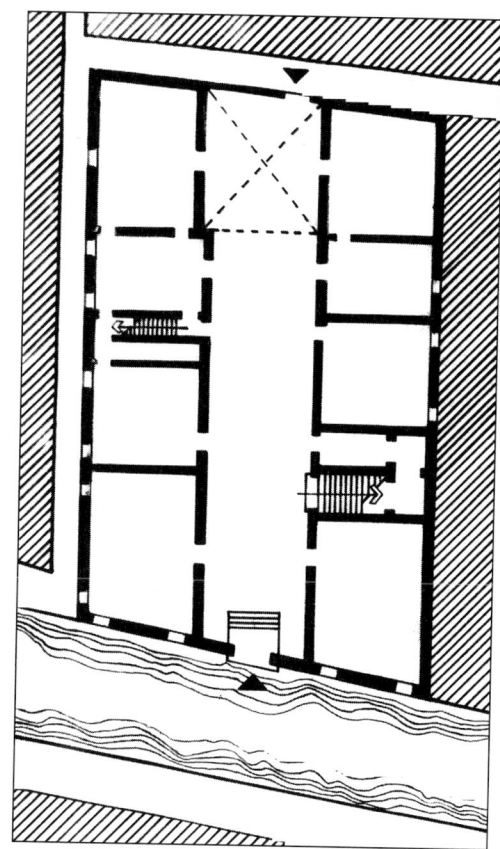

**7.2** *Venice—Gothic palace floor plan, illustrating dual entry from canal and street. After Maretto.*

doors giving onto street or backyard. Such attributes encouraged certain uses by offering a fit location: one with warmth, light, a view to the street, a place to withdraw. Each architectural element invited small acts of settlement, which created territorial zones within the large rooms.

Thus, architecture supported inhabitation by offering a varied topography of spaces and forms. At times, the very entities to which people linked their activities—fireplace, window, sleeping alcove, and so on—were themselves like lower-order forms, inhabiting the larger building.

## Territorial Occupation

In the Pompeiian house, cultural and cosmological function dictated that the ancestral shrine be placed on axis within the atrium, in an area marking the transition to a more private zone of the house, the *tablinum*. Yet that niche also served as reception area and repository of family mementos (see figures 12.2 and 15.2).

The Chinese ancestral shrine is located in a similar position, this time on axis with the center of the pavilion located at the rear of the main courtyard. This pavilion was also where the family gathered, where visitors might be entertained, where meals might be shared. At the same time, it also served as the daytime abode for the patriarch of the house. Such multiple capacity for varying use was intrinsic to the architecture; it did not result from programming multipurpose space.

The notion that form should precisely accommodate inhabitation in a tightly engineered and optimized fit—that it must mirror or be molded by a program—simply did not exist in prior epochs. The architecture of the large medieval hall, rustic barn, or palace defined form

with spatial character. Specific locations for the daily functions of life, with all of their human-size territorial claims, were not predefined. Territorial boundaries between individuals and groups of people were accordingly more complex and fluid, far less dependent on walls and doors, than those which modern functionalism supports.

The historical absence of functional specificity in architecture was by no means attributable to poverty of means or of inventiveness. Reading the duc de Saint-Simon's elaborate memoirs, we conclude that even in life at Versailles, the richly decorated and generously apportioned spaces defined nothing more specific than a regal context.[3] Smaller-scale settlement came from later decisions and territorial claims, supported by furniture and smaller utensils. The four-poster bed and chair were not merely furniture placed in a private space: they created private space. As a means of inhabitation unto themselves, they claimed territory that frequently occupied only part of a large room.

In perceiving acts and objects—no less than walls and doors—as territorial delineations, we begin more fully to understand elaborate salutations, compliments, bows, and other customary gestures. These inordinately complex social acts also represent probings, assertions, and readjustments of invisible boundaries, both spatial and psychological. People populated Versailles's vast halls as they would have populated a landscape, strategically positioning themselves and their furniture to claim and domesticate it and accompanied by no less strategic gestures and language.

The contrast with contemporary functionalism is stark. Current architectural practice first formulates and fixes highly specific program prior to design. The program is derived or projected from a single point in time. Function-specific spatial translation then generates the initial form diagram. Rather than suggesting broad architectural possibility for inhabitation, the resulting form may seek to limit capacity to the one function that is intended, in an approach that ignores the iterative nature of the process of mutual self-definition of form and inhabitation.

Each act of settlement relies on articulated form to stimulate further interpretation. Given the increasing fluidity and variety of contemporary life, the functionalist approach may prove to be a short-lived phenomenon. Inhabitation remains fundamentally territorial, and architecture may return to the articulation of space that is open to acts of inhabitation.

## 7.4 Territorial Hierarchy

### An Asymmetrical Relation

Territorial control is the ability to exclude, to shut the door, selectively admitting only who and what we desire.

But while territorial power can legitimately shut out, it may not confine. Unrestricted freedom to exit is implicitly understood. Conversely, such restriction represents a rude and unconventional act. Under many circumstances, it is illegal. Thus the curfew represents an extraordinary exercise of power: negation of the order established by territorial convention.

The relationship existing between spaces on opposite sides of a gate is therefore asymmetrical. One may always exit: from bunk bed into bedroom, from bedroom into house, from house into street, from city into surrounding countryside. But moving in the reverse direction, one is subject to scrutiny at each door or gate, unable to simply enter wherever one pleases. Strangers seeking admission to a compound may be refused. Once granted entry into the street beyond the gate, they may not randomly enter any building. Moreover, permission to enter a given house does not convey permission to enter any bedroom, nor to occupy any desk or bed.

This asymmetry implies hierarchy. Territories situate themselves within larger territories; conversely they may contain other territories. Thus the town, which is situated in the county, contains the house. The occupant of the house may accept a boarder, in which case one room becomes an included territory within the house.

At each boundary, the asymmetry holds. Someone living in a boardinghouse maintains the right to shut the door of her room: even the landlord must ask permission to enter. Although the landlord may refuse to let pets in his house, and therefore into the boarder's room, the boarder also maintains the right to exit her room any time, to enter the landlord's space and proceed toward the exit door, to enter the street.

## Hierarchy Based on Inclusion

Territorial organization is founded on the principle of inclusion within other territories. A simple diagram presents the basic territorial situation.

Given the territory of a boarder, a rented room that is in turn within a house included in the larger territory of a neighborhood, it is clear that the landlord's territory, *A*, in figure 7.3 encompasses the boarder's room, *B*. The total territory of the house—the sum of space behind the front door—remains constant, whether one, two, or no rooms are rented. The boarder's room is part of the larger territory, within which it constitutes an included territory.

In the same diagram, *A* may represent the neighborhood or town and *B* the house in it. Again, no matter how many houses there are, they all are contained within the same, constant territory, *A*.

## Territorial Depth

Situations of variable territorial depth can be depicted, adapting the diagramming technique of figure 7.3. Figure 7.4 adds included territories *C* within territory *B*. Territorial depth is measured by the number of boundary crossings (indicated by arrows in figure 7.5) needed to move from the outer space to the innermost territory.

## Private and Public Space

Should house *B* in figure 7.3 be demolished, and the lot converted into a public playground, the total size of neighborhood *A* does not increase. The neighborhood, as one territory, exhibits two kinds of space: space occupied by houses (*B*) and space not so occupied (*A* minus *B*). We tend to call the latter *public space,* and houses with their lots *private space.* But fixed definitions of *private* and *public* are illusory, as

137

**7.3**   *The territorial principle of inclusion—The existence of included territories in A also results in the presence of public and private spaces there.*

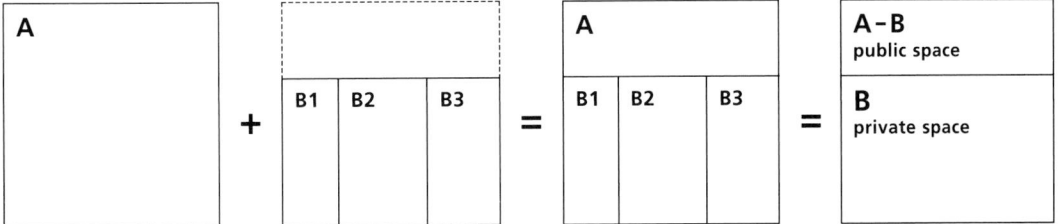

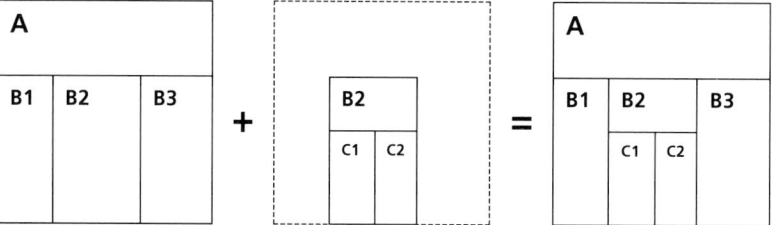

**7.4** *Territorial inclusion occurring in increasing depth—Territory B may include territories C, resulting in the presence of public and private spaces in B.*

becomes clear in examining situations of greater territorial depth, as in figure 7.5.

The terms are quite relative. If a hotel guest quits her room and joins a colleague in the foyer, she clearly enters public space. When she exits the hotel, she again enters public space. At the end of the day, she returns. Stepping out of a cab, she leaves the city streets and passes through the hotel's doorway, returning to the foyer: this time, the foyer represents private space, relative to the street.

The fact that privateness and publicness are not static conditions causes much confusion. Architects and planners confronted with territorial depth tend to classify space as *private, semiprivate, semipublic,* and *public.* In fact, whether a given territorial space is private or public depends entirely on one's perspective: the same space is simultaneously private to those not yet admitted and public to those from included territories, who are free to enter at all times.[4]

By observing a certain discipline in terminology, we can avoid misunderstanding. *Territory* refers to a unit of spatial control. *Private* and *public* refer to space, but not to territory. Within territory, we find two kinds of space: *pri-*

*vate space* is that which is occupied by included territories, and *public space* is whatever remains after such inclusion. While territory itself is neither public nor private, each territory contains spaces that are public, private, or both. A territory can simultaneously occupy a private space, included in a larger territory, and contain public space, relative to its own included territories, as is the case with a gated community.

Finally, there is a clear distinction between the designation of space as *private* and the degree of *privacy* it affords. The first term is territorial, the second is not. Neither backyards without fences nor bedrooms without window curtains may afford much privacy. But both spaces are clearly private, relative to street and alley.

## Territorial and Form Hierarchies as Control Hierarchies

Like the Order of Form, the Order of Place is a control hierarchy. In form hierarchies, we control physical parts and configurations of parts. In territorial hierarchies of inclusion, we control space. In both hierarchies, agents controlling higher levels dominate agents controlling lower levels.

Dominance in hierarchies of form is manifested in the ability to transform, forcing lower-level configurations to adjust to that transformation. In hierarchies of inclusion, dominance is expressed by refusing admittance to included territories. Goods and parties cannot pass through en route to lower-level territory. Massachusetts does not admit handguns into its commonwealth; therefore, citizens may not transport firearms across its border to their homes. If a landlord does not admit cats in his house, the boarder cannot keep a cat in her room: it is contraband.

When higher-level agents control what goes into included territories, included agents must, as a rule, accept the imposed limitations on what filters through the higher level.

## Moving Through the Territorial Hierarchy

All space is continuously linked by the combined principle of selective entry and unrestricted exit. In moving from one place to another, we go freely up the territorial hierarchy and then down again somewhere else, where we may be permitted to enter. In visiting a neighbor, one typically steps out the door, up into common public space, then down again through the neighbor's gate, as one is admitted back into a more deeply embedded territorial level.

There are good reasons, therefore, why landlocked countries are disadvantaged. They lack access to the highest level of territory: to the public space of the open seas and their unrestricted skies, and to all of the realms that those seas and skies touch.

139

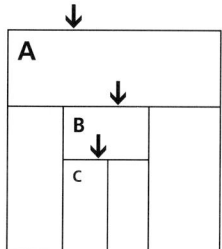

**7.5** *Territorial depth—The territorial depth of A, as shown in figure 7.4. Three crossings are needed to move from outside A to the deepest included territory.*

$7 \cdot 5$ Horizontal Relations
Are Avoided

## Territory Precludes Horizontal Interaction

In abstract diagrammatic representation, "vertical" relationships create hierarchy. "Horizontal" relationships in no way determine formal structure. But in a real world composed of physical parts, the horizontal is not so easily discounted. Neighboring territories abut, and one's neighbor is frequently closer than the public street. We have already observed that dominance and dependency are unpredictable and inherently unstable in horizontal interaction among configurations (see chapter 1.5).

Dominance among forms of enclosure, for instance, is established by confinement. Thus, city blocks segregate groups of houses; rooms formed by partitioning segregate configurations of furniture. But some same-level configurations inevitably find themselves sharing space. Buildings share available space within the city block. Likewise, within a room shared among co-workers, several live configurations of furniture may be found. When configurations on the same level relate horizontally, the rules of territory take over, continuing separation by means of boundaries. Horizontal territorial boundaries may be invisible, but they nonetheless form an impenetrable membrane, preventing configurations from interacting.

Often there exists no physical constraint of gravity, enclosure, or supply network to preclude horizontal connection between territories. Yet instances where gates connect two territories horizontally, or where configurations on different sides of a territorial boundary interact directly, are few. Abutting houses along the street frequently turn blind walls toward one another. In suburbs, trees, shrubs, lawns, and other outdoor elements are confined within invisible setback lines. Crossing a horizontal boundary—for example, directly entering an abutting neighbor's backyard through a side gate—is an informal and intimate exception.

In short, when the higher-level configuration does not separate live configurations on the lower level, territorial structure will. The separation has no technical or functional rationale. It is a matter of control. Territorial order maintains vertical organization where physical order leaves off.


## Large-Scale Territorial Boundaries

It is only at a scale far above the perceptible built environment that horizontal territorial relationships become unavoidable. Unlike the vertical gate connecting private and public space, gates between nations are strictly symmetrical. Goods flow over borders in both directions, regulated by customs officers. In contrast to vertical gates, under the control of a single agent who determines what comes in, horizontal gates open only when parties on both sides agree. Otherwise the boundary remains closed.

Horizontal territorial traffic between countries spawns elaborate procedures of exchange and mutual control, as well as frequent disputes. Nations may force or intimidate others to open gates: Finland, during the cold war, was in no position to refuse entry to Soviet goods. But usually gates open by mutual consent. European countries are currently involved in a prolonged process of permanently opening up borders while maintaining territorial autonomy.

But to return to the experiential scale of place, far removed from the scale of nations: built form reinforces equilibrium where people settle together. At the scale of human inhabitation, territory serves to segregate what physical form leaves open.

Chapter 8

# Observing Territorial Structure

## Territory Varies with Form

Territorial inclusion is remarkably consistent throughout varied physical circumstances. Environmental form, in all its richness and variety, always interprets the same basic set of territorial principles. The following illustrations compare two very different examples.

## Row House Urban Tissue

The European bourgeois row house runs the gamut from thirteenth-century French bastide towns, to Dutch seventeenth- and eighteenth-century canal towns, to terraced residential districts of seventeenth- and eighteenth-century England. Basically, each individual house gives onto a single, uninterrupted public space comprising all streets, squares, and canals. The urban territorial structure of these environments is simple.

The spatial hierarchy characterizing street networks on the urban level is clearly distinct from its remarkably flat territorial structure. Urban space exhibits pronounced hierarchy. In Amsterdam, there are the major canals, major streets perpendicular to them, and secondary streets running alongside canals. It would seem reasonable to assume that, paralleling hierarchy observed in the order of form, secondary streets constitute a lower territorial level. Yet no evidence supports this.

On the other hand, clear street and neighborhood territories that have no formal indi-

**8.1** Territorial Structure in Different Environments

**8.1** *Paris, 1739—Detail from the "Turgot Map" by Louis Bretez, showing buildings set tight along the streets. Their deep lots feature extensive rear gardens (page 142).*

cation are established throughout the built environment: it is simply understood that certain blocks, neighborhoods, or even driveways are not entered without express permission from inhabitants. In many large cities, there are some quarters into which neither police, building inspectors, nor tax collectors venture. There are urban areas in which shopkeepers must pay scheduled "protection" fees to local gangsters or be driven out. Local enforcement, formal or informal, establishes territorial depth within broader urban fabric.

Territorial interpretations of house form vary greatly. Included territories created by acts of dwelling do not correlate to any specific house form. The lower end of the territorial structure may be far more diverse than the form initially suggests. In the Dutch canal house, for example, we commonly observe a basement entrance; when not used by upstairs inhabitants for warehousing or other commercial activities, the basement frequently becomes an independent shop or dwelling. The building then contains two or more noncommunicating stacked territories, each directly related to the street (figure 8.2).

The house, although built as a single configuration, lends itself to varied territorial use. Thus built form is an accumulation of acts of building followed by acts of inhabitation: the making of territory follows and interprets the creation of form.

In another Dutch variant, a rear house is accessed via a small alley between the original house and the lot line, as portrayed in Ver-

**8.2** Amsterdam—Canal house, showing three separate entrances: to the main house, to an upstairs dwelling, and to a basement dwelling.

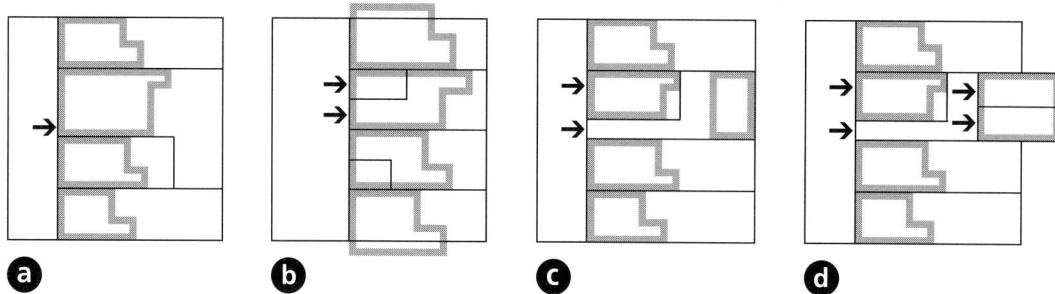

**8.3** *Varying territorial interpretations of the row house:*

*(a) A single house is a single territory.*

*(b) A single house is not a single territory.*

*(c) The back house with access to the street exists at the same territorial depth as the other houses.*

*(d) The back house comprises two territories with a common entry garden. The back house is consequently at a deeper territorial depth than houses on the street.*

meer's *A Street in Delft*. There exist two territories on the same level, each maintaining direct access to the street (figure 8.3c). However, the narrow dead-end alley may access two back houses on adjacent lots, in which case territorial depth increases: the alley now provides public space for the two back houses. Since it can be shut off from the street with a door, the alley itself is private space relative to the street (figure 8.3d).

Within the house, we earlier noted a lack of isomorphism in the relationship between built form and fluid territory, the latter being established by people and their furniture in relation to fireplace, window, alcove, and the like. While we may generally categorize entrance halls and stairs as minimal public space for inhabitants, we also note that individual territorial situations are in fact quite variable. There may be no obvious physical signs of a highly complex reality.

## Traditional Middle Eastern Tissue

In comparison with European row house urban tissue, spaces within traditional Middle Eastern urban environment display deeper territorial structure. The historic quarter of Tunis shows dead-end streets with their own gates. A number of individual houses are reached via each of these streets. In this way, bi-level territory is firmly established within urban space.

**8.4** *Tunis Medina—Urban fabric with superimposed house plans. The first territorial level is indicated, showing hole-in-the-wall shops, houses entered directly from the streets, and territories constituting a dead-end street together with those houses accessed from it. Note that the house bounded by the rue de la Kasba and the rue des Tamis connects to two impasses, Bou Machem and la Paysanne. This is an example of territorial overlap. Base map courtesy of the Association Sauvegarde de la Medina, Tunis.*

The houses themselves, like many courtyard house types, are almost perfect territorial forms in plan (see also figure 17.4). The courtyard is entered through a gate, from a street or dead-end alley. Individual rooms cluster around it. The courtyard reads as the public space of the house's territory. Each room comprises a wide and shallow private space, with three niches large enough to hold a bed, couch, or bench: one directly opposite the door is recessed into a deeper zone that also offers storage spaces; the other two are located to the right and the left of the door. These niches echo the courtyard pattern: the relatively public center of the room is surrounded by privacies.

In Tunisian urban space, shops give directly onto streets, thus occupying the same territorial level as dead-end streets. Courtyard houses may also find themselves on this level (see figure 8.4). The same forms—in this case, courtyard house or shop—generally recur on very different territorial levels. Again, there is no rigid isomorphism in the relation between form and territorial structure.

A cursory comparison of Dutch and Tunisian tissue demonstrates how differently territorial structure and urban form may relate. Within a flat urban territorial structure, historic Amsterdam's canal house form functions like a well-articulated container. Because it reflects no predetermined territorial model, it easily accommodates a range of lower-level territorial situations. Courtyard house environment, as typified in Tunisia, exhibits more depth in the urban spaces, while the houses are very territorial in form. It is hard to see how occupancy can deviate very much from a predetermined territorial interpretation.

The Tunisian example is, indeed, an almost immediate reflection of the act of inhabitation. Its lack of overarching geometric form suggests bottom-up growth. Dwellings come first, leaving open public space to be formed as density increases.[1]

In general, the Middle Eastern form is more "territorial" throughout, while the European model seems more governed by geometry and building structure.

## Party Walls and Territorial Boundaries

Walls between neighbors are another aspect worthy of comparison. In the Middle Eastern tradition, abutters frequently cooperate in shared party walls. Whoever builds first must be prepared to accept and accommodate the neighbor's beams in what then becomes a common wall.[2] In terms of form hierarchy, the total configuration of party walls within the block becomes a higher-level form. Whereas in Olynthus a similar higher-level structure was premeditated and built in one intervention, the higher-level common courtyard wall structure in the Middle East typically arises out of many cumulative individual acts.

In the western European row house tradition, shared party walls are unknown. As early as the medieval bastide towns, each house has its own load-bearing walls just within the territorial lot line. Walls are thus doubled, perhaps just a hand's width apart, to allow water collection from both roofs. This reflects a predetermined territorial structure of lot divisions. It allows live configurations to transform freely within their territorial boundaries. Each building may be independently erected or demolished. Interaction, interference, and negotiation between neighbors are thus kept to a minimum during the building process.

Such different approaches to building party walls reflect profound differences in conceiving the environment. The western European model accommodates separate acts of settlement, utilizing a geometric structure that includes house lots. It creates a predetermined framework of relatively shallow territorial depth. The Middle Eastern model, devoid of predetermined geometry, recognizes only the act of settlement and produces over time a relatively deep territorial structure.

Externally, one is a form containing settlement; the other is settlement generating form. Inside the houses, however, the reverse holds true. There, the courtyard house form lends structure to minor acts of settlement, while the canal house leaves settlement to create its own order.

## 8.2 Urban Form as Territorial Form

### Paris, 1736

The Turgot map of Paris (figure 8.1) portrays an environment in which most buildings are about five stories high, about as high as people could climb every day. Continuous perimeter walls at each street's edge define urban blocks. Public space is minimal: even the extensive Jardin de Luxembourg is entirely removed from view behind high buildings and walls. It does not participate in the public environment.

Within discrete blocks are found precursors of the Parisian communal courtyards. The fabric is typical of a high-density urban environment. Streets are of minimal width, even though they must serve all of the teeming territories behind the façades.

Such crowded, narrow streets may be deceptive: toward the edge of the city, buildings retain their height and remain situated right at the street edge proper. But there we find much lower density, for the buildings have extensive backyards—primarily for agriculture, sometimes fashioned as pleasure gardens.

Further into the outskirts, within the *faubourgs,* houses appear only intermittently. Yet they still crowd the street, even when fronting expansive cultivated fields. Moreover, the fields are walled in. Even there, public space is rigorously separated from private outside space. Green space is always private.

### Buildings on the Edge

Thus, buildings were developed with many stories, even when their large lots were sparsely developed. This may signify that land was slated for other purposes—for growing vegetables and fruits; for raising sufficient animals to feed a large city, thereby maintaining its autonomy. But buildings that always stand at the street edge, jealously guarding open space beyond, clearly adopt an assertively territorial stance toward public space.

The minimal public space of the streets and squares was lively and crowded. Accordingly, ground-floor space along street frontage was predominantly earmarked for commercial and work space. Domestic space was concentrated more inside and upstairs. Public space was also dangerous, uncontrolled, and dark at night, a place to separate from the more peaceful and regulated private realm in which all inhabitants were known and specifically admitted.

## Dutch Townscape

For millennia, jealously guarded private open space behind buildings and walls, creating a walled-off domain, was typical of urban form throughout the world, regardless of population density.

In historic Dutch cities, we find that although the urban network of public space, with its canals lined with trees, is more generous, most open space remains invisible from the streets or canals. Despite sixteenth- or seventeenth-century Delft's unmistakably urban character, population density may well have been lower than that of a modern Dutch suburb or garden city.[3]

Space is used differently in contemporary urban environment. The proportion of public space is larger, no doubt because of the car. In addition, private exterior space is displayed publicly. Historically, there was no point to setting back a building: front yards were, for all practical purposes, useless.

## When Territory Precedes Form

The eighteenth-century *Complete Map of the Capital City during the Qianlong Era* reveals an urban structure in Beijing based on walled-in compounds that are accessed through clearly articulated gates (see also figure 5.8). The wall,

**8.5** *Beijing, ca. 1750—Detail of the* Complete Map of the Capital City during the Qianlong Era, *showing main street and residential streets. Most of the latter have gates. Ceremonial gates are seen at the crossing of two main streets. Houses typically exhibit an entrance court followed by one or more courts, each having pavilions at three sides. Reproduced courtesy of the Harvard-Yenching Library.*

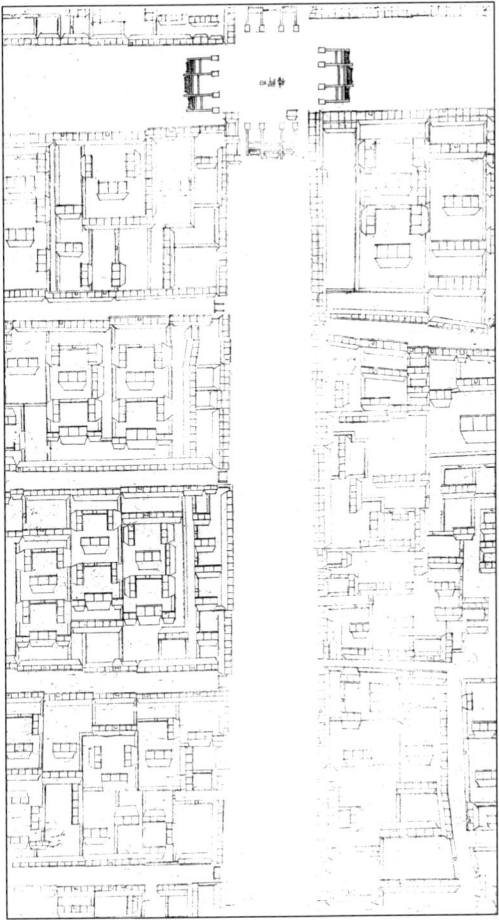

151

a primarily territorial demarcation, stands on its own, initially defining the compound within which pavilions, under separate roofs, are then arranged to form a sequence of courtyards. Whereas in the Tunisian fabric (figure 8.4), it remains ambiguous whether territory or form was there first, in Beijing territorial demarcation preceded the buildings.

Large-scale environmental creation in which territory precedes form is universal and still very much alive. We find walled territory in urban compounds in the informal sectors of Latin American cities (see figure 5.9). There, too, settlers first build walls around their territory, with a gate to the street.[4] In warm and dry climates like those of Mexico and Peru, it suffices for a family to live inside the walls with just a primitive shack to sleep in. Gradually, a large two-story house with several courtyards emerges.

Comparing the maps of Tunis and Beijing reveals another difference in the relationship of territorial structure to hierarchy of form. Within the Tunisian fabric, territorial depth is found in the street system as well: dead-end streets shared by a handful of houses will have their own gates giving onto the network; secondary streets may have gates toward major streets. Whether individual houses have a single courtyard or many, territorial depth is found only between a courtyard and its surrounding rooms.

In the Chinese model, territorial depth within the compound can be extensive: courtyard after courtyard after courtyard may be arranged hierarchically, sometimes connected by alleys. In the street network, territorial depth is implied by the existence of gates at the entrances of the alleys and at some intersections of the streets.[5]

## 8.3 House and Territory

### Overlap of Form and Territory

House types do not necessarily represent any specific social entity. They therefore cannot be equated with any specific territorial interpretation. Thus, the Dutch canal house demonstrates how the row house, although typically a single-family bourgeois dwelling, can accommodate different occupation. Nor does this diversity necessarily result from change of use over time: some seventeenth-century duplex canal houses have two original façade doors, one of which leads to an upstairs dwelling.

Such variation is not limited to residential uses. Within one building type we find shops, bakeries, and many other residential-scale commercial activities. These patterns of variable use and occupancy may occur anywhere and are not limited to a particular house type. The Pompeiian courtyard house, although oriented inward, for commercial purposes consistently opened rooms onto busy streets (see figure 15.2). While the suburban house type and fabric do not typically support pedestrian storefront service retail activity, a building suggesting single-family use may in fact hold two or more households, or, more commonly, a business office at home.

There exists no strict parallel between the social unit of a certain culture and any one house form, although some relationship clearly exists. The first purpose of the Chinese courtyard compound, so susceptible to expansion by erecting additional pavilions, is to shelter an extended family. The first purpose of the western European row house is to enable dwelling by a single family.

Variations of territorial and functional interpretation within such general themes suggest that house form results above all from conventional acts of building repeated in thematic variation, out of which urban fabric is also woven. Such thematic variation is related, not surprisingly, to the social structure that brings it forth. Building types commonly associated with housing do not so much represent dwellings as forms created to accommodate common patterns of occupancy, with which given social groups specifically identify.

Dwelling, as already argued, is a territorial act of occupation. It may involve a space smaller than a house: the boarder's dwelling is a room. House building, on the other hand, is a form-making act within acquired territory. The resulting house form always remains open to territorial interpretation.

Extreme changes in social organization following initial occupancy may trigger unforeseen variations. In a detailed study of nineteenth-century courtyard houses in Santiago de Chile, Fernando Domeyko records deliberate reordering to establish clear new territorial demarcation, permitting higher density. The house, initially built for a prosperous extended family, has now become a small village, occupied by a number of working-class nuclear family households. The territorial organization so clearly suggested by the courtyard form is scrupulously retained. But private rooms around the courtyard are now clustered in twos and threes by small front patios carved out of the larger courtyard. Public space remaining in the courtyard is reduced to an alley.[6]

**8.6** *Santiago de Chile—Partial view of a turn-of-the-century house with two successive courtyards. The house is shown as presently occupied by several families. Inhabitants have fenced off parts of the courtyards to make private yards, leaving a narrow public alley in the central axis. The house is thus transformed into a little village, known as the "Cité Knossos." After Domeyko.*

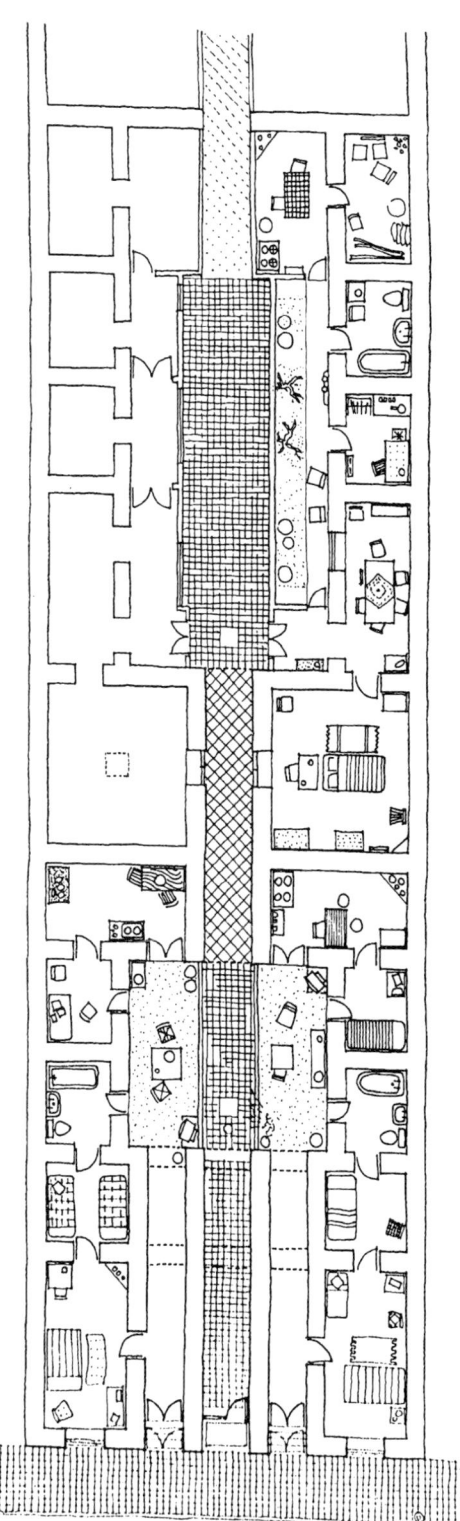

155

This example, while extreme, is by no means an exception. Once form is present, life makes use of it, adjusting it and adjusting to it, offering ever-changing territorial interpretations within its relative constancy.

Similarly drastic changes are observed in affluent residential neighborhoods of Cambridge, Massachusetts, as grand Victorian mansions set in substantial gardens are converted into condominiums. They still accommodate only those who can afford to dwell comfortably near the center of the city; new entrances are created at sides and rear to provide private access. These houses are subdivided vertically and horizontally, offering stacked dwellings front and back as well as one or two beneath the eaves. The backyard is now a communal parking area that provides access to multiple dwellings in the house, increasing territorial depth.

type its name and developed its characteristic architecture of wooden columns and banisters, sometimes elaborately carved.

Mansion conversions like those in Cambridge have more recently provided an image for new construction. Large "houses" recalling single-family mansions are now designed to contain a number of smaller dwellings from the start. In Europe in the 1920s and 1930s, there similarly emerged "two-under-one-roof" houses. Such duplexes share a party wall and a single roof, with entrances and garages at opposite ends, recalling the familiar single-family house form. This further supports the notion that house form is one convention, occupation another.

## Territorial Conversion

Territorial interpretation of a given form may lead, in turn, to new forms: following a massive influx of workers into nineteenth-century Amsterdam, its fabric was extended (see figure 4.4c). The new neighborhoods contained buildings that retained the width and height of the canal house. But each floor became a separate dwelling, connected to the street via a communal staircase. Although the architecture was reductive and the technical quality was poor, this variant could be understood as the final transformation of a historic building type.

The Bostonian single-family gabled urban house with porch, set on a narrow lot, was transformed into the "triple-decker" type still in evidence throughout surrounding cities. Here too, each floor became a separate apartment with its own porch. Stacked porches gave the

## 8.4 Public Space

### Use vs. Control of Space

A living room may be under the firm control of a single family member, or it may be controlled more implicitly by communal consensus. In either case, it follows that those who use the space—children, friends, and guests—need not be in control of it.

Public space is, by definition, space used by those who do not individually control it. Users of public space may come from either included or higher-level territory. Entering the public realm from private space is a fundamental right: the door to public space is always open, and there must always be a public space we can move out to. In doing so, one is still on "home turf": public space is communally shared among those from similarly included territories. Household members access and share the living room. Residents in a development may share clubhouse privileges. Further up the territorial hierarchy, that sense of proprietorship fades. Yet interstate highways in the United States, as well as the Mall in Washington, D.C., are spaces held in common by all American citizens.

Public space is also used, without exercise of control, by those admitted from outside, who have a different attitude than those entering from included territory. The outsider enters from another (higher-level) public space as a guest. There always remains some possibility that entry will be barred to the neighbor, the out-of-towner, or the foreigner. Use from outside is specifically granted, and temporary in nature.

## Use of Space and Contents

Once entered into public space, by right or by admittance, one is free to walk in public parks, enter public museums, drive public roads, sit on public benches, and use, for a fee, public phones. In addition to using space, we also use things. To a certain extent, we can actually manipulate configurations we do not control, just as we can enter a space we do not control. But there are clear limitations. The house guest is invited to sit in a chair, perhaps to pick up a magazine, but is not expected to rearrange or remove furniture. With respect to actual physical transformations, the visitor is given little leeway.

Control of things is an immediate, hands-on affair. In the Parisian Jardin des Tuileries, visitors may sit in iron garden chairs arranged around the pond. But a fee is exacted for this privilege, by a matron who continually restores the arrangement as each visitor departs. The park constitutes a large public space, but the circle of chairs is the matron's configuration, as she will pointedly inform you.

We move "upward" to use spaces of increasingly "public" character in the order of place. But to use and manipulate things, we move downward into the territory of the person in direct control: a person who is actually there. The unhappy fate of uncontrolled telephone booths and public toilets offers proof that this territorial reality cannot easily be denied.

**8.7** *Cambridge, Massachusetts—Triple-decker house.*

## Claiming Territory through
## Use of Space

The use of things occurs at the scale of the body. It inevitably implies occupancy of sufficient space—an instant territory, however temporary and transparent—to exercise this use.

Configurations do not float freely in space; and control implies territory. Thus control of a configuration simultaneously implies a territorial claim. The subway musician stands against a pillar and places a hat in front of her. People respect the claim and maintain a distance, entering her space sporadically to toss a coin. The hawker admitted into the flea market must be granted a corner to display his wares. The traditional market exhibits instant territorial arrangements in town squares throughout the world. Many temporary territories are included for only a few hours, a cyclical increase and decrease of territorial depth that in some towns has gone on for centuries. In the living room, we see the same phenomenon: when books or toys are brought to occupy a corner or a couch, some depth is added to the territorial situation of a communal space.

The human body implies territorial presence. Therefore, being in a public space is partaking in a game of instant territorial reconfiguration, shifting as people use things: sitting on benches, waiting for buses, parking cars, entering telephone booths, standing by the sidewalk. A game of fleeting spatial claims and territorial inclusions follows the flow of use within the contextual setting of a given public space.

160

**8.8**  *Jogjakarta, Indonesia—Sidewalk barber.*

Chapter 9

# Territory and Buildings

## 9.1 Street and House

### The Suburban Yard

The mansion standing free in its own estate may offer some visual connection with the public road. But the space between is open land. Even when landscaped, it is not shaped to extend either house or street. The entry gate marks the territory, not the house: the territorial claim is quite separate from the building. Sometimes there is only a post or a stone to indicate a boundary.

The suburban house (figure 9.2a) bears witness to a somewhat more spatial, architectural engagement. Street and house keep their distance, but stand in close enough proximity to provide a certain tension between the built form inside a larger territory and the public space outside that territory. The suburban front yard is the mediating space in between: the property of the inhabitant but open to the street, contributing to the public realm. Houses are separated just enough to be perceived as individual forms, and set back just enough to create a sense of independence.

"Suburban" aptly describes this arrangement. In a fully urban environment, building and street are closely married: the façade forms part of a street wall, at the edge of domestic territory. In the suburb, that street wall is dissolved and a front yard mediates between house and territorial boundary. An architectural complement to the dignity of the public realm is sometimes preserved in the way the entryway or façade addresses the street. But bungalows and ranch houses typically seek to deny the closeness of the street, appropriating imag-

**9.1** *Venice, ca. 1339—Detail of map by Jacopo de Barbari (page 162).*

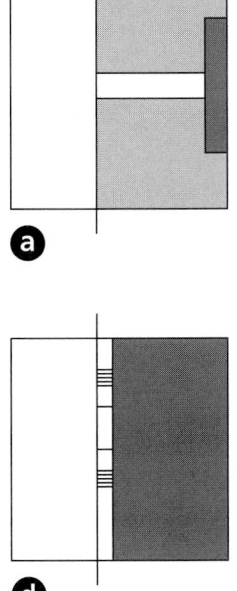

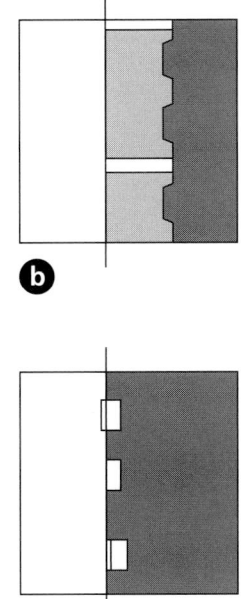

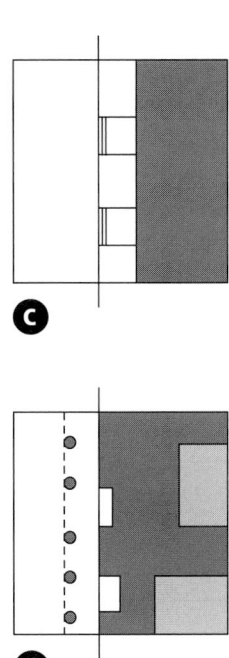

165

ery to suggest a freestanding cottage in the wilderness.

## The Urban Yard

As we move from the suburb toward the city (figures 9.2b and 9.4a), the distance between building and street decreases, until the diminished front yard requires architectural reinforcement to sustain itself as a strip of nature between house and street. Victorian houses of Boston's Back Bay, for instance, have front yard depths of at most fifteen feet—just large enough to plant a tree and maintain a few feet of lawn between shrubs at the foundations and those along the street. Assertion of the ter-

**9.2** The relation of territorial boundary to building (vertical lines extending beyond the square indicate the territorial boundary):

(a) The suburban house in its garden.

(b) Urban houses fronted by narrow gardens, forming a street wall.

(c) The British terraced house with an "area" between sidewalk and building.

(d) The Dutch canal house with a zone for stoops between pavement and building.

(e) Perfect coincidence of territorial boundary and building façade.

(f) Northern Italian arcades, such as those in Bologna, with the territorial boundary located behind the line of the façade.

**9.3** *Kampong near Jogjakarta, Indonesia—House in sub-urban setting in a kampong with fence between public and private space.*

ritorial boundary now becomes necessary: the street is too close and the small strip of yard too vulnerable. Hence, in the Back Bay, low walls with iron railings, together about knee-high, are found along the sidewalk. They form a modest but essential architectural element.

Because these fences are similar in composition and uniform in height, they form a continuous element, de-emphasizing the individuality of the houses, joining them in response to the street. Jointly, the fences define the sidewalk as much as they demarcate individual yards.

In this configuration, house façades begin to merge into a street wall. The Back Bay street wall is particularly successful in that it is formed with bay windows. While their widths may vary, their projection beyond the façade and into the yards is always the same, such that they too are perfectly aligned in plan.[1] In this

way, the street wall, standing behind the shallow front yards with their greenery, undulates but remains anchored to urban geometry.

## The Six-Foot Yard

The urban front yard (figure 9.4b) of limited dimension is found in endless variation in the nineteenth- and twentieth-century city. Some five or six feet of separation between garden gate and house door are sufficient to evoke the presence of a garden. Demarcation of the territorial boundary becomes essential to preserve the garden's integrity. Boundary forms vary from slender three-foot iron fences to elaborate combinations of masonry wall and railing. In Holland, citizens commonly keep boundary forms low, to preserve a view of the street from the living room.

**9.4** *Distances between public space and building in an urban setting:*

*(a) Boston Back Bay, nineteenth century—Narrow front yards with buildings aligned in a continuous wall.*

*(b) Apeldoorn, the Netherlands—Minimal front yard with low iron fence and freestanding house.*

*(c) London—The "area" of an English terraced house, showing the bridge from the sidewalk to the main floor and steps down to basement floor.*

*(d) Amsterdam—Canal house stoops.*

### The Georgian Terrace

Urban infrastructure in Georgian terraced housing (figures 9.2c and 9.4c) elevates the street with fill cut from house lots. The front sidewalk is a few steps below the main floor; the rear garden is roughly at basement level. In front of the house is the "area": several yards of space between house and sidewalk, through which light and narrow steps descend to the basement. A bridge over the area connects main entry to street, linking territorial edge to built space.

Iron railings protect pedestrians from the private depth below, adding to the unique elaboration of the margin between house and public space. This pattern sets the house only a few paces from the sidewalk. The entry door, at the end of the bridge, is often framed by a pediment and columns. The whole exhibits a certain friendly detachment but remains unmistakably urban.

### A Four-Foot Masonry Margin

The essence of urban architecture is how it negotiates the narrow margin available between territorial boundary and building façade. In the Amsterdam canal house (figures 9.2d and 9.4d), the main floor is raised four or five feet above street level. Thus the entry is approached via a half-flight of stairs. (The water table is only a few feet below the pavement.) When the basement is used for warehousing goods, these are brought in via a steep half-flight of steps hidden under bulkheads, at street level.

All of these elements occupy a four-foot margin between façade and street. This margin clearly forms part of the domestic territory. It was sometimes used to extend basement space,

a venerable tradition still occasionally in evidence today. The area in question would be paved by the home owner, frequently in costly stone, contrasting with the brick paving in the public street. The territorial boundary was often asserted by small granite columns, sometimes connected with iron chains, placed four feet from the façade.[2]

### The Minimal Yard

Six to eight feet is probably a reasonable limit for retaining the identity of the garden between house and street. Yet in Japan, a small tree and some shrubs may be wedged between a territorial wall and the house two or three feet behind it, to hide ground-floor windows. The symbolically not-quite-urban house alludes to affluence and freedom. With such a strong configurational meaning, dimensions become secondary: as long as the proper elements are there, in the proper relationship, the image and the message are conveyed.

### The Courtyard House

When territorial boundary and house wall do coincide (figure 9.2e), a certain tension is lost. The streets of Roman Pompeii and Greek Delos give us examples of such isomorphism. Middle Eastern townscapes such as Tunis are similarly walled in. The street becomes an enclosed space devoid of civic expression beyond occasional recessed house gates, with perhaps a small sculpted seat near the doorway. There are no architectural façades, just unadorned walls. Windows are few, appearing at the second floor.

Such walled-in streets suit the introverted nature of the courtyard house, which requires no light from the public space. Pedestrians move inside a long continuous form, rather than past individual buildings. The street comes alive only where shops and work places open toward it, where sounds and goods spill out into the sunny public space from dark holes in the wall.

## Lines Crossing: The Arcade

The convergence of built form and territorial boundaries allows further variety in relations between the two. The porticoes of medieval and Renaissance cities like Bologna and Padua reveal a pattern in which houses are built above the sidewalk, supported by columns and vaults (figure 9.2f; see also figure 14.4). Together, they form a shaded walkway sandwiched between a bright public street and bright gated courtyard. Here, the lines actually cross, locating the territorial boundary behind the building's upper-level façade and allowing public space to penetrate the building on the ground floor, where gates inside the arcades open onto domestic courtyards.

## Varying Form within Fixed Territory

Form is interpreted in different ways, and different occupation and territorial boundaries result. As a rule, form is generally more stable than its territorial interpretation. However, given a fixed territorial structure, different forms can be placed in it. Accordingly, all diagrams in figure 9.5 represent identical territorial organization: within a territory $A$, two lesser territories $B$ are included.

In examples (b) and (c), building forms lie within the territory $B$ and constitute part of it. This is the most common form of either the freestanding house (c) or the townhouse with its own party walls (b).

In (d), the house is owned by an absentee landlord and therefore lies outside the control of the inhabiting territorial power $B$.

Example (e) has a shared party wall. Neither $B1$ nor $B2$ can control that wall independently; hence a third power constituted by $B1$

# 9.2   Territory and Building

**9.5**   *A single territorial diagram representing varied buildings and uses:*

*(a) Initial territory diagram without buildings.*

*(b) Abutting houses with blind walls.*

*(c) Freestanding houses in gardens.*

*(d) House as in (c) above, when rented by occupant.*

*(e) Houses with a common party wall.*

*(f) Houses as in (e) above, when rented by occupants.*

*(g) A single building within which apartments are rented.*

and $B_2$ together is in control of it. Other than that, the two $B$ powers control their own houses.

In (f), the whole duplex house is under control of an absentee landlord. Territorial powers $B$ do not control any part of it.

Finally, (g) represents a housing estate in which both the building and the surrounding landscape are controlled by a housing authority, $A$. Renters $B$ merely control space within the building.

In (d) and (f), the property owner is not an agent in the given territorial context. Therefore, we have three territorial powers—$A$, $B_1$, and $B_2$—as well as another new agent controlling the form.

Thus, the environmental game is played in a variety of ways. Various built forms and variable control distributions may go with the same territorial structure. The building can operate in either territorial depth ($A$ or $B$) but also can be controlled by outside agents.

171

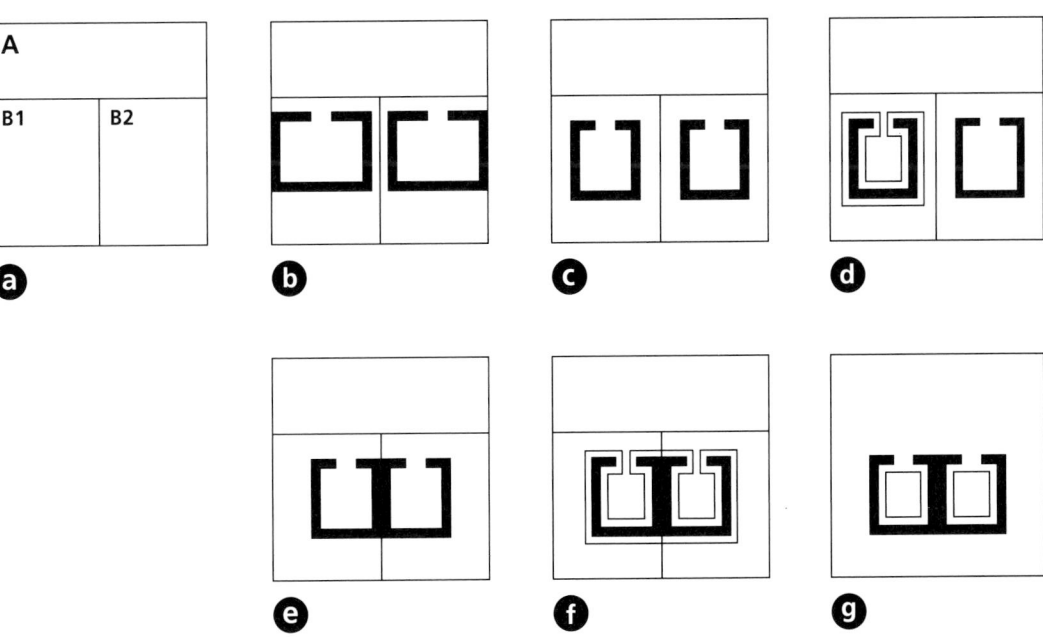

## 9.3    Within the City Block

### Varying Territorial Structure

The common organization of city blocks places buildings that ring the street perimeter shoulder to shoulder. They thus form a continuous street wall and an internal open space invisible from the street. The arrangement of this internal open space and its connection to the street network merits scrutiny: to a large extent, they determine the character of urban fabric.

The pictograms in figure 9.6 represent a minimal arrangement of this form: for purposes of diagramming, four territories coincide with four houses. (In reality, many more houses compose a block.) Differences observed all have to do with the way space inside the block is treated. Together, the series of emblematic pictograms allows for discussion of numerous generic situations in territorial structure.

In the most common version of (c), we find alleys several feet wide connecting to backyards. The alley is handy for bringing bicycles into a back shed; and it provides a much-appreciated way for children to visit from backyard to backyard. Unless the alley is gated (d), it is territorially part of the general public space,

**9.6** *Territorial variations on the urban block—Pictograms diagramming houses around a block. All have access to the surrounding streets that form the block. Variations on the space internal to a city block can result in territorial differences.*

*(a) Territorial diagram applicable to cases (b), (c), (g), and (h).*

*(b) Internal open space is subdivided into private gardens.*

*(c) Private gardens have access to a back alley, which is part of the public street network.*

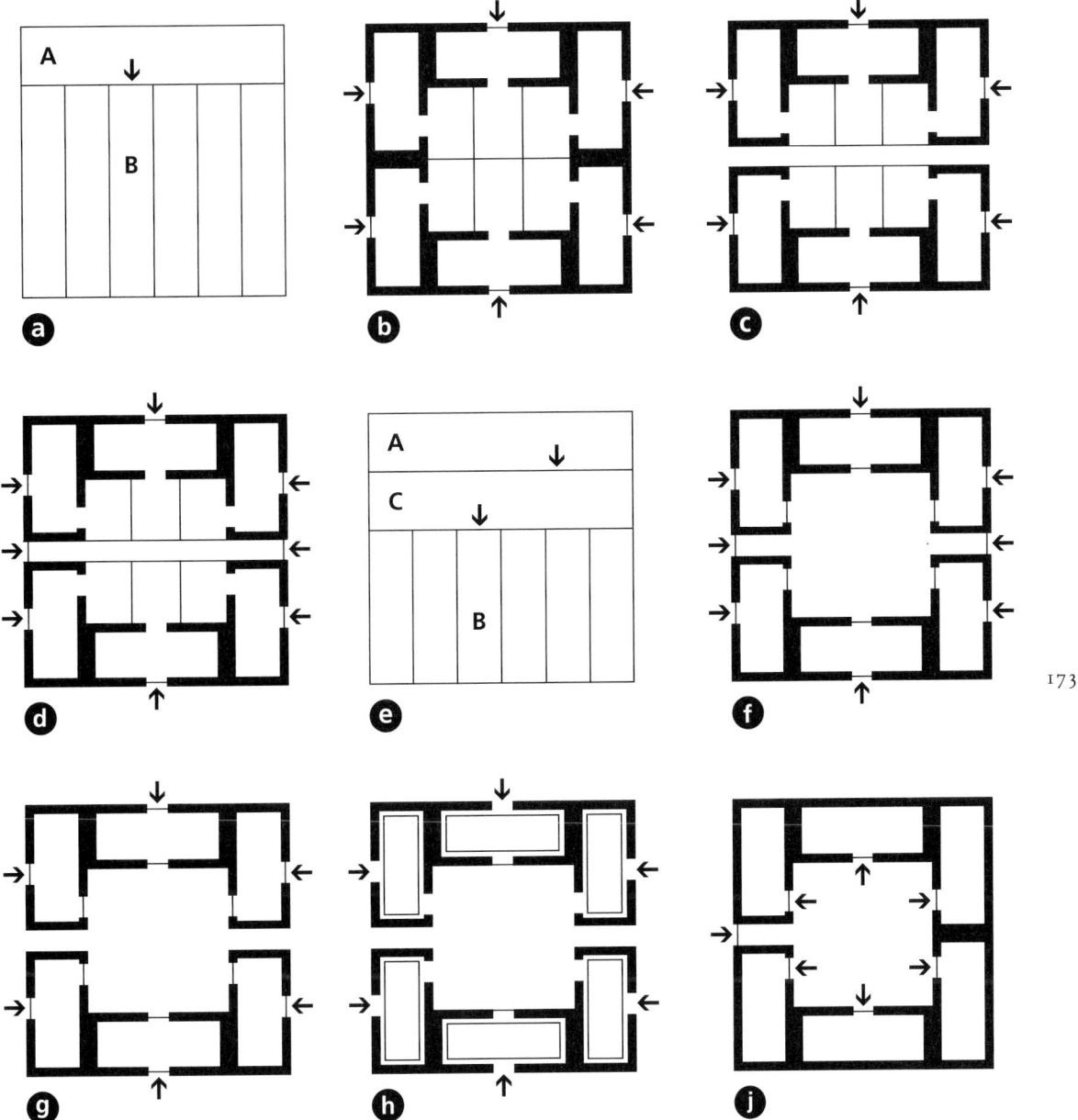

(d) The back alley, when gated, becomes a public space for the surrounding houses.

(e) Territorial diagram applicable to (d) and (f)—provided that depth is traced through the backyard—and to (j).

(f) Private gardens are merged in a single gated communal yard.

(g) Private gardens are merged in a single ungated communal yard.

(h) Houses are rented from a party who controls both the buildings and their communal yard.

(j) The communal yard forms a courtyard between house and street.

on a par with the streets. There exists only one territorial depth (a), while in terms of form we find perhaps three levels—street, secondary street, and alley.

## Dual Orientation

In (c) and (d), house territory manifests dual orientation. Public space may be entered by two gates: one at the street, another at the alley. Because alley and street are so different in character, a potentially ambiguous environmental structure remains clear and thus disorientation is avoided. As a result, the scheme is eminently workable. Dual orientation of house territory need not be confined to the narrow alley. More elaborate and sophisticated examples can be noted.

In British terraced housing, the *mews* was specifically designed to provide access to carriage houses built in back of private yards.[3] From the outset, servants' quarters were also

found in buildings at the mews, adjacent to or on top of the stables. As society changed, outbuildings were commonly converted into or replaced by independent residential buildings. These formed their own territories back-to-back with that of the main house, thereby terminating the dual exposure of the latter. In this way, the mews became a modest and intimate residential street, in contrast to the more formal streets of the block proper.

In the Venetian urban fabric (see figure 7.2), dual orientation is more sophisticated. Houses connect to the network of canals on one side and a network of narrow streets, alleys, and squares on the other. Visitors are received with appropriate dignity on a gated landing at the ground-floor gondola mooring. Arriving from the canal, one passes under the house and up a (frequently elaborate) staircase in the middle of the house, to reach a large central, main floor space once again facing the waterway. A second stair at the back of the house connects the main floor to a courtyard. This courtyard has a gate,

**9.7** *Bath—Section showing the* mews, *a secondary street behind the main street. What used to be stables and servant quarters, accessed from the back street, have now become private houses. (After Hamdi and Edgerly). See also the partial reproduction of Edinburgh New Town, figure 18.1, for a similar situation.*

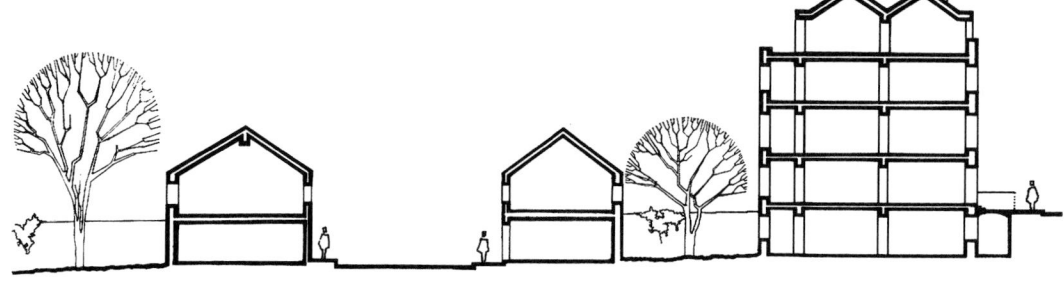

which also provides a service entry, opening onto the pedestrian street.

The two networks in the Venetian urban fabric are separate worlds, engaged with great freedom and improvisation. Pedestrians occasionally arrive at a purely urban environment of streets and squares, with no waterway in sight. Conversely, crossing a canal, or walking alongside it, may lead to a square at water's edge. There are no urban blocks whatsoever here. But the street network remains, behind and between buildings, hidden from major waterways. Houses span between the two. Only along secondary canals do water, buildings, and pedestrian space become more intimately intertwined.

In Suzhou and other cities of the Yangtze River delta, houses also mediate between waterway and street. But major streets are wide and often lined with trees. They are laid out in a more geometric pattern, accommodating horses and carts as well as pedestrians. Therefore the two realms—waterways and street network—are almost equally balanced in practical importance and in physical size. It is the street side on which the houses front formally; but at the water side, life may be equally intense.

As the case of Radburn—a modern, but less convincing model of dual orientation—seems to indicate, success in dual orientation requires differentiation between the two realms to which the house relates. In Radburn, single-family dwellings situated within their gardens front on one street with another secondary street in back. The latter, clearly intended by the urban designers as a communal space, connects to parking. It is no longer clear precisely which side of the house is the front.

The ambiguity seems as much related to form as to use. The same dual functional relation is found in traditional back alleys such

175

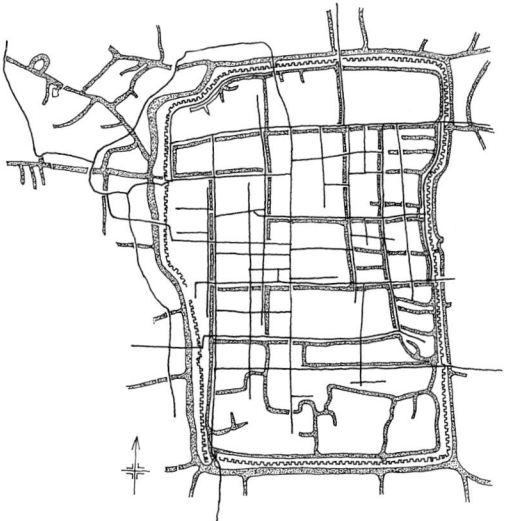

**9.8** *Suzhou, China—Diagrammatic map showing the relationship between two interwoven networks, streets and waterways. Estates and houses usually span between the two.*

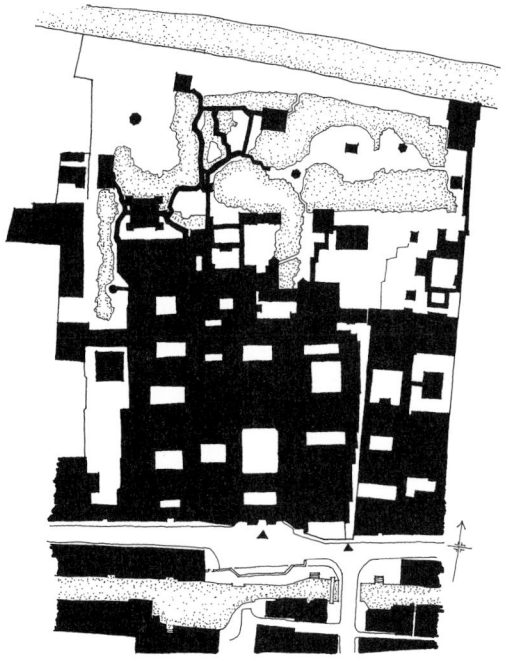

**9.9** *Suzhou, China—Waterfront. A large compound of several houses belonging to an extended family. Each house is composed around a sequence of courtyards— there are six such strings of courtyards in all—and spans between street and waterway. The triangle on the left marks the entrance to the main house; that on the right marks the gate of a narrow lane leading to the Zhuo Zheng or "Humble Administrator's" Garden (figure 10.1). On the other side of the street, modest shops also span street and water networks.*

as in Boston's Back Bay. But there, the physical distinction between the two sides is quite clearly articulated, and the front façades face a busy street. In the garden city of Radburn, any such distinctions remain minimal.

## Territorial Overlap

The back alley or service street of figure 9.6c is a straightforward extension of public space already formed by the streets. In terms of form, there exists, therefore, a tri-level street network organization: major residential street, side street, and back alley. But with respect to territorial structure, there is just one public space, with no evidence of gates or other means of closing off alleys from secondary streets or the

latter from major residential streets. For that reason, at the point where back alley reaches street space, no gate is indicated. There are now two gates from each territory of depth $B$ into the public space: one from the front and one from the back. But these two gates are equivalent, as territory goes. The territorial diagram itself does not change with the introduction of the alley.[4]

Sometimes, we do find gates at the end of the alley (d), for which only inhabitants of abutting houses have a key. This usually happens where alleys are very narrow, clearly intended to help the inhabitants reach their backyards and not at all for general access. In this case, the alley serves as another public space for the territories already included in $A$, adding another territorial level. Territory $B$ is now connected to two distinct public spaces (public relative to *B*). When *B* is entered via the back alley, it is two gates removed from *A*, whereas entering via *A* requires only one gate. Relative to *A*, territory *B* may be one or two levels deep, depending on the route we choose to reach it.

We may say that two territorial situations, those in diagrams (a) and (e), overlap in *B*. From one perspective (e), *B* lies in *C*. The alley is *C*'s public space. From another perspective (a), territory *B* lies in *A*.

Similar overlap is found when a corner house fronts a major and a minor street. If the latter exists behind a gate (as in historic Beijing), it constitutes private space relative to the major street. Yet because there are entrances on both streets, a similar territorial overlap occurs. In general, such cases of overlap are exceptions or involve physical situations of lesser significance, such as minor service alleys. (In the Middle Eastern fabric, cases of houses connecting to two different gated dead-end streets are somewhat more frequent, although by no means the rule; see figure 8.4.)

## Communal Backyard Space

Pictograms (f), (g), and (h) diagram backyards merged into larger communal space, in order to create shared space for communal activities in a more protected, less public setting than is offered by the street network. This shared space in (g) would be accessible to others coming in from the larger public domain, a situation that is clearly not as desirable as (f). Though this form suggests a more private space, its implementation in practice is rather ambiguous. In (h), communal space is actually controlled by an outside agent: a public housing authority or

municipality. Here, the houses are presumably rented, with all real estate controlled and maintained by the authority.

The outcome of such quasi-community space is seldom positive, for reasons that become readily apparent: in (g) and (h), the commitment of inhabitants living adjacent to the space can only be minimal. Successful communal space is communally controlled and maintained. Here, adjacent inhabitants are not in communal control.

In (f), the space is controlled by inhabitants who can close the gates. The design and actual use of the space may be determined collectively by inhabitants or delegates. If they are truly in control, they will have the option of carving public space up into private outdoor spaces, thus returning to model (d). Experience indicates that, given the choice, people often prefer subdivision. Either way, the scheme will work.

In all cases, the communal backyards of (f), (g), and (h) create ambiguous dual orientation and concomitant disorientation. The more pronounced the communal backyard space, the more unclear it becomes which side is more formal and important. The distinction between a formal front and a more protected and informal back is very much ingrained in territorial consciousness. Large communal space at the back weakens that distinction.

Courtyard organization, as represented in schematic (j), is an ancient form, providing more communal space between the domestic and the truly public. Both territorially and architecturally, it is unambiguous. But it represents a totally different urban type than the terraced house model that is the essence of examples (b) through (h). The courtyard turns itself away from the street. It is, generally speaking, an urban model, highly suitable for high-density, low-rise living. Yet territorially similar situations are also found in Indonesia and Africa in informal residential neighborhoods. In those cases, groups of families live in compounds behind a single gate, maintaining their own little gardens but also a communal open space. While these are not urban situations, their territorial disposition is equivalent to the one in (j).[5]

## Continuity of Territorial Depth

The final pictogram, figure 9.10, represents a shared, communal space totally separated from the street network. It occurs when the backyards of figure 9.6b become unified communal space. It is a purely theoretical design, unobserved in real life. (By its very nature, its existence would be known only to inhabitants sharing a space.) But as a rule, there is little reason for inhabitants living on four different streets to share space within a block.

Of more importance, this final scheme is anomalous because it suggests discontinuous territorial depth: its backyard public space is nowhere connected to a more public space. Coming out of the house into the shared communal space, one can only go back, but not to a more general territory. This violates territorial structure. Environmental order, regardless of its particular form, is always a continuous chain of public spaces of increasing territorial size.[6] We either go continuously up in the territorial chain, or we go continuously down. All environmental space, in fact, is one.

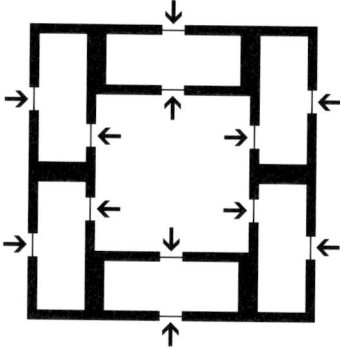

**9.10** *An anomalous territorial variation on the urban block—A communal backyard not connecting to any larger public space. This form is purely theoretical.*

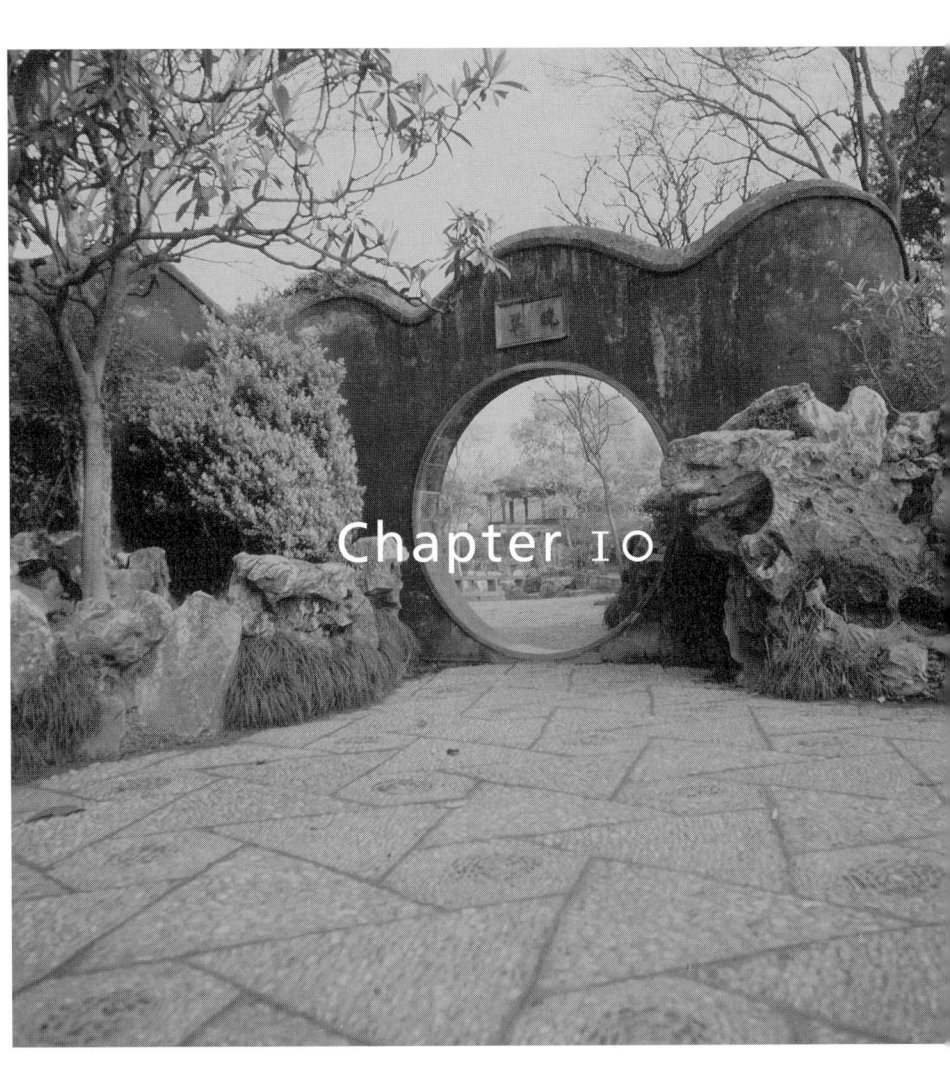

Chapter 10

# Gates

## 10.1   Seven Gates

### Territory and Form Combined

The gate simultaneously engages form and territory. It encloses and connects physically defined spaces. The way in which settlement draws boundaries will determine whether or not it has territorial meaning.

Even when the gate does not constitute an actual entrance into territory, its form conveys protection, separation, seclusion, or the beginning of another space. In the suburban house, for instance, the entry door is not the territorial gate. Nonetheless, as the entry into a home, it is sturdier, more solid than the interior doors. Even when other perimeter doors present vulnerable glazing to terrace, garden, or yard, the front door is treated as a symbol of strength and security, belying its lack of territorial function.

Exploring the roles a gate can play between form and territory reveals the multiple interactions between form of enclosure and control of space. A matrix will server to organize our inquiry, to map the range of meanings related to the gate form.

Gated space, when covered by a roof, is denoted as "inside"; otherwise, it is "outside." This terminology conveys strictly physical—nonterritorial—meaning. Combinations of "inside" and "outside" establish the three columns of the matrix. Examples, in sequence, are the exterior house door (in/out), the door between two rooms (in/in), and the garden gate (out/out).

Ambiguous situations will predictably be encountered; some interpretations that rely on conventional wisdom may prove debatable at

**10.1**  *Suzhou, China—Moon gate, Zhuo Zheng (Humble Administrator's) Garden (page 180).*

the limits of the definition. Thus, the interpretation of what constitutes "covered" space may vary. What, for instance, is one to make of the glass-covered street, the *passage* of nineteenth-century Paris, with its celebrated equivalents in Milan and Brussels? Is the exterior door opening onto a partially enclosed covered porch an inside/outside gate?

The horizontal rows correspond to three ways a gate may be territorially defined. It is either a gate with territorial meaning, or it is not. If territorial, it may establish a vertical connection (i.e., between public and private space) or a horizontal connection (i.e., between neighbors). Accordingly, nine kinds of gates can be distinguished.[1]

## Seven Gates

The top of the matrix highlights the reluctance of built environment to allow horizontal relations: two cases have not been numbered because they are extremely unlikely to occur:

Internal doors between neighbors (in/in horizontal) rarely exist. The closest environmental approximation occurs in communicating doors between hotel rooms, permitting them to be joined into a single suite. The horizontal nature of their relationship is confirmed by the presence typically of two opposing doors set within the single frame: to open passage in a horizontal territorial situation, both parties must agree. Yet the example is weak: once the doors open to create a unified suite, territorial and vertical distinctions vanish. Otherwise, the doors remain closed.

Gates or doors giving directly onto a neighbor's garden or courtyard from within one's own house (in/out horizontal) may exist here and there. But this form is neither present in any thematic way nor specifically articulated in any architecture.

The open-air horizontal territorial gate (1), however, does serve a clear purpose. The border between nations, guarded by customs agents if not by the military, is also doubled, opening only when both sides agree. On a lower level, this kind of gate is atypical and anecdotal, and it is not developed thematically. Between friendly neighbors, a garden gate or an opening in a hedge may offer unrestricted passage, particularly for children and pets. Adults may casually visit as well.

Thus, of the nine possible gates, two do not generally occur, because they destabilize environmental balance. Our world therefore knows seven gates, which seems just right.

183

**10.2** *Matrix of gates.*

|  | in/out | in/in | out/out |
|---|---|---|---|
| **horizontal territorial** |  |  | 1 |
| **vertical territorial** | 2 | 3 | 4 |
| **not territorial** | 5 | 6 | 7 |

## 10.2   Territorial Gates

### Inside/Outside, Type 2

Gate 2, leading from the outside in, crossing a vertical territorial boundary, appears to be the most straightforward example of what gates are about. Yet unambiguous residential examples, in which one passes into the building right at the boundary, are not easily found. As discussed in chapter 9.1, the territorial boundary seldom coincides exactly with the physical gate. In decidedly urban environmental fabrics such as the Amsterdam canal house, the Georgian terraced house, or the Bolognese arcade house, territorial boundaries simply do not coincide with the door or gate into the building.

Shops and zero setback townhouses, as in the eighteenth-century Paris of Turgot (see figure 8.1) do create a street wall with doors leading directly into houses, shops, and workplaces. Within that urban environment, which consistently exhibits such gates, there are also many courtyard building types, which do not: in the latter, the gate is usually of the outside/outside type.

Architecture generally recognizes both the territorial boundary and the actual gate, and creates distance, some transition zone, between them. This zone combines architectural articulation and territorial meaning. The complete coincidence of territorial boundary and gate eliminates the possibility of meaningful architectural elaboration.

Examples of such coincidence are found in the otherwise exuberant residential architecture of the Amsterdam School. In many cases, house doors are placed flat into the plane of the street wall, without mediation between public and private space. This poverty of expression is initially surprising, because the overall architecture is so highly articulated—consistently elaborated and expressively detailed at windows, corners, roofs, chimneys, and so on. But on reflection, we realize that the complete coincidence of boundaries at the door is a territorial tip-off: the architectural elaboration does not represent inhabitation. Rather, we see architects engaged in lively, but purely formal, demonstrations of design prowess.[2]

## Inside/Inside, Type 3

To label the inside/inside passage a "gate," with all of the territorial meaning that implies, does not follow common daily usage. Yet even the boarder's modest door constitutes a true territorial passage. The landlady must knock before opening it. She is not to cross its threshold uninvited. It is equally reasonable to also attach territorial meaning to a household member's bedroom door. Adolescents as well as parents have personal territories that others may not casually penetrate.

Unambiguous inside/inside vertical gates abound in the workplace. Offices along a corridor all have vertical gates. These doors have nameplates and will be closed or opened to the public as the inhabitant decides. Similarly, we see inside/inside gates in the shopping mall, where each shop abuts covered public space.

Finally, still discussing examples of type 3, we have the apartment door. Typically, there is no ambiguity: territory begins at the apartment's gate. Corridor, stairs, and elevator landing constitute public space in the building. Both public and private space are inside. Oc-

**10.3** *Amsterdam South—Amsterdam School entrance doors to apartments. The building's edge coincides exactly with its territorial boundary.*

casionally, recesses in the corridor wall may constitute private space, separating territorial boundary from actual gate.[3]

## Outside/Outside, Type 4

Doors set flat in a street wall are also found in outdoor covered spaces of courtyard houses, whether in Tunisian urban fabric, classical examples from Pompeii and Delos, Chinese compounds, or French *hôtels particuliers*. Determining whether the transition from covered passage to street constitutes an outside/outside gate will depend on the way the passage is configured as much as on individual judgment.

In Spanish colonial courtyard houses of Latin America, the *zaguán* or connecting passage provides unobstructed views between courtyard and street. The passage is perhaps a room deep. A dark space connecting two lighter spaces, it constitutes an extended gate. Indeed, the Spanish word *zaguán* denotes the entire configuration. The entrance itself is often a double wooden door, each leaf of which has a hinged wooden plank behind a single pane of etched glass. To facilitate surveillance from within, the kitchen door is often placed on axis with the *zaguán,* at the rear of the courtyard. The *zaguán* configuration allows visitors to gaze within as much as it allows inhabitants to monitor the street: an unblocked view through the pane signals that inhabitants are at home.

The Middle Eastern courtyard house, by contrast, can best be classified under type 2. Here, the passage from street to court is never straight, for reasons of privacy. Visitors turn two times before arriving in the courtyard. This transitional device reinforces the experience of leaving the street and entering a building, although the actual distance between court and street may be no more than we find in the Latin American *zaguán.*

In fact, the passage may not lead male visitors to the courtyard at all. Before reaching it, there may be a door, or a flight of stairs, leading to the room where the master of the house entertains guests and conducts business. Frequently, only relatives are allowed into the courtyard.

The classical Beijing courtyard house clearly fits in type 4. Its gate leads directly into the first courtyard, where a gate building stands in the axis of the main court. The two gates—one at the street and one between forecourt and main court—are not aligned on axis. The resulting offset prevents evil spirits from entering. The Chinese entrance gate is a beautiful example of an architectural gate in an otherwise unadorned wall. It is usually decorated and in more elaborate cases has a curved roof of its own. In rural areas, the house gate also enters directly into a yard.

Town gates throughout history may also be classified under this type. Medieval gates of smaller towns in France and Italy often stand in the axis of a major street. But there are also more elaborate examples; one may first be led into a forecourt, from which the town is entered through a second gate. Invaders who penetrate the first gate, trapped before they can proceed, can be assaulted by defenders atop the massive walls. This common ancient defensive principle shaped the Lion Gate of Mycenae and is also found in the remains of the gates of Pompeii.

However, as already noted, municipal territory generally extends beyond the town's perimeter walls, just as the estate extends territorially by virtue of its open lands. The town gate's defenses are real, but become territorial only at night, when the actual boundary withdraws to coincide with the town wall.

**10.4**  Left Bank, Paris—View from the street into a courtyard.

**10.5**  Village near Teheran, Iran—Entry gate to courtyard house. Within the entrance building a Z-shaped path ensures visual privacy for the courtyard.

**10.6**  Village near Taiyuan, Shanxi Province, China—Gate leading to the yard of a newly constructed home. From the air, scores of new rural villages in the surrounding land can be seen. All houses faithfully follow an age-old vernacular typology.

**10.7**  San Gimignano, Italy—Town gate.

## 10.3 Gates without Territorial Meaning

Doors opening onto a balcony are clearly inside/outside nonterritorial gates. A minimal interpretation of this variant is found in the "French window," a narrow double door that opens inward and leads out to a balcony, reduced in depth to no more than a foot.

Patio and garden doors are familiar renditions of the inside/outside nonterritorial gate. They mediate inside and outside living space and invite various methods of softening contrast. Awnings, vines, or trees may shade the opening. Flagstone, tile, or wooden planking may separate grass from carpet. Glazed doors, folding or sliding, may open entire wall sections.

Lack of territorial meaning may dissolve the gate form into a transition zone. In other cases, such a zone may become quite extensive, tracing a building's entire footprint, as is beautifully articulated by the overhanging eaves and the extended platform surrounding the traditional Japanese house, sitting in its own garden. Recessed paper sliding doors, combined with sliding shutters, perform the physical gate function.

This transition zone can become more and more immaterial. In Malaysia, woven bamboo screens allow the tropical breeze to pass through the house and also filter light. Here enclosure itself articulates transition, in a different way than in the Japanese house. Among the more formal pavilions is the *pendopo*, used by Javanese royalty for audiences with commoners, courtiers, and foreign dignitaries, as well as for performances of dance and music. In the shade of a large tiled roof, held up by slender wooden posts, screens have dissolved: there is only a cool tiled floor raised a few feet above ground, open to all sides. The last vestiges

**10.8** *Paris—Boulevard elevation with so-called French windows. The windows reach the floor and have double casements opening as doors behind a metal banister.*

of a gate form have disappeared. But the transition from one place to another remains unmistakable.

## Inside/Inside, Type 6

The inside/inside variant includes any household door devoid of territorial meaning. This type becomes particularly interesting when it ritualizes the uses of space. In the Victorian house, we often find pocket doors between the parlor and dining room. An opening no more than six feet wide is sufficient to make a single space out of two. The pocket doors are drawn together or apart to serve daily family life as use demands. But they also allow more ceremonial interpretation—as, for instance, when entertaining guests, the doors are thrust apart to display an artful and elaborate dinner service.

The inside/inside gate serves purely symbolic purposes. It neither responds to territorial needs nor provides shelter. In many Catholic churches, the choir screen and screens in front of chapels serve this function.[4]

## Outside/Outside, Type 7

The final type is, as much as the previous one, an invitation for architectural play and pomp. The Arc de Triomphe, adapted from the Roman ceremonial gate, clearly belongs to this type. So do many of the arbors, pergolas, and additional gate forms found in gardens solely for reasons of spatial delight.

The ancient Chinese, who mastered the subtleties of the gate form, invented the "moon gate" by making a circular opening in a garden wall. This pure and delightful expression of the nonterritorial external gate type cannot be closed, which is appropriate for a gate without territorial meaning. In making the wall continue by our feet as well as above our head, the designer lets us know that the opening enters into another world.

Chapter 11

In and Out of Territory

## II.I  Supply Form and Territory

### Interaction Between Territory and Supply Forms

The relationship between form and territory is inherent in forms of enclosure: housing compounds, halls, and rooms are defined by perimeter walls. Network forms, such as the street net that defines urban blocks, still represent enclosure forms. But at a scale larger than physical enclosure, networks and supply forms may invite territorial interpretation in their own right. In the city, real estate desirability and value increase with proximity to a metro stop or access to a freeway. In the country, we build close to highway, canal, or railway station.

Settlement adjusts to link with favorable topography: the flow of a river, solar orientation, prevailing winds, and site slope all inform territorial decisions. New development similarly sites itself to link with existing settlement infrastructures, in anticipation of tapping into access and supply lines. As new settlements develop, lines extend to feed from existing infrastructure, which is itself extended.

Connections to nearby supply forms are inevitable. In formal development, roads, sewage lines, water, gas, and communications are made available right after lots are subdivided and put up for sale. But at the informal fringes of the urban world, territorial decisions occur well in advance. Settlers dig wells and waste pits, and tap nearby power lines illegally, while building a power base to eventually demand extension of the infrastructure. Though the time frame for the meeting of territory and supply varies greatly, the process remains the same: territorial decisions come first, in response to

*11.1*  *Chicago—Inbound approach from the highway.*
*Photo by Landslides. Printed with permission (page 192).*

many factors, including proximity to existing infrastructures of supply and transportation.

Decisions regarding supply form follow. Once territory has been decided on, the appropriate connection to existing supply systems—adding a branch at the lowest possible level to an existing tree—will somehow be achieved. Configuration and reconfiguration of dependent branches do not disturb existing supply form at higher levels.

The infrastructure of supply thus informs the establishment of territory. Territories connect to existing forms of supply, thereby triggering lower-level supply form extensions. To directly correlate supply form and territorial hierarchies remains impossible: the two exist in distinct, overlapping domains. Nor does supply form directly echo territory. As the cycle progresses, supply form must ultimately increase capacity, affecting all levels of its hierarchy.

## Crossing Territorial Boundaries

Territory is containment: the forms we control are kept within the space we control. But supply is conveyance; supply forms transport things from one territory to another. Crossing territorial boundaries in the process is, by definition, inevitable. In branching distribution from a single source or line to many, numerous boundaries are crossed.

It seems natural that the supply form should spring from a source in a greater territory, branching to distribute itself to many lesser territories. Power produced at a regional plant must eventually service every room in every building. A sewage treatment plant, conversely, must be reached from every bathroom and kitchen.

In a conceptual branching diagram, service supplies flow vertically from greater territo-ries into lesser ones. Tree forms accordingly branch out over territory. Supply form and territorial levels roughly correspond at lesser levels of territorial structure. Sewage pipes, telephone lines, and power lines run from the house into the street, then toward major branches in presumably greater territorial space. Just as horizontal crossings between neighboring territories are avoided in built environment, so similar territorial caveats apply to establishing permanent cross-links between utility lines occurring at the same level.

Supply lines that traverse private lots may come from easements controlled by public or private utility companies, which are protected by law. Utilities need not be owned by the municipality that controls the public space they use, but they are of necessity granted some spatial control within territories they do not own. Thus, changes in control would not be synchronous with branching, even if supply form did physically echo territorial form (which in fact it seldom does).

Ideally, changes at each level of supply form hierarchy would coincide with changes in territorial depth: as we move from slender waste line to thicker stack, to still thicker house collector, to increasingly larger mains, each would correspond to a territorial level. But such isomorphic disposition of two hierarchies simply does not reflect reality: supply form hierarchy is determined by technology. The capacity of pipes, lines, and cables is one thing; the territorial depth they operate in is another. Control distribution over the supply form is yet a third independent factor. Nor are supply nodes coincident with territorial boundaries. Urban residential water lines commonly connect to the main under the street, not at the boundary of private lot and public space.

Agents in control of supply forms frequently operate in foreign territory. In other words, supply forms are commonly *foreign elements* in each territory ("foreign" relative to the territory they traverse). Utility companies claim access to the spaces where these elements are found. At the regional and municipal level, contracts, laws, and regulations protect the supply form from threats of interference throughout the various territorial jurisdictions in which it must reside.

The power distribution line that runs to the building is owned by the electricity company, up to the distribution panel. Only after compulsory inspection and approval of the internal installation (and its installer) may private manipulation of the form be permitted at the deepest levels of the private building.

As technology becomes more foolproof and as a globally networked citizenry becomes more technologically savvy, such authority is shifting. Thus, Dutch and American telephone companies have finally relinquished control of telephone lines and systems within the building. The user now freely strings together a network from a single access point, removing the utility, and any service obligation, from that deepest territory. Power, gas, and sewage systems, however, pose hazards that make the relation between technical control and territorial control more complex.[1]

Supply form and territorial structure do ultimately correlate on the scale of the small building and the street, however contrapuntal or syncopated their combined rhythm may be. But the parallels entirely disappear as scale increases. This is nothing new. In gently sloping to maintain water flow, aqueducts have crossed valleys, roads, and private estates for millennia. As part of the landscape, they operate on a scale that transcends small settlement boundaries. Even imperial Rome's geometric subdivisions of land were likewise ignored.

Large-scale utility infrastructures continue to move across and through settlements with similar autonomy. In the countryside, high-voltage power lines are strung as the crow flies: steel towers march straight across landscape, undeterred, from one horizon to the other. Where land ownership has not been consolidated under the power authority, they matter-of-factly cross lot after lot of private land, sanctioned and even invited by easements. Above a certain scale, supply forms inevitably interrupt human-size territorial structure, exhibiting true dominance by higher-level form. They do not therefore escape territorial structure but rather relate territory on a provincial and national scale.

## II.2  Supply Form and Dwelling

### High-Rise Apartment Dwelling

Territorially, the high-rise apartment building represents a neighborhood, encompassing a number of included territories. But supply form distribution does not suggest any such model, as horizontal boundaries are continually crossed. Sewage lines from an apartment commonly occur in the territory of the downstairs neighbor, running horizontally above the ceiling, toward a stack. Whenever repairs or maintenance are required, the downstairs neighbor's territory is entered; should leaks occur, her property will be damaged.[2] Central hot-water heating systems in apartment buildings also commonly run supply and return lines vertically behind the façade, looping to and from horizontal mains in the basement. Again, a single supply or return line runs across a number of territorially horizontal boundaries.

Inhabitant and professional alike still model the large apartment building conceptually as an overgrown and overcomplicated house. Therefore, these forms of deployment appear as logical as they would be in a single-family residence. But when the building is perceived to be a three-dimensional neighborhood containing a number of independent dwelling units, technological deployment differs. Thus, European hot-water heating systems were developed to serve each individual apartment from a heating unit that fits easily in a closet, providing a perfect match between territory and supply form. Distribution occurs within a single territory, and the unit is under the control of the inhabitant. Water and gas are piped from a main in a communal vertical chase that is, ideally, both an extension of and accessible to the public corridor. As this system has rapidly overtaken older alternatives, it has also turned out to be the most cost-effective solution.

Alternative systems that distribute sewage lines within the territory they serve, avoiding encroachment on downstairs neighbors, are currently being instituted experimentally in the Netherlands. Inhabitants' demands for autonomy in deciding on layout within territory, for the right to customize dwelling interiors, is providing the incentive. The new technology that makes this possible is also proving more efficient and cost-effective than current systems.

Building technology research and development to date have focused primarily on the performance of appliances and systems. Clearly, in the large building, whose structure of territorial control and inhabitation resembles that of a small neighborhood or street, the paramount issue is redistribution of control. Where this has occurred, it has also entailed rethinking a complex process of professional intervention that has been in operation for a long time.

## Row House Dwelling

The model of the traditional urban row house on its own lot offers a clear relation between supply, territory, and enclosure form. Utility supply forms run in the street or above it. Each house has its own branches. Ideally, a solitary agent within each house controls subsequent distribution.

This standard arrangement forms the basis of much of our technical and legal handling of supply forms. The house unit thus served is conceptualized not as a territory but rather as an object. Relative size and contents of the object do not substantially affect residential engineering. Nuclear or extended families, reluctant or aggressive electronics consumers, are all supplied according to generous universal rules

of thumb. As long as the house remains a single household territory, the match is near perfect. But when it behaves more like a large building containing many territories, a gross mismatch between the house and its supply forms easily comes about.

Territorial considerations sometimes override efficiency in civil engineering solutions. In the row house, downstairs bathrooms and kitchens are usually located in the center or rear of the house. Running sewer collectors across backyards along the rear façade, and simply increasing their width incrementally as total drainage volume increases, would dramatically reduce pipe lengths and diameters. Yet repairs to the sewer main would then occur at back doors, patios, decks, and gardens, necessitating territorial encroachment. Moreover, running the sewer mains horizontally across territories would create an unattractive chain of dependency among home owners.

Neighborhoods of private owners therefore readily adopt the "less efficient" solution, in which relationships between hierarchically equivalent branches are mediated through a higher-level branch occurring in public space, under control of a public authority. For example, streets in the Netherlands are generally public property under municipal control, whereas yards remain quite private. Utility companies accordingly install all lines under the street, categorically refusing to enter private territory.

In the United States, the suburban developer responsible for sewer lines and in control of both levels of form—of street and house lots—will routinely run the lines across lawns (preferring backyards to front yards, where driveways must be crossed). Even then, easements occur only at lawn's edge, where their presence constitutes a minimal territorial in-

199

fringement. In public housing schemes, however, sewage lines frequently do traverse backyards, as close to the buildings as possible, on purely economic grounds. Implicitly, the housing authority considers all backyards to fall within its own territory and will operate there with impunity whenever repairs are needed.

The conflict between territorial interests and installation costs is thus resolved in various ways, depending on the control pattern at hand.

## II.3 Limitations of Territorial Autonomy

### Continuous Foreign Elements

As we have seen, technology, economics, and situations of control all play a role when local territory is occupied by extraneous elements of infrastructure including supply systems. Such *foreign elements* may occur on all scales and need not always be damaging. A distinction must be drawn between those supply forms that spill over from neighboring territories, in defiance of horizontal boundaries, and those that belong to larger territories and serve general communal interests (or even specific local interests). The former are problematic, while the latter foreign elements may be inevitable or even desirable, constituting an integral part of environmental organization.

In apartment buildings, vertical chases for utilities are ideally positioned in public space, accessible from the corridors. In Japan, this constitutes general practice. Elsewhere, such a solution is often considered too expensive. It is also often technically possible to place all bearing structure in public space, avoiding freestanding columns within dwellings. But the increased expense of long span construction produces no sizable benefits in relation to interior articulation.

In the case of federal highways running through states and counties, there rarely exists alternative public space available on that territorial scale. Highways and the land they occupy thus must be carved out of included territories to become public space, and solutions are seldom found to the satisfaction of all involved. This holds true more generally for all infrastructures distributed throughout state, county, and municipal levels. Recent vast increases in the variety, extent, and density of supply and web forms have added a new dimension to this venerable phenomenon.

## Discontinuous Foreign Elements

Discontinuous foreign elements deliberately arrayed in diverse territories include conglomerates of subsidiary manufacturing facilities, dealerships, retail outlets, chain franchises, representatives of religious and political networks, and military bases. Such configurations of discrete and dispersed foreign elements are by definition under control of a single agent outside the territory of their location. That agent can unilaterally decide to withdraw them.

In the United States, businesses that originate elsewhere require no specific permission per se from local authorities in order to cross jurisdictional boundaries and establish themselves locally. Commercial enterprises enjoy certain universal and inalienable common law rights to settle freely among all entities. They are thus constrained only by local zoning, planning, and other environmental control entities, banking boards, licensing boards, and so on. Distribution of such "foreign elements" is often seen as mutually beneficial, bringing jobs and "outside" money to be spent locally. Municipalities offer substantial tax benefits to woo outside commercial investment and job creation.

But external control of local shops and facilities has its price. There is frequently little confluence of interests between local territory and the far-flung commercial network. At the very least, territorial power remains vulnerable to sudden withdrawal of the very benefits that made inclusion so desirable.

## Territorial Access for Goods

Admission into territory may be required to import goods for use, consumption, or trade. Goods sold extraterritorially must move up

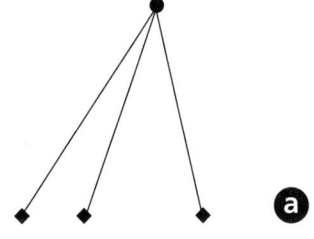

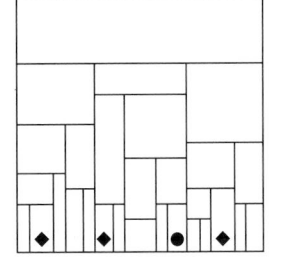

203

**11.2**  *A conceptual model of distribution of foreign elements within a territorial structure:*

*(a) Foreign elements organized according to hierarchy of management.*

*(b) Location of elements within territorial structure.*

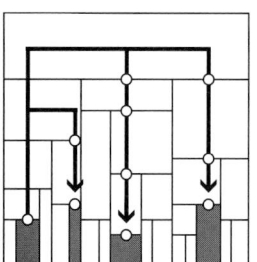

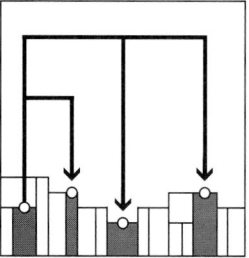

through territorial structure then descend again into included territories. When the distance between the point of departure and point of delivery is increased, so too territorial depth to be crossed may increase. The issues related to this movement, paralleling those having to do with foreign elements, are as old as trade.

On overland routes, each crossing into a local municipality or fiefdom occasioned taxation, if not harassment. In the Netherlands, for instance, medieval castles were strategically placed along delta branches of the Rhine and Maas rivers to extract rights of passage. Ancient ships therefore plied the Mediterranean coast, and even the open seas, of necessity: whatever the risks, they were preferable to the hazards encountered in repeated overland boundary crossings.

For commercial enterprises seeking to maximize distribution of consumer goods, there is no merit in territorial structure. The ideal diagram for consumerism exists at a single level: that of the nuclear family which consumes within a unified network of global markets (see figure 11.3b). All intermediate territorial crossings represent only potential barriers.

## A Shifting Balance

Configurations of foreign elements serving all manner of commercial and institutional purposes have become ubiquitous. Vast contemporary supply forms, webs and networks, and widely dispersed institutional and commercial configurations are increasingly apparent.

Higher-level forms are coming to define and control all levels of physical environment. Traditional gradations of territorial structure appear to shape the emerging contemporary environment less and less.

**11.3** *Access lines and crossings:*

*(a) Lines and crossings in deep territorial structure.*

*(b) Lines and crossings in shallow territorial structure.*

Paradoxically, the proliferation of extensive and unmediated large-scale infrastructure has gone hand in hand with explosive growth in acts of settlement at the small scale of a single room, house, or neighborhood. The two are closely related, feeding and justifying one another, indeed to a large extent creating one another. Territory experienced as an environmental structure—rather than as a political, market, or military domain—occurs at the relatively small human scale, tied to such fields of common settlement.

Everyday personal experience of small-scale settlement is usually limited to places in which we or our relatives, close friends, and colleagues live, work, or shop. When we exit into the public realm, the world seems to comprise giant infrastructures and ubiquitous institutions. While traveling, we do not easily venture beyond familiar networks. Visiting distant cities and countries, we seldom penetrate into small-scale domestic worlds where we do not know anyone. We may not even notice their vast extent as we fly over them. We experience the modern world as increasingly public and large scale, while in the actual occupation of the earth's surface, the small scale and the local is growing at a tremendous rate.

We have a good deal of anecdotal knowledge of a profound and fundamental change in territorial autonomy. While we tend to equate such change with the large scale, we may do well to scrutinize its small-scale manifestations. In historical perspective, we begin to note several important phenomena affecting modern territorial structure:

1. The increasing number and variety of supply forms penetrating down to the room level, with a concomitant increase in complexity of environmental systems.

2. The increasing number, variety, and preeminence of dispersed foreign elements, evidencing growth in global networks of commercial and institutional organization. This also signals diminishing scope of local territorial control.

3. The increasing size of buildings. Three-dimensional expansion of the urban field brings both a disorderly array of supply forms and a denial of territorial autonomy on the smaller domestic scale. An increasingly complex field is thereby rendered more rigid.

It is too soon to assess the long-term meaning of these trends. The observed phenomena are at present intensifying, but not entirely new: in environmental matters, new structures always grow and transform out of the old. Whether present conditions jointly herald a permanent structural shift to an as-yet undefined and unprecedented environmental hierarchy, or are merely generating temporary local disturbances while shifting a fundamentally unchanged environmental structure into a new balance, remains unknown.

205

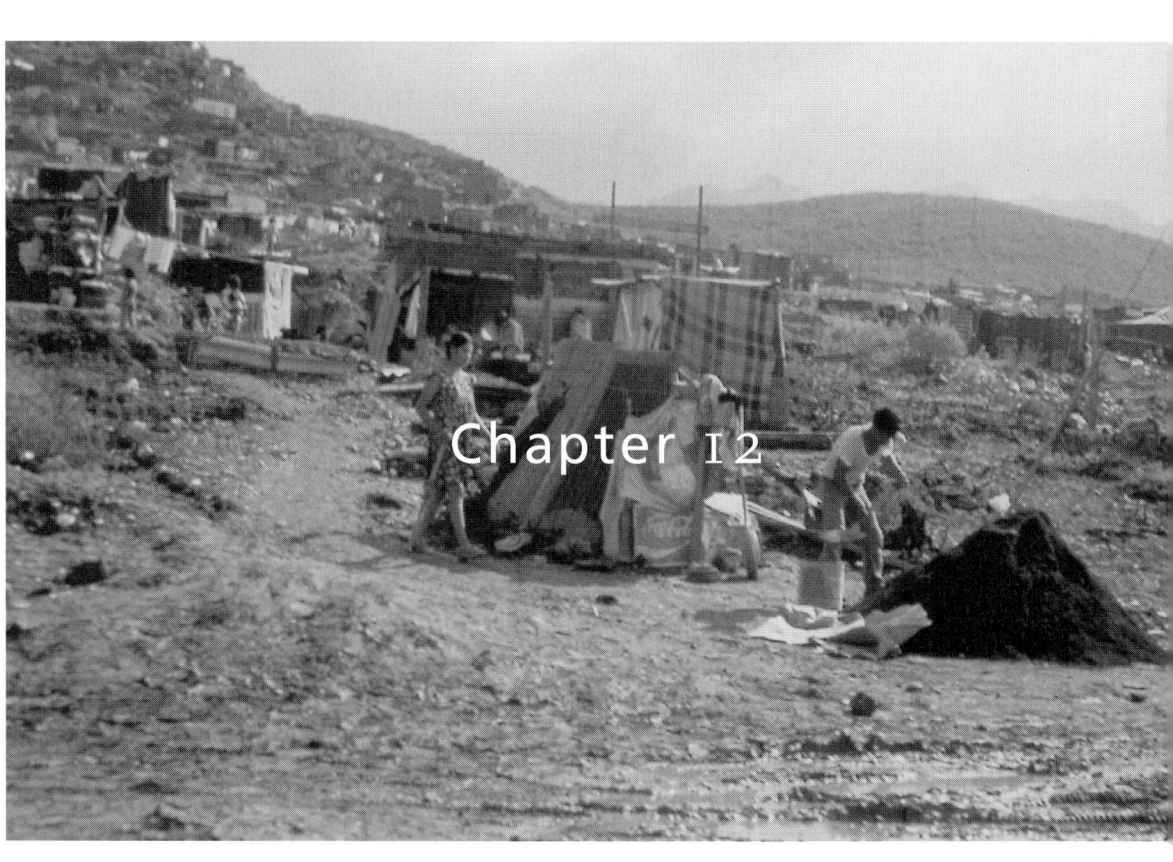

Chapter 12

# Shifts in Territorial Structure

## 12.1 Horizontal Shifts in Territorial Division

### Shifting Boundaries

Horizontal shifts necessitate negotiation among neighbors. On an international or tribal scale, negotiation may be replaced by force. On the urban scale, tensions and disputes between neighbors are common. But shifts negotiated in good faith to the advantage of all parties also occur with great regularity.

The urban block's inherent flexibility is readily apparent. In place of the initial uniform lot division, there may be sales of double lots or larger. Two lots make for a large house, three lots may be divided in two, and so forth. Similar moves can be made in the course of time after initial construction, leading to new building.

But exchanges can be more piecemeal. Johannes Overbeck's map of Pompeii portrays Roman courtyard houses conceived in a very clear and obvious typology.[1] Upon closer scrutiny, we suspect rooms have shifted from one house to another. They show a blind wall to the abutting courtyard onto which they would once have opened. A door now links them to the other side of the presumed demising line.

We can safely assume not much has changed in this regard since Roman times. In the historic centers of Dutch canal cities like Amsterdam and Delft, we find houses with rear yards extending behind the house next door; in all probability, a prosperous owner bought part of his neighbor's backyard to extend his own.

**12.1** *Squatter settlement near Monterrey, Mexico—This picture was taken several days after the land was first invaded (page 206).*

## Increasing Density

Incidental individual horizontal shifts frequently reflect broader patterns of intensification. Throughout Latin America, towns were usually laid out with lots large enough for free-standing houses and gardens. Blocks often eventually ended up with townhouses on much narrower lots.

During the nineteenth century, European historic urban centers were under intense pressure. Urban population grew, while the city's territory (and its legal possibility for expansion, throughout much of Europe) remained severely restricted. Intensification resulted in backyard infilling. Hidden behind older downtown buildings we find large new ones: workshops, theaters, and schools.[2] These buildings required dedicated access from the street. Sometimes entry was achieved by transforming an existing sideyard into an alley, or else the ground floor of an older building provided access. Sometimes a townhouse was demolished, providing narrow street frontage for a wide building.[3]

209

*12.2* *Pompeii—Fragment of urban fabric. Rooms tend to line up along territorial boundaries facing the atrium, peristyle, or garden. At various places, the territorial boundary shifts, causing one or more rooms to then face in the opposite direction. This been interpreted as the result of negotiations between neighbors, causing a horizontal territorial exchange. After Overbeck.*

*12.3* *The Hague—Part of the nineteenth-century fabric. Density increased during the industrial revolution, while city limits remained inflexible. Schools, factories, and even public buildings were built in backyard space with a narrow entrance to the street. Drawing by H. Reijenga, courtesy of SAR.*

## 12.2 Vertical Shifts in Territorial Division

### Increase of Public Space

The balance of power between a greater territory and its lesser included ones is not necessarily stable. It is normal, for instance, for public streets to be widened over time under the pressure of increasing traffic. The implications of this move, already discussed in the context of changing higher-level form in an existing fabric (see chapter 2.1), are inevitably territorial.

In the fabric of Cambridge, Massachusetts, we can still read evidence of the original late-seventeenth- and eighteenth-century estates and can trace their gradual subdivision to accommodate more and more individual territories. Sometimes this resulted in adding a new street to the public realm, as was the case with Appleton Street, carved out of the Lee estate. Sometimes a dead-end street, like Clement Circle off Sparks Street, was introduced, the better to utilize the deep gardens of the original estate. In such cases, a portion of the private space was surrendered to make the remaining land yield more revenue.[4]

An increase of public space may thus result either from pressure from above or from intensification of available land within included territories.

### Increase of Included Territories

In the Western urban tradition, the division between public and private space is generally structural. Although the dominant territorial power may increase public space by asserting rights of eminent domain, citizens in control of included territories do not commonly usurp large portions of public space. By contrast, historic Middle Eastern urban tissues frequently

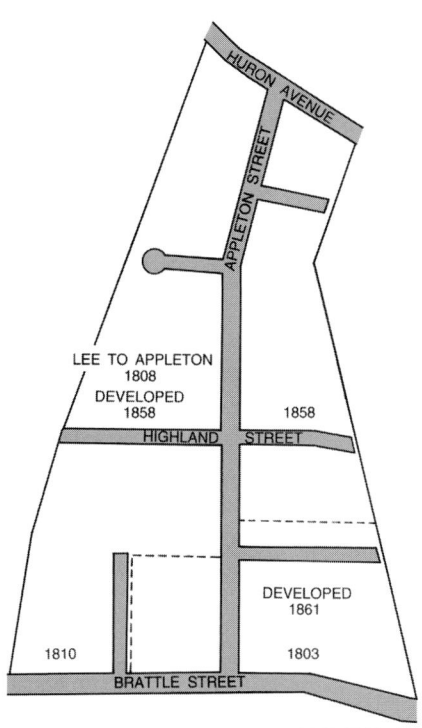

LEE ESTATE

211

witnessed citizens extending structures—and with them, territory—by building into the street. Sidewalks were commonly occupied, or whole streets were built over at the second-floor level, straddled with columns or walls to carry the new construction. The resulting pattern of partially covered streets is characteristic of much traditional Middle Eastern urban environment.

Such small-scale interventions formed part of a remarkably sophisticated and deliberate process. In broad general terms, a major formal principle in this urban culture was that anything was permitted, as long as one did not harm one's neighbors. In other words, if neigh-

**12.4** *Appleton Street, Cambridge, Massachusetts—The street was laid out across the original Lee estate, thereby extending the public space of the urban fabric. After a drawing by Susan M. Fogel.*

**12.5** *Tunis, ca. 1900—Postcard showing overpass. Courtesy of Jamel Akbar.*

bors tolerated the proposed change, it was done. It was ultimately possible to block off a street by simply building across it. Jamel Akbar reports such actions continuing in newly constructed Saudi neighborhoods, though no longer sanctioned by the Westernized laws of Saudi Arabia. Where informal traditional control remains active, age-old territorial transformations still occur, albeit with concrete Western-style buildings.[5]

## Sidewalks under Occupation

The Middle Eastern example is the result of a bottom-up process. Dominant top-down control inevitably implies increased proportion of public space. Preoccupation with public space was already noted when we discussed Amsterdam School architecture (see chapter 4.3). Cooperatives imbued with the ideals of a socialist society were design clients as well as end users of these celebrated neighborhoods. Their vision of a new world was shared by their architects and by the enlightened technical bureaucracy of the Amsterdam municipality. Size and quality of public space were greatly emphasized. Many streets exhibit very broad sidewalks.

By the 1960s, the Amsterdam School neighborhoods' original population of blue-collar workers was gone. Inhabitants no longer shared the original occupants' pride in the renowned social housing experiment. During the era of student revolts, administrators controlling the inner-city housing estates were suddenly put on the defensive. Inhabitants defied the anonymous municipal bureaucracy and its assertion of control of all outside space.

In a clear and deliberate invasion of public space, sidewalks were converted into gardens. No ground-floor apartment doors open

onto them. To this day, gardeners climb down from windows to reach their territorial extension, or else detour through the communal hallway and street.[6]

## Expanding Rearward in Public Housing

Public housing throughout the world is, by definition, a top-down process. As agents routinely seek to solidify and expand their realm of control, public space in such estates is maximized. Following the modernist canon, public estate dwellings are designed to stand amid unfenced lawns and gardens.

Maintaining that much public greenery is difficult even for the affluent European state.

For a developing country, it is well-nigh impossible. A state of general neglect inevitably comes to characterize such spaces. Scorched by the hot sun, they are at best sandlots for soccer and other ball games. At worst, they quickly become dumping grounds for trash and broken-down cars.

Enterprising inhabitants of adjacent apartments sometimes invade. Surrounded by otherwise barren waste, we then see fenced-in gardens within which vegetables and fruit trees are cultivated. As the fences go up, the vertical boundary in the territorial balance is shifted, but no depth is added. In other cases occupants of mass housing actually build out, claiming territory for rear extensions from the surrounding wasteland.

**12.6**  *Amsterdam South—Gardens, carved out of the sidewalk space by citizens in the 1960s, were subsequently accepted by the municipality as private territory. No communicating doors exist between the gardens and spaces within the building.*

**12.7**  *Cairo—Public housing occupants have extended their apartments to the back of the building, which overlooks a street servicing the front of the next building. Clearly, cooperation was required for neighbors to build extensions on the second and third floor, supported by columns.*

## 12.3 Increase in Territorial Depth

### Top-Down Action

Increasing density in an urban environment leads not just to the intensification of available private space, as witnessed in previous chapters; it may also lead to an increase in territorial depth. Two processes may be distinguished here. In the first, a territorial power, in a "top-down" action, will subdivide its own space to create increased depth, usually to enable more intensive use (moving from figure 12.8a to b1). In the second, action is "bottom-up": a number of included territories join forces and appropriate their own public space from the more general public space, thus increasing depth (moving from figure 12.8a to b2).

To examine the first process, we may consider the dead-end streets created to subdivide large private landholdings in Cambridge, Massachusetts. Initially, these were privately controlled. To reach the inhabitants, one first had to enter a communal dead-end street, whose creation constituted an actual increase of territorial depth. Eventually, the dead-end streets were placed under control of the municipality and became an extension of general public space, with consequent loss of territorial depth.

A similar move, in a more dense urban environment, has been observed in central Mexico City. Courtyards of large nineteenth-century urban houses provide access to backyards, now converted into a narrow alley with houses one room wide on either side.

Here the forces that created the infamous "back-to-back" houses of nineteenth-century industrial cities like Birmingham and Glasgow still remain at work. There, too, the type was born in the gardens of larger houses. Later, it was utilized in new construction, because of the extremely high densities it yields.

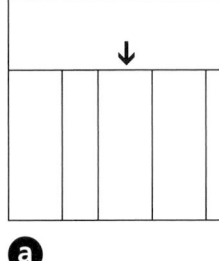
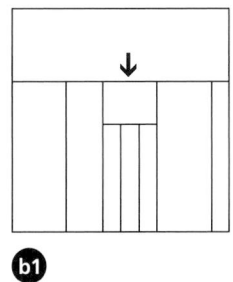
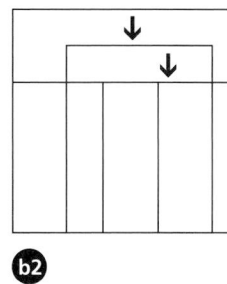
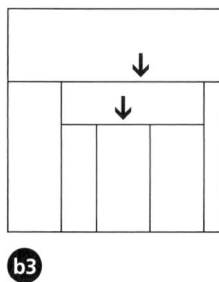

**12.8** Increase in territorial depth—Principal schematic diagrams.

Transformation from (a) to (b1): An included territory may in turn encompass included territories.

Transformation from (a) to (b2): Included territories occupy public space to make it their own.

Transformation from (a) to (b3): Included territories sacrifice some of their own space to make shared public space.

**12.9** Mexico City—Back-to-back housing. Built in the backyard of an older residential building, the houses are two rooms deep and one room wide. Light must enter through the front door. The high back room accommodates a wooden loft for children's beds or storage.

In discussing territory as interpreting form, reference was previously made to patio houses that had become small villages containing a number of individual households (see chapter 8.3 and figure 8.6). This way of increasing territorial depth is familiar: conversion of single-family mansions into apartment buildings is part and parcel of urban intensification. The patio house, being a highly territorial form, allowed this change with minimal physical change.

In Santiago de Chile's turn-of-the-century fabric, alleys now give onto entire neighborhoods erected in backyards. Alleys within such "cités" are often separated from the municipal street network by well-articulated gates.

## Bottom-Up Action

The second way to increase territorial depth occurs when those controlling existing territories act jointly, claiming part of the general public space and converting it into their own public space at a lower level (see figure 12.8b2). In St. Louis, Missouri, for instance, neighborhood home owners organized to purchase their street from the municipality. In return for tax abatement, they agreed to maintain the sewers and paving at their own expense. In effect, they created a virtual condominium. Before long, the newly created territorial level was closed off at both intersections by wooden booms, operable only by inhabitants.

Wherever adjacent territories join, common public space must be created. Individual territories can each contribute a part of their own to the common space, but more often public space on the new level is carved out of the larger public space already there. Such moves often result from overextension of the public claim, occurring when public authorities can no longer control public space.

A similar development of the 1960s created the Dutch *woonerf;* inhabitants lobbied municipalities to discourage through traffic on residential streets, making them safer for local use. The municipalities obligingly relandscaped the streets to discourage traffic, facilitate parking, and render public space safe for children at play and for adults washing and repairing their cars.

Compared with the straightforward territorial shift in St. Louis, the *woonerf* is ambiguous. Residents undoubtedly consider it their territory. But ability to prevent entry is the ultimate territorial test, and the *woonerf* fails it. Nor was there a shift in responsibility. Rather, a benevolent accommodation was agreed upon, and control remained in the hands of the municipality. *Woonerfs* are found in upper-middle-class professional neighborhoods whose inhabitants have access to those in control of public space.

Another bottom-up way to increase depth occurs when included territories each sacrifice some of their own to jointly create common space (changing figure 12.8a to b3). But examples are uncommon. Though neighbors might convert portions of their private backyards into a gated communal yard, actual occurrences have not been documented.

## 12.4  Decrease in Territorial Depth

### Bottom-Up Change: A Dearth of Examples

A decrease in depth does not come about easily. The bottom-up process implies that lower-level agents invade shared public space and reapportion it in its entirety to enlarge their own territory. The next level up becomes their new public space. Consequently, one gate providing access to the original common space is replaced by as many gates as there used to be at the bottom of it.

Although easy to posit in diagram (figure 12.10, moving from (a) to (b1)), it may be topologically difficult in practice. For instance, when the communal space to be usurped is a dead-end street, every house on that street may not be able to maintain direct access to public space beyond it. Another case could be the reverse of one cited earlier: neighbors might convert a gated common backyard space into private yards.

Yet another variant involves a single lower-level territory first annexing all others with which it shares the use of common space. Subsequently, there is only one included territory. Common space consequently loses its purpose and is easily incorporated as well. Again, it is difficult to find clear peacetime examples.

### Top-Down Demolition of Gates

A decrease in territorial depth is more easily conceived from the top down, as a greater territorial power appropriates public space common to territories on the level now removed (figure 12.10, moving from (a) to (b2)).

In the case of Tunis, demolition of the gates in dead-end streets occurred during installation of an urban sewage network. The municipality assumed control based on maintenance requirements. Given the contemporary primacy of technology, it is not surprising to find technical grounds supplying the rationale for appropriation; but it remains an exercise of power all the same.[7]

More than one and a half centuries before a municipal utility altered territorial structure in traditional Tunis, Napoleon's army did so in Cairo. Cairo's many territorial levels were invariably marked by gates: in addition to individual residential entry doors, gates closed off the dead-end streets shared by these houses. The collector streets from which these dead-end alleys branched were also gated, marking neighborhood boundaries along major urban thoroughfares. Street gates were not symbolic, as was the case in imperial Beijing. Instead they were sealed every night, to be opened again at dawn.

In 1798 the occupying French army set about establishing a single unified public space by demolishing all intermediate gates. Their intent was to extend public space without interruption from the main town entry to each residential front door. Although the act is clearly documented, the impact of this drastic territorial restructuring is not. Moreover, the French missed many gates of dead-end streets because they mistook them for more familiar forms: entrances to private courtyard houses like those in Paris.[8]

The French occupation was short-lived, but throughout the surviving fabric of historic Cairo, gates are invariably missing or not in use. Although their absence must in part reflect the gradual attrition of lower-level territorial control in conjunction with modernization, the Napoleonic action that preceded these changes was a deliberate attempt to bring about precisely such flattening of territorial structure.

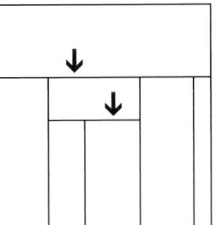

**a**

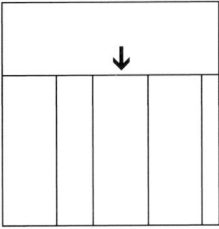

**b1**

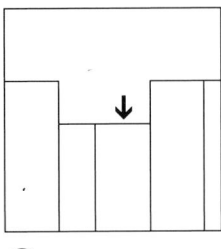

**b2**

219

**12.10** *Decrease in territorial depth—Principal schematic diagrams.*

*Transformation from (a) to (b1): Included territories jointly annex and divide existing shared space between themselves.*

*Transformation from (a) to (b2): Encompassing territory invades and annexes included territory.*

## Napoleon's Perspective

The drastic intervention of Napoleon's army prefigured the highly centralized mode of operation characteristic of many contemporary governments, within societies aspiring to the administrative power to control citizens on all social levels. The architecture of Claude-Nicolas Ledoux gave clear expression to that assertion of bureaucratic power, which was already in evidence before the French Revolution.[9]

The Salt Works at Arc-et-Senans demonstrates an architecture of absolute and centralized control. Its concentric layout placed the director at the center. As much as it actually facilitated visual control, the design symbolized the presence of the all-seeing eye—so graphically depicted by the architect himself—at the center of this artificial universe. Inside, the buildings have corridors leading to large multipurpose rooms. Within their confines, several families frequently came to dwell together.

The concentric layout of this executed plan relates it to another architectural icon of the Enlightenment, the Panopticon of Jeremy Bentham, revealing similar conceptions of space: it was to be centrally controlled and of minimal territorial depth. Certainly, Bentham's variant of this model is perverse: gates that lead to lesser territories are sealed from without, violating the most basic principle of territorial structure.[10] But Ledoux's formally superior Salt Works architecture is only a shade removed from such perversion.[11]

The corridor connecting numerous rooms is of equal interest. It signals another means to flatten territorial depth. Earlier, we observed that large buildings in the past, such as Versailles, frequently comprised relatively simple forms. But they could contain complex and dynamic territorial structures brought forth by inhabitation. Their very lack of functional determinism made this possible. Examples as diverse as the Loire Valley chateaux, Diocletian's palace at Split, and the remains of Knossos suggest spaces arranged directly and sequentially. There may be stairwells and service corridors, but the architecture is one of procession, of a sequence of spaces.[12] Although it is sometimes hierarchically ordered, it always creates a virtual landscape for inhabitation. Such built environment possesses rather open-ended monumentality, always suggesting further possibilities of territorial depth.

This quality begins to waver in the Enlightenment, then abruptly disappears with modernism's first large institutional buildings. It is instructive to compare the territorial structure of the Salt Works, the Panopticon, and Napoleonic Cairo with the territorial structure of the modern institutional building, in which, for the first time in history, the corridor acts as the primary structuring space. It connects to all other floors and entrances via stairs or elevators, as a rule running continuously along each floor. Be it office building, laboratory, hospital, or school, the contemporary building features a corridor spine that arrays rooms as expediently as possible. Its form expresses the shallowest possible territorial structure in so direct and immutable a manner that acts of settlement cannot increase territorial depth.

Corridors manifestly result from a centralized process of design, reflecting centralized social organization. They have now established an institutional typology enshrined in codes and regulations as much as in custom. A full understanding of their ubiquitous emergence as a trademark of institutional building will require historical perspective.

Only in those commercial buildings where fit-out between façades is left to the tenant do we begin to find plan layout of a more open-ended nature. When interior subdivision of large floor areas is customized, territorial depth may emerge. But this trend toward Open Building practice has not been uniformly adopted, nor is it compatible with all institutional building types.[13]

III

# Understanding, The Cultural Order

Chapter 13

# Common Understanding

## Coherence

It is difficult to find any environment that is not highly coherent, initial impressions notwithstanding.

To foreigners, forays on foot into ancient back streets in Tokyo or cruises through American residential strip development may prove equally bewildering. Familiarity brings an apprehension of implicit structure: as recurring features and rhythmic repetitions are recognized, seemingly random environment becomes "readable."

For a long time, Western observers found traditional Muslim towns chaotic, or at best "folkloric," because they did not present an immediately familiar structure. We have now come to admire those same environments for their unique and very powerful unity, for their clearly recognizable structure and thematic use of a handful of typical elements.

Such environmental coherence is ubiquitous, and it is not fully attributable to the presence of hierarchical structures of form and place.

## The Social Dimension

Environments are artifacts. Their overall coherence ultimately reflects a social dimension, as do the two orders previously considered.

## 13.1 Beyond Control

*Amsterdam gables—The nonstructural façades, composed of timber frames and brick fill, extend upward to make a decorative profile (page 223).*

**13.1** *San Francisco, 1972—Suburban tract houses display varied façades in front of identical units (page 224).*

It is consistency observed throughout a society that makes definition of level structure possible. Form hierarchies ultimately reflect the common values of agents who, within certain generally accepted constraints, mutually interact with external material, technical, and economic conditions. Each shapes the other, and environmental structure changes accordingly. In noting that one environment exhibits a fully developed furniture level while another, although equally sophisticated, does not, we cannot always rationalize precisely why these differences occur.

Human beings seek signs of formal coherence among grouped artifacts, overlaying comprehensible structure on seemingly random form. Environment that randomly mixes courtyard house and apartment building types is extremely unlikely. When an example is discovered, we hypothesize about its significance in ways that assume and develop coherent structure: *Perhaps it represents an environment in transition, from one form to the other, as has occurred in some coastal towns overrun by sudden beach resort development.* Deeply engrained experience has taught us that environmental structure and consistency of shared values go hand in hand.

Within the constraints of levels and territory—common physical and biological constructs to which agents adhere—a good deal of freedom remains. Within a suburban environment, for instance, each house on its own lot might be idiosyncratically designed, without altering either level structure or territorial organization. Yet even within eclectic American suburbs, extensive distribution of wildly dissimilar forms is rare.

Amos Rapoport has argued convincingly that vernacular house forms are not fully explicable in terms of available materials, level of technology, climate, or other environmental or economic constraints.[1] There always remain options to be determined by individual preference. Vernacular forms represent such preferences adopted communally. But as agents exercise individual preference, their acts typically conform to a socially determined framework.

Even within contemporary societies that emphasize individuality, there exists little formal evidence to suggest that this has substantially changed. Citizens still seek to settle into environments where they "belong." Settlement begins with reading formal signals indicating shared preferences, to determine to what, within a fabric, we can potentially relate.

Thus, agents act as social beings in exercising control in built environment. This, in combination with physical constraints and gravity, creates the Order of Form. In combination with territorial necessity, it creates the Order of Place. Out of the infinite possibility remaining, the desire to relate to fellow agents via common structure creates further coherence. This third order establishes mutual preference, without hierarchy. It is based entirely on human understanding.

227

## 13.2   The Implicit

Common understanding about form ranges from clearly explicit bylaws and building codes to deeply implicit customs and habits. Between these two extremes there exists all manner of ongoing rule making, agreement, and consensus. What remains unspoken, what is taken for granted, makes for the strongest bonds. True coherence resides in the implicit.

Why aren't North American suburban front yards walled in, as is the norm almost everywhere else in the world? To the native suburbanite, that alternative is, literally, unthinkable. Built environment is all about the unspoken— regularities, customs, habits, conventions. These assumptions are taken for granted by those who have always lived with them. The profoundly familiar remains unquestioned. Conventions are so self-evident that it generally takes an outsider to frame the questions that define them.

Not so many generations ago, rural communities on both sides of the Atlantic still shared a common understanding about the single-family dwelling. When a new house was needed, the client sought out a carpenter or mason. They might jointly visit the site and discuss size, budget, schedule, and perhaps a few particulars. Little more information was needed before a handshake sealed the agreement and construction began.

There were no architectural contract documents, no design drawings, no building codes. Although form varied from place to place, each social group implicitly understood what they intended by *house:* they knew the internal layout, how the building would be constructed, what the windows and trim and surface treatments would be, and how great an impact on neighboring territory would be acceptable.

Social agreement—what is self-evident—obscures alternatives.

## Becoming Explicit

It may come to pass that the implicit no longer suffices. What was customary may no longer be taken for granted. When custom is challenged, achieving consensus may require regulations and bylaws.

For example, as a suburban environment becomes urbanized, density and traffic increase. Security and privacy become concerns. Finally, someone fences in her yard. Indignant neighbors protest the flagrant violation of a common understanding. The violation surfaces an implicit agreement that had never been discussed. Suddenly, many shared assumptions are questioned.

Over time, the aberration may become accepted, even widespread. If it becomes the norm, a new pattern of fenced-in yards emerges, superseding the old. Shared understanding about how to enclose territory may sink back into implicit self-evidence. Otherwise, the challenge may lead to legislation. Neighborhoods may explicitly prohibit or regulate yard fences. What had been self-evident is thus formalized as a rule.

## Increasing Complexity

In environmental dynamics, formalization remains rooted in the informal, without which it becomes moot.

Today, building requires all manner of regulation, formally recognized industry standards and technical specifications, drawings and contracts. We objectively document agreements about building for good reason: increasingly complex technology, diversifying population, and new ways of building trigger formalization.

Architectural interventions now involve architects, engineers, and consultants for plumbing, heating, ventilation and air-conditioning, electric power and communication systems, landscaping, interiors, and so on. Legal, financial, and marketing strategies, implemented by yet other specialists and committees, are continually coordinated within the design team. The ultimate project execution—building—is yet another process involving many different experts. Agents continually make judgments in ongoing dialogue.

Social and technical complexity necessitate the degree of formal documentation now required. Nonetheless, environment does continue to get built. There is reason to assume that unspoken understanding and customary behavior are commensurately increasing among those who act. That environmental design and building remain fundamentally implicit and social processes is reflected in the intensive socialization and "guild training" that accompany professional studies and internship, and no less clearly in the deeply embedded social tradition of complaining about "overregulation."

### Forms of Understanding

Form is shared in different conventionally accepted and generally applied ways. *Patterns, types,* and *systems* have been recognized as three distinct ways in which parts are combined to convey agreement. These concepts are loosely defined in daily usage, but sufficiently distinct to demonstrate how form is coordinated among agents.

Patterns, types, and systems may be collectively called *forms of understanding.* Other conventions of formal agreement may eventually be recognized by observing transformation in the built environment.

### Thematic Environment

## 13.3   Ways of Sharing Form

Patterns and types are not templates to be carelessly repeated. Systems are not recipes: they provide rules within which variations are made. Forms of understanding jointly establish *themes.* We appropriate and improvise upon them to make new instances of our own. In using the theme to create a unique variation, we define ourselves within the context of that society; thus the act of choosing a theme connects agent and society. While built environment manifests itself by our exercise of control, such control is expressed thematically. In each variation, we conform in order to create.

The environmental order of levels and territorial hierarchy are deep-seated human constructs, shifting gradually over millennia as culture and language change. They are the themes of which we are least aware, those least susceptible to individual influence. But in the Order of Understanding, themes are subject to our active social participation.

It is in this third and cultural order that forms add meaning to the variations we make.

## 13.4  Words and Forms

Making form is hard work. Limited by the fact that masonry, wood, and steel respond only to force judiciously applied, we must nonetheless overcome gravity. Yet speaking of form is easy: we readily name parts and properties, describe how form is made. Speaking and abstraction help effect action: they are the wellspring of formal architecture.

Sharing of physical things is apparent in the first sign of common understanding of form: the names we choose. From the moment of creation, forms await naming and appropriation by a social group. Without common names, spaces formed by architectural elements and assembled configurations remain undifferentiated, unrecognized.

Remarkably, standard building parts have always had precise names. Every building supply item, from the smallest carriage bolt or knife thread insert up, has its own designation, for social and technical reasons. Although the making of buildings requires technical jargon, common names for architectural form as wholes are shared by laypeople and professionals alike. The word *atrium* surely conveyed a world unto itself to the Roman citizen, requiring neither explanation nor description among inhabitants of Pompeii. The *iwan*, a recessed space overlooking a private courtyard in the Muslim house, is another example of named form that requires no description within its appropriating social group. Similar examples on the urban level are *alley* and *boulevard*.

Shared form names like *attic* and *porch* denote environmental forms rather than functions. They prescribe no particular use, although they may become habitually associated with certain usages. (Conversely, functional names such as *bedroom* or *dining room* do not indicate specific forms.) Form names convey a particular kind of space and built form in a particular context. Familiarity with such forms requires holistic experience within socially defined daily life.

Vernacular architecture describes architectural configurations with a richly textured nomenclature: there are names for particular entryways, particular rooms, particular windows, particular courtyards, and so on. Common understanding thus allows continuously inhabited houses, villages, and towns to grow and evolve with great formal coherence and variety for centuries, or even millennia.

Most shared form names continue to draw upon the past. Thus far, contemporary environments have not yielded many new nonfunctional and nontechnical physical forms similarly shared and named throughout a culture. Sometimes new formal content is self-consciously grafted onto old names like *atrium*, but new environmental names fully shared in a social body do not seem to have appeared.

## Building and Speaking

Forms of understanding, like language, transmit knowledge. To signal verbal understanding, words may be repeated in paraphrase. To signal formal understanding, variants of pattern, type, or system are built.

In both cases, knowing is communicated by acts of structuring, by doing. But speaking and building are not interchangeable, nor are they directly translatable. Knowledge situated in words can be translated into another language, and understanding embedded in one built form may well be conveyed in another. Yet there is no reason to believe that implicit meaning or understanding within form can be fully translated into words, or vice versa.

The term *language*, when describing formal structures, is at best metaphorical. Form is more meaningfully judged on its own merits as an autonomous medium of human exchange, one whose structure parallels but fundamentally differs from that of language. Rather than parsing lexical, grammatical, or discursive meaning in apprehending form, we examine and understand patterns, systems, and types.

## Meaning

Form is its own visceral, physical, inherent meaning. It is irreplaceable in our lives because its concrete common understanding cannot be otherwise conveyed. The inadequacy of words becomes clear when those who share form seek to speak about its meaning; for each, the terms are different. In attempting to distill and translate the common meaning of form in words, we voice only individual experience.

One may want a tree for shade, for the view of spring blooms framed by a window, or perhaps simply for the experience of nurturing it. When neighbors jointly decide to plant a tree within a common courtyard, their consensus concerns the tree and its presence, not its meaning or its rationale. A consensus regarding form implies no other consensus.

Forms stand in our midst as autonomous presences, participants in our lives in their own right. Thus, when the critic speaks of what a form makes her feel and think, we may recognize echoes of our own response. But such an experience is quite different from that of the agent who engages form, putting hands to it to transform it.

233

Chapter 14

# Patterns

## 14.1 Relations among Parts

### Relating Parts in Different Configurations

House façades throughout the Veneto traditionally feature narrow windows in stuccoed walls. The windows are characteristically placed apart, toward the building or room corner, leaving a stretch of solid wall in the center. The configuration incorporates a rule of selection (narrow windows) and a rule of distribution (windows are placed close to the edge). It is found in the modest houses of a fishing village like Burano, as well as in proud palaces along the Canal Grande, in Venice proper.

In chapter 10.2 we examined the *zaguán* pattern relating kitchen and front door (territorial gates, type 4). We are familiar with the implicit pattern of North American front porches, which seeks to establish a specific relation between porch and street. In much of the traditional Middle East, to give another example, neighbors on opposite sides of the street stagger their entry doors. To place entry doors directly facing one another would constitute a gross breach of privacy.

In general, a *pattern* consistently and repeatedly relates a few parts in the same way.

### Alexander's Pattern Language

As observers of built environment, Christopher Alexander and others have extensively documented how patterns, as consistent relations between two or more parts, play an important

*14.1  Bologna, Italy—Fragment of the 1724 version of a 1637 woodcut by Matteo Borboni, showing the arcades under houses along the street (page 234).*

role in our structuring and understanding of environment. We owe to such observers our public awareness of patterns—what Alexander calls a "Pattern Language."[1]

For an inquiry that focuses on recognizing environmental structure, discussion of whether form is good or bad has little point. Yet for Alexander and other advocates deliberately attempting to transform built environment, it

*14.2*  *The Veneto—Gothic palace façades on Venice's Canal Grande, and the façade of a fisherman's house in Burano. Placement of second-floor windows follows a similar pattern in both examples.*

remains the central question. Where we seek to understand how actors transform form and, through form, act on one another, *A Pattern Language* seeks to convince actors which forms are good. Where we find a "true" pattern to be one consistently applied within a social body, the pattern's goodness for Alexander seems to be embedded in the form itself, in some autonomous and objective way.

Among broadly grouped and repeatedly observed formal relations, configurations of different kinds—systems, types, and patterns—vary in complexity, field, manner of organization, and degree of universality or specificity. Society clearly employs a variety of vehicles of understanding. We need not promote just one as the universal building block of environmental structure, as is suggested in Alexander's *Timeless Way of Building.*[2]

In what follows, the term *pattern* refers specifically to relations among a few parts; its application reveals a common understanding among actors. These actors may not necessarily share other, more complex forms of understanding, like those embodied in systems or types.

## Relating Live Configurations

Patterns that relate porch to street, or front door to opposing neighbor's door, denote minimal configurations that are not *live* (under the control of a single agent). Each part of the pattern may be perceived to belong to a separate configuration. Indeed, patterns frequently seem most significant when they prescribe relationships among individual parts of separate live configurations. Such patterns predefine the interaction between two or more agents in the environment.

Clearly, relationships governed by patterns need not occur between configurations on the same level. Staggered opposing doors belong to separate configurations at the same level, and therefore relate horizontally, while porches relate to the street vertically. Patterns simply incorporate relations deemed important enough to be applied consistently, without the agent considering control or hierarchy. They represent an environmental formulation entirely directed at achieving an agreed-upon quality. As such, they manifest considerable architectural power.

The Veneto window pattern does relate parts within a single live configuration. But its consistent application, house after house, reveals another way in which the pattern links different live configurations: repetition. As we will have occasion to observe in more detail below, the pattern is most powerful when applied repeatedly within a given locale.

## Nonstandard Parts in Fixed Relation

Windows in Veneto homes differ greatly. In the humble houses of Burano, they are simple rectangles surrounded by broad bands of color to set them off from the painted façade wall. Along the Canal Grande, the windows have Gothic arches and borders of elaborately carved stone. Despite similarity of selection, positioning, and distribution, the pattern clearly does not imply standardization. In specifying a relation between identifiable objects, it does not prescribe the character of the objects themselves.

The pattern represents a continuity: the deliberate application of something already done. Yet each instance of the pattern may involve a different decision, agent, place, or time.

Over time, different interventions introduce variation as a natural by-product of freedom of execution and interpretation, within the rules governing each pattern.

## Virtual Operation on a Higher Level

Combined continuity and variety within the pattern are particularly beneficial when a pattern is consistently applied within a given environment. Consider a North American street lined with rhythmically spaced maple trees, and porch after porch set back about the same distance from the sidewalk.

This cumulative effect of a pattern is also well illustrated by the stoops in front of seventeenth-century Dutch canal houses. Along the façade wall there exists a zone for steps. A margin of about four feet is populated by sculpted stoops in stone and brick, ascending and descending into the houses. These stoops are outfitted with wrought-iron banisters and sometimes incorporate narrow benches. Matching detailing and materials link the stoops to individual façades. But together they introduce a varied and lively string of sculpted forms between the pedestrian and the street wall. In this way, the pattern individually adopted by each house adds up to a virtual infrastructure on an urban scale.

Their varied repetition along the street wall introduces a consistent rhythmic element, reinforcing the powerful horizontal sweep of the canal and punctuating the strong linear quality of continuous street walls formed by opposing rows of houses. Individual façades combine to form extended screens of flat glass and brick silhouetted against the sky.

The cumulative effect of repeating a pattern is also evident in the Parisian entresol, a narrow intermediate floor suspended between

239

**14.3** *Boulevard Saint-Michel, Paris—Façades with entresols and gateway extending upward through entresol.*

ground floor below and the first residential floor above. The entresol forms a vertical margin between two zones. It is used as an extension for shop and work spaces below, often providing a place for offices or storage. But the entresol can also be connected to apartments above, or it can constitute a separate apartment floor.

The combined height of ground floor and entresol provides a continuous one-and-a-half-story façade distinct from the floors above. This effectively relates to the pedestrian space and scale of the street (and hence to the urban fabric). Pedestrian space is further reinforced by trees on the sidewalk, the lower branches of which are at about entresol height.

Behind the façade, shop height is sometimes increased by pulling the entresol back from the street, to become a mezzanine balcony within a one-and-a-half-story space. Courtyard entry gates are often built to the maximum height of the entresol, even when, further back, the entresol extends across the passage from street to courtyard.

As with the Amsterdam stoops, consistent application makes this pattern operate on the urban level. Along nineteenth-century Parisian boulevards, its combined one-and-a-half-story façade helps articulate an urban structure many blocks long, lending it scale and proportion commensurate with the surrounding urban tissue. But the entresol is, in fact, a quite old pattern in Paris. It is consistently found in seventeenth- and eighteenth-century buildings in the Marais, on the Left Bank, and on the Île Saint-Louis.

The pattern by itself, as a rule of selection and distribution for a number of parts in the built environment, does not prefigure any cumulative effect. It is only when the pattern is applied with consistency in a certain place that it can add identity and structure to common space, with an impact extending far beyond that of a number of isolated events. Thus, great strength is added when patterns run in local populations and groups, together forming entities on a level higher than their own.

As we will later observe, other signs of understanding, such as types and systems, do not necessarily diminish in meaning when broadcast across different locations via a network. The pattern, in that respect, seems more bound to a particular place.

## 14.2 Formalization of a Pattern

### The Italian Portico

For centuries in Northern Italian cities like Padua and Bologna, each house would cover the sidewalk by means of columns supporting the upper façade (see also chapter 9.1). The resulting portico would align with neighbors', thereby contributing to the continuous covered pedestrian network throughout the town.

Thematic interpretation varies at each house. Columns differ in shape, spans vary, and so do the heights and spring points of the arches. But throughout the city, these individual acts add up to a collective product, building a virtual urban infrastructure of great architectural power and intricacy. The resulting form bears the qualities of two levels. It structures the townscape by virtue of continuity, but it retains variety in size, detailing, and arcade span, hallmarks of individual interpretation. Façade alignment makes the whole more than the sum of the parts.

The territorial origin of the urban portico is ambiguous. It is unlikely to have resulted from voluntary universal ceding of territory to the public realm. This suggests that the origin of the pattern was instead expansion into the public space by overbuilding it. However, this interpretation assumes the initial creation of streets far wider than medieval conditions generally supported.[3]

The Bolognese porticos are of Renaissance origin and do not consistently occur in the medieval core. Here it is entirely possible that wide streets were laid out and citizens encouraged to build over the sidewalk. Whatever the motivations and mechanisms through which this consistent pattern emerged, it remains a form of understanding of great force.

**14.4** *Bologna—Typical street with arcades.*

## The Path to San Luca

The pattern's presence as a virtual urban infrastructure in Bologna seems to suggest the next step. In the seventeenth century, citizens built a portico from the city gate into the countryside, covering an ancient walkway to the shrine of San Luca. This portico, like those in town, is open on one side and has a blind wall on the other. But it had no buildings above or behind it. The continuous surface is relieved by an occasional niche with statuary, and in several instance by gates connecting to a country road.

Conceived as a single intervention, the three-and-a-half-kilometer portico follows the road to Florence for a while, crosses it with an elegant covered stone bridge, then ascends a steep hill, culminating in the baroque chapel designed by Carlo Francesco Dotti.[4]

Thus, the familiar urban phenomenon left the city and moved into the landscape, now operating as an autonomous form, a portico without a building. What had always been a collective form now was a single infrastructure on a par with the road and canal. Over time, near the town, buildings eventually were appended.

**14.5** *Bologna—The "portico" outside the town gates, heading toward the shrine of San Luca, begun in 1674. Along the first kilometer, buildings were later built behind and atop the arcade.*

As in the town, the buildings are all different. But the portico remains rigidly uniform, as any extended single intervention is bound to be.

Thus, the same form, during successive centuries, passed under sequential control of different kinds of agents pursuing different objectives. Beginning in the collective imagination of inhabitants, it passed into the realm of bureaucratic regulation of an urban fabric, ultimately ending in a symbolic gesture professionally executed by a prestigious architect. The development took centuries to unfold.

Thus the common gives rise to architecture.

245

**14.6** *Bologna—Continuation of fig. 14.5. The "portico" begins to switch back across the hills, as it approaches the shrine.*

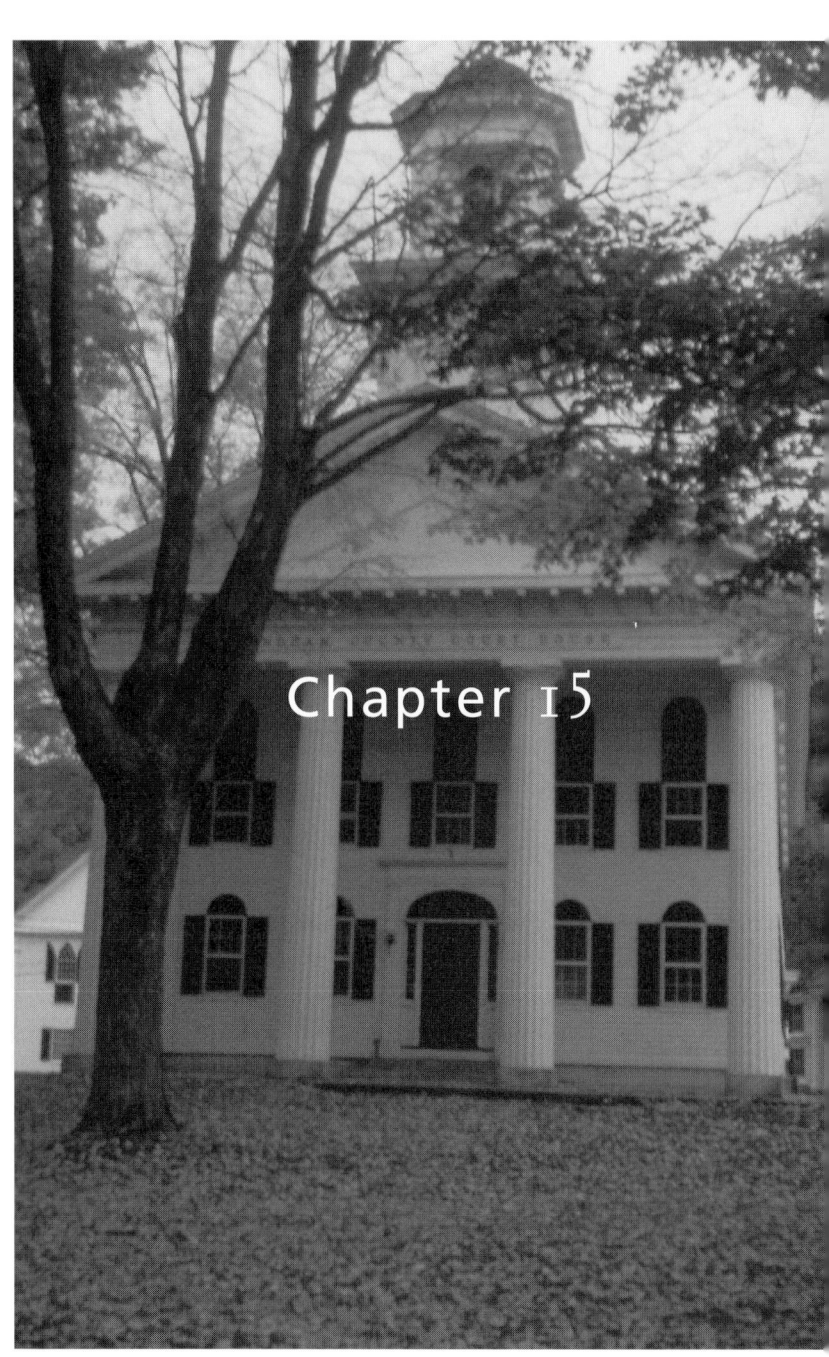

Chapter 15

The Systemic Environment

## 15.1 Thematic Systems

### Systems, Variants, and Structure

Two buildings varying in size and plan may both be built in classicistic style. Two other buildings with quite different architecture may both be built of load-bearing brick walls with wooden floors and roof. In each case, dissimilar configurations share a common *system*.

Classicistic styles demand that we use certain elements—column, entablature, and so on—assembled in certain ways: there are rules about the selection of parts and the relation of these parts to one another. Likewise, the composite construction system of load-bearing masonry and wood has certain kinds of parts, related in certain ways.

In any system we may distinguish two aspects: configurations and structure. Same-system configurations relate similar parts in similar ways, manifesting *variants* of the system. Rules of selection and relation define what the variants have in common: this is the system's *structure*.

System, variants, and structure imply one another. In positing the existence of a vernacular system with rules of selection and relation, we must test and demonstrate the potential of the system's structure by providing examples of variants. In positing that an artifact represents a variant within a system, we must define the structure of that system.

*15.1 Newfane, Vermont—Windham County Courthouse (page 246).*

## Thematic Systems

The systems concept is quite general. It is equally applicable to phenomena in nature—the composition of plants out of stems, leaves, roots, flowers, and fruits; or the composition of molecules out of elements—and to human artifacts like buildings and cars. Systems of the latter kind, which develop out of human understanding, are *thematic systems*. Such systems tend to develop and eventually transform over time in a thematic way.

Structure, as a construct we intuit by observing phenomena in nature, is itself an artifact. When nature does not follow the rules of the structure we have proposed, it is the rules that must adapt and be "corrected." New theories and classifications result. Thus, the platypus forced a redefinition of what it means to be a mammal, just as a series of archaeological finds have redefined the relation of great apes to humans.

In forms of understanding as well, a given rule structure may be challenged by particular instances, as we saw in the earlier example in which a front yard fence was built within a suburban environment of uniformly open lawns. But exceptions do not necessarily prove the rule structure wrong. Given a consensus, the challenge can be rejected: human beings can jointly act to make variants follow the structure.

Within thematic systems, structure and variants alike are artifacts. When a configuration poorly fits the structure of the thematic system of which it is assumed to be a variant, several avenues are open. We may establish the aberrant variant as the beginning of a subsequent trend, effectively adapting the rule system. Or we may reject the variant, preferring to stick to time-tested ways. Gradual change within thematic systems is a product of human deliberation and consensus.

## The Freedom of Systems

Patterns may appear to be variants in a simple system, but they have additional constraints. In systems terminology, a pattern has strict "selection rules." It generally concerns a relationship between not more than two named parts. Patterns determine not only the parts used and how they relate, but also where they must be deployed and what configuration they must form; rules of *distribution* are provided as well.

The pattern is, in short, a recipe intended to produce a certain outcome. Systems, on the other hand, allow far greater freedom to make any configuration desired: what matters most is the relation of parts, not the particular configurations. In a building construction system, for instance, we may know exactly how the ends of wooden floor beams must be fire cut, then laid into the grouted masonry beam pocket. But there is no inherent specification as to length or number of walls or floors. We are free to make any configuration as long as we observe the relational constraints. In a pattern this would not do: the configuration itself, with due allowance for variations in dimension and in some aspects of selection, would be largely predetermined.

The system is thus a means to achieve a variety of results. Just as a given building system allows us to make a wide variety of buildings, all built in the same way, so the system of classical composition similarly allows the design of very different buildings, all composed "in the same manner." Systems are by no means neutral, but they allow more freedom to create . . . in a specified way.

## Systemic Variation:
## The Pompeiian House

A case in point is the system of linked open space in the Pompeiian house. The major open spaces are the *atrium, peristyle,* and *garden,* always ordered in that precise sequence. These selection rules are rather restrictive, and might well form a pattern, were players limited to recombining three spaces.

But smaller houses need not have the full sequence. Instead one, two, or all three spaces may be selected: houses may forgo a garden, and some have only an atrium. A rule may be formulated: *The third and/or second open spaces may be eliminated, but never the atrium.*[1] Whether one or two spaces are omitted, the sequencing order remains. Moreover, the sequencing rule does not provide positional constraints. The axis along which the sequence develops need not be straight. Directions may shift. Thus, the variety of possible distributions is again much wider than a pattern would allow.

This example also demonstrates that systems are not architecturally neutral. The spatial organization of the house, in spite of its many possible variants, remains quite distinct: there can be no doubt that the building is a Pompeiian house. In the same way, we recognize a classical building or a building of load-bearing masonry construction.

*15.2* *Pompeii—Pompeiian houses observed in a variety of sizes show the systemic consistency of the type. Room sizes are fairly constant, but sizes of larger spaces differ. Application of the peristyle and/or the garden behind the atrium may vary. Note also the hole-in-the-wall shops (*tabernae*) along the street, with stairs leading to a loft space above. After Overbeck.*

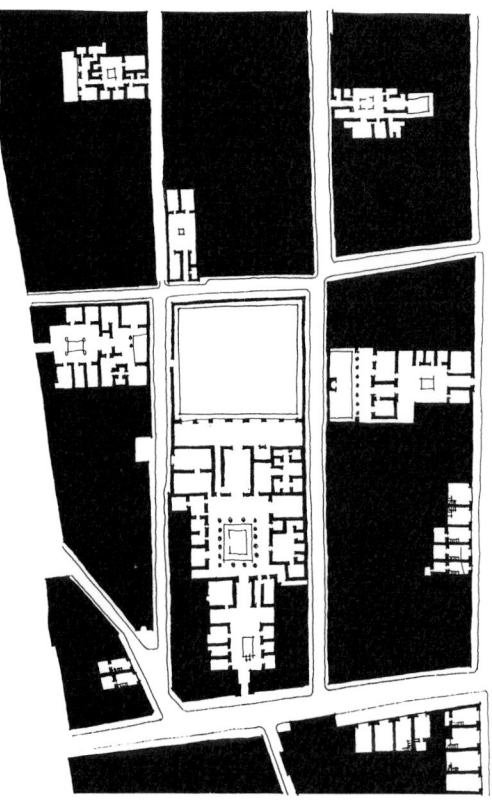

## 15.2 The Social Roots of Systems

### Systems Reside in a Social Body

Pompeiian houses, like other historic and vernacular types, suggest systemic knowledge shared among those who built and those who inhabited. A good deal of systemic knowledge, no doubt, can be shared between layperson and specialist. But of the three vehicles for understanding—pattern, type, and system—the system is the most technical and professional. Because it relates more to the question of *how* things are done than to *what* is done, mastering the system requires a certain knack, more specialized experience, and detailed know-how. Designing a steel frame requires explicit and formal know-how, but also what Schön has referred to as "knowing-in-practice"; designing a classical or international style building does as well. To a significant extent, the system represents an understanding among specialists.

In many cases a thematic system is equated with a specific group or combination of teams of specialists. Thus, for the composite system of brick masonry and wood construction to exist, both masons and carpenters must be available. For almost every subsystem we may find in the modern building—ranging from steel structure to curtain wall, flooring, partitioning, and all technical equipment and utilities—consultants design it and specialized subcontractors install it.

The relationship between systems and trades is reciprocal: masons and carpenters are identified by the systems they sustain. When supporting conditions for the system disappear, no social body can maintain its identification with that system. For centuries there existed a guild of plasterers. As their labor-intensive technology has become outmoded, decorative and ordinary plasterers, like stone masons and tin smiths, have become an endangered species.

## The Social Basis of Systems

The fundamentally social basis of systems explains why formal description and encoding are inevitably limited. Although books, manuals, codes, and regulations may accompany a system, there is no reason to equate that system solely with a formal description of its structure. For a system to exist in the built environment, a social body must first *appropriate* it. Formal description may or may not result, depending on the nature of the system and the circumstances in which it becomes manifest.

Consequently, systems of great sophistication, like those which created the Romanesque churches of France, have prospered for generations without much formal codification. To be sure, there was a great deal of knowledge and experience passed on from master to apprentice. Certainly knowledge was distilled and perpetuated in a sophisticated lexicon. But this all took place within a human context, within a people.

Formal description often follows late in a vernacular system's life, portending its imminent demise. In maritime history, the first Dutch manuals on shipbuilding appeared only once hegemony in overseas trade had already peaked. The most innovative ship types had been in use for generations. Dutch flat-bottom fishing boats, marvels of sophistication and craftsmanship, continued to be built until well into the twentieth century without any formal description whatsoever. Similarly, the first books describing the building of Dutch windmills were produced at about the time that the steam engine was invented in England.

In contrast, as is examined in more detail below, modernism's preoccupation with systems approaches to building produced numerous highly detailed and minutely documented technical and architectural systems of great logic and invention. But such systems were rarely fully appropriated into a larger social body. Consequently, they were never implemented. That failure cannot adequately be explained solely on technical or economic grounds.

The relationship between social body and system is yet another way in which people and form merge. We previously found territorial structure to be closely related to inhabitation. Live configurations represent agents as players who control the existing built environment and trigger change. In systems, we now observe a melding through the act of making: systems represent and unite the varied social bodies that share in implementing and sustaining them.

## Explicitness and Social Structure

Technical systems within the contemporary built environment are exhaustively documented in manuals and regulations. Indeed, the modern building seems almost fully described in every regard except its meaning. Compare the skyscraper with the medieval cathedral. The latter's process was not informal; there were rules, principles, and exhaustive knowledge at play. But these were not formally documented—certainly not in standard practice, and hardly for any specific project. Compared to present practice, the medieval process seems overwhelmingly implicit.

Sophistication by itself does not explain this difference: it is difficult to ascertain which typology is more complex overall. The same goes for other historic ways of building. The Japanese traditional house, which continues to be architecturally prestigious, is perhaps more linked to modern sensibility in its systemic qualities. But historically, although a precise vocabulary existed, building knowledge was again passed from person to person with a minimum of formal documentation and codification. When we compare systems, we find that the extent of documentation required is determined by social not technical factors.

Romanesque and Gothic cathedrals, like traditional Japanese houses, were single systems, controlled by a single guild. The modern building, in contrast, is a combination of many technical subsystems, each related to its own body of specialists. Although the modern steel structure of a tall building may be a primitive form compared to the intricate masonry vaulting system of a Romanesque church, the former is fully documented in drawings, manuals, and codes. Each new variant must be exhaustively described in plans, sections, elevations, and countless details and specifications.

Whereas the historical systems existed under unified control, the contemporary system is subject to dispersed control. The structural frame is typically designed by one party, following the architectural design of another. Systems rules for calculation, detailing, and overall design may be controlled by yet another body. The parts are fabricated by other parties, and frequently erected on site by others still.

Thus in steel construction, variant design, variant execution, and system structure are each controlled by different agents. No one party is cognizant of all phases or aspects of the system. Overlap of knowledge and experience is partial. Exhaustive codification and documentation are therefore absolutely essential to make it work.

In contrast, the Japanese wood frame house, no less sophisticated or complex a system, was designed, manufactured, and erected by a single responsible party, making the exchange of documents unnecessary. The same can be said of the Romanesque masonry system. Hence patterns of control cause modes of systematization and degrees of implicitness to vary significantly.

In the contemporary building, a large number of subsystems must also be combined. The way they are combined, and what is combined, may vary from case to case. Among socially diverse players combined in an ad hoc manner, coordination of action is inevitably required.

## Coordination

Coordination of subsystems, by itself, was not altogether foreign to historic processes. Only a few generations ago, the Dutch contractor ordered any window by simply stating the type of window, and its size: vertically in number of brick courses, and horizontally in number of "headers." This simplified transfer of technical specifics required no standardization of parts.

Such effective coordination between carpenter and contractor depended on two conditions that no longer universally pertain. First, brick masonry had to be the stable and universal construction method. Coordination could not work if precast concrete panels might be readily substituted. Second, both parties had to operate in the same place and local culture, in socioeconomic interdependence.

Contemporary buildings integrate numerous diverse subsystems, many of them proprietary. Parties controlling subsystems are now interchangeable and geographically dispersed. Logistical coordination is of the essence in contemporary building: sequenced processing of parts and managed coordination of social bodies in play. But all depends on a prior determination of selected subsystems, how they are distributed in space (and over time), and how their parts are located relative to one another.

These plans are made by designers and consultants: disparate parties cognizant only of parts of the whole, who must ensure the exact location of actual parts in space. Their judgment must reflect the impact of control patterns on the combination of subsystems, and they in turn determine how subsystems affect control patterns. This dynamic interaction is addressed largely implicitly.

Hence thematic systems merge social and material organization, explaining the one by the other. At issue is not how systems can be better described, but how the inevitable implicit coordination among parties is best achieved. This question leads to the discussion of typology—the third form of understanding—below.

## 15.3 Traveling Systems

### Systems Travel Among People

Systems may be technical by virtue of the skill and knowledge necessary to use them, yet readily recognized and appreciated by laypeople. Stylistic choices are based on values with little technical content: to recognize and appreciate a classical façade does not require the ability either to design or to build one.

The choice of technical systems may likewise demonstrate extrinsic values. Viollet-le-Duc often rationalized his preference for the Gothic style in terms of its intrinsic technical clarity and logic of construction, but his preference was also based on Gallic self-identification and national pride. Bruno Taut, speaking for modernism, rejected brick, because that material had been compromised by extensive use in the slums of nineteenth-century industrial cities. To him, steel and concrete represented the clarity and honesty promised by the modern age.

Thus, system preferences express all manner of social values apart from the particular skills and knowledge needed to execute the systems. The choice of thematic systems expresses profound common understanding above and beyond inherent systemic qualities. Tied to social meaning and identification, systems accompany people wherever they go. The first Dutch colonists in Jakarta built smothering brick canal houses along newly dug canals that were infested with malarial mosquitoes. Doubtless, they did not at first know how to build otherwise. But a familiar environment, however dangerous for their health, also provided emotional security in an incomprehensible foreign world.

Systems, as ways of working and being, travel with people. They can accordingly connect to social networks serving populations dispersed in time and place without diminishing their power. The same system is thus found in very different locations, its variants always produced by agents who share the values invested in them.

## The Classical System

Classicistic architecture is an extensive system that has represented specific values connecting people in very different places. An architectural style tracing its roots—via Andrea Palladio—to the ancient Romans and Greeks, classicistic architecture ranges from courthouses and churches scattered throughout historic settlements of the North American continent, to British colonial architecture throughout the empire, to czarist Russia's architecture of the wealthy and the cultured. It also trickled down to find expression in the middle-class townhouses of Georgian London.

The initial elements of this thematic system came to full bloom within a few generations, during a brief period of widespread Athenian cultural hegemony, several millennia ago. Over time, in successive stages embraced by successive cultures, it continued to combine great dignity of form with remarkable adaptability to varying contexts.

The cultural, technical, and aesthetic associations of its elements, particularly the anthropomorphic presence of the column, made it endure as an image of human refinement. Identification with Hellenic conquest in the East and later with the hegemony of Rome made it synonymous with power. Ultimately, its combined beauty and power proved irresistible to various peoples and cultures for two thousand years. Foreign publication of Palladio's illustrated books made the classicistic way of building widely accessible. There was no need to visit Rome or the Veneto. As is characteristic of thematic form, classical architecture was continually redefined as it was emulated, though kinship to the original always remained visible.

Since the eighteenth century, the social body identifying with things classical has remained an elite of power and culture distributed across the world, ignoring national boundaries, though many Palladian elements have been appropriated subsequently into regional vernaculars. Architectural qualities aside, this thematic system is of particular interest because it resides in a social body without a clear locus: its adherents belong to a network, not to any place or territory.

## The International Style

In this respect, the classicistic thematic system is comparable with modernism, the stylistic system that largely supplanted it in the first decades of this century. The network identifying with modernism again comprises a society operating across national and geographic boundaries. Thus, while the so-called International Style was certainly innovative, its provenance was not: in fact, both styles were championed by an international power elite.

Subtle differences distinguish the networks that respectively spawned the classicistic and the modernist. Classicistic architecture represented part of a broader culture deeply rooted in history. It was common to those sharing a particular education, which included the classical languages, certain classical texts, and a code of values and beliefs.

Modernism, in its infancy, seems to have rested on a more fragile alliance between a professional elite and a commercial/bureaucratic one, each having its own reasons for maintaining a worldwide network. The International Style initially traveled among architects, via personal connections, conferences, exhibitions, publications, and, eventually, educational institutions. In housing and urban design, it became connected with bureaucratic institutions, many of which themselves maintained international links.

For a long time, the mainstream wielding political and commercial power remained suspicious of modern art and architecture, clinging to historical styles. But connections between modern architecture and international political power, as exemplified in the United Nations in Manhattan, or in Chandigarh, strengthened rapidly in the wake of the Second World War. Eventually, with widespread adoption of modernism in the United States, a link with corporate culture was forged.

## Network-Based Systems

In antiquity, environmental systems traveled with people. Thus, Greek colonizers exported their environmental structure, their ways of building houses and towns. Those ways were transplanted into new soil, creating new settlements. The colonial environment would transform over time, adopting new forms in response to new local conditions and influences. A people could not simply appropriate alien structures or forms yet maintain its identity. For example, as Islam spread over North Africa, Islamic environmental form traveled and transformed together with its culture of origin. Spanish colonial town building in Latin America witnessed a similar pattern of exportation, growth, and transformation.

But during the era when classicistic architecture proliferated throughout the Western world, something else happened. The Palladian style was imported by a variety of peoples to serve as a cultural and formal overlay, to graft onto older local building traditions. The Palladian system seemingly traveled autonomously, spreading from one local culture to another, without an accompanying movement of populations.

The vehicle by which it traveled, and in which it permanently resided, was a networked social body without a locus, distinct from any local culture or group. Aided by printed examples to emulate and by graphic explanations of the systemic elements supporting it, this way of designing was adopted by an international elite spanning a good deal of the globe.

Certainly, systems traveling via network have always existed. As traders and technicians spread technical systems, distant societies adapted to new manufacturing techniques. Dutch traders brought Chinese earthenware to Europe, resulting, eventually, in indigenous Delft blue pottery. Chinese silk-making came to Persia; spaghetti came to Italy. In such instances, transplanted technical systems took root in new localities and were able to sustain themselves without further support of the network that delivered them. In fact, local adoption of foreign technology was often a means to become independent from such networks.

Current technical systems, by contrast, increasingly seem to depend permanently on the technological and social networks within which they reside. Local manufacturing depends on the flow of proprietary information and knowledge sustained by specialists and technicians. Whereas in the past, environmental form was usually not affected by network-based systems, we now find systems for plumbing, electricity, and steel and concrete structures penetrating even the *barrios* and *favelas* of environments exclusively controlled by informal local powers. Although there are local variants of these systems, their structures are sustained by a network society. Parts from which the variants are composed are most likely manufactured elsewhere. Factory locations are, themselves, network dependent.

The network-based environmental system, which first came to full fruition with Palladian architecture, is now evident not only in high-rise technology and large precast concrete panel construction, but also in more humble modern technical systems that serve settlement, such as water, gas, electrical power, sewage, sanitary equipment, telephone, and television. The latter, being less weighted with social and cultural values, penetrate much more deeply into environmental form and are found in places that otherwise display a distinctly local architecture.

The irrefutable innovation of the modern era lies in systems of all kinds being sustained permanently by network—as opposed to local—societies. Of this phenomenon, building systems and architectural styles represent only a part. It seems to encompass all ways of producing and signals a more fundamental shift than mere increase of scale and frequency in manufacturing and commerce.

259

**15.3** *Squatter settlement La Reina, Santiago de Chile— House with television antenna.*

## 15.4 The Abstractness of Systems

### Stud Frame Construction Dematerialized

Systems knowledge involves much factual data: which physical parts are available, how they perform, and how they assemble. But the systemic also has its abstract, immaterial properties, as becomes evident when we scrutinize the North American stick-built frame system.

During a century of use, every subsystem within the wooden stud wall-building system has been changed. "Two-by-fours" are currently standardized at slightly less than $1^{1}/_{2}'' \times 3^{1}/_{2}''$. Nominal eight-foot wood studs are often pre-cut to $7'\ 7^{1}/_{2}''$, or routinely replaced by steel or aluminum studs. "Wood" sheathing may take the form of plywood, reconstituted wood by-products, or structural insulation board; "wood" siding can be achieved in composite, aluminum, or plastic panels. The lath-and-plaster interior wall finish is now routinely constructed in boards made of gypsum sandwiched between layers of paper. Of course, the nails have become "fasteners," shot or screwed rather than hammered.

Although every subsystem has been completely reinterpreted, the whole remains intact, recognizable as the evolving composite system created a century ago. While each individual interpretation may vary, relations between parts remain constant. These parts, themselves, are again systems, reflecting constant relations among yet other parts. Parts may change, as long as the relations among them do not.

The system's sophisticated and abstract understanding of spatial and functional principles—independent of material selection—is familiar to all who actually build, though it is never documented or explicitly expressed. It is a prime example of knowing by working and doing, rather than by description or definition: a knowledge without words. Words are thus reserved for naming parts and describing the systems formed with them; that is to say, the words occur to specify conditions of transformation and variation.

The implicit relations are never mentioned, because they do not change.

## Classicistic Architecture in Different Materials

A similar dematerialized understanding of a system occurred over time in the classical orders. The Greeks built temples in marble. Unfinished column drums were stacked on site with great precision. Masons would measure them in position, subsequently calculating and executing the required entasis, finish cutting, fluting, and polishing the monumental shafts.

But the Romans built their classical columns of brick, pargeted with a cement plaster finish, a technique later adapted in the Renaissance by Palladio and others. Later still, in North America, we find beautifully proportioned and executed classical columns fashioned of wooden staves. And in late-nineteenth-century American cities like New York and Baltimore, we find classical façades executed in cast iron. Here again, the system passed on from generation to generation was dematerialized. Not bound to any single mode of production, the shapes and proportions of its parts and the relations among them remained constant.

## Dematerialized Systems Shared by Nonprofessionals

When dematerialized concepts are shared among laypeople and craftsworkers alike, the latter bear more responsibility for their actual materialization and for the structural integrity of the whole. Classicistic architecture, as a conception of relations between abstract forms, is old enough to have passed fully into the general culture. As with vernacular systems, specialized knowledge and general knowledge, although distinguishable, are inseparable.

With respect to stick-built systems, we know that the balloon frame was actually invented around 1850, in response to improved timber milling and the introduction of the wire nail. But that invention was limited to the frame. Many other subsystems subsequently became attached. Together, these structure the contemporary North American house. The integration of all these subsystems cannot be seen as one specific invention. It was an outcome of using the balloon frame. In this exceptional case, we can trace the emergence of a system that operates as a true vernacular from the moment of its birth.

In both examples, fairly complex systems have become part of a more widely shared understanding of the built environment. Abstract understanding in both cases—without material specification or knowledge of technical details—extends far beyond the body of specialists, to clients and users.

There is good reason to conclude that these examples are by no means the exception: for a system to pervade the built environment, it must settle into the broader society of inhabitants. This process seems to go with its translation into a more abstract notion of relations of forms in space, as its systemic qualities are separated from particular materials and technologies.

261

Chapter 16

# Systems Misunderstood

# 16.1 A System's Image

## North American Timber Frame Houses

As conceptual systems executed in a variety of materials, the classical orders depend almost exclusively on social appropriation for their survival. Modernism's sweep through Western architecture accordingly tolled, albeit temporarily, the death knell of classicistic architecture. That system became moribund, cast off by society, only to be resurrected when its social value returned.

During succeeding waves of eclecticism, the acceptance or rejection of architectural styles based entirely on symbolic meaning and social identification is easily understood. It happens with technical systems as well. Once the symbolic and aesthetic qualities associated with a way of building are again appreciated, its technical system may adapt and reanimate. A case in point is the current timber frame revival in North America.

Houses had long been built in heavy timber frames. Then wood stud construction appeared. Uniform two-by-four studs are milled from cheaper lumber. They are easier to transport, to mill, to cut to length, and to handle on site. Kiln dried, they do not require long warehousing to establish dimensional stability. "Stick framing" is easier to build and easier to design. It requires less knowledge and less skilled labor. It is a comparatively forgiving and easy-to-correct system, even after construction.

Wood stud construction rapidly permeated home building technology. Old-fashioned

**16.1** *Cairo—Housing blocks: typical products of European prefab concrete panel systems. Their aggressive exportation to developing countries coincided with rejection of the systems in Western Europe (page 262).*

timber framing simply could not compete with the new technology. It disappeared for obvious technical and economic reasons. Yet this way of building, updated and with factory precut timber, is now experiencing a resurgence, in spite of its drawbacks. Clients who can afford it now specify exposed post-and-beam structure. Timber frame designers and builders are proliferating.[1]

Paralleling developments in wood frame construction, modern subsystems now easily combine with timber framing. In-system exterior walls and roofs now frequently consist of industrially produced stressed skin panels. Nonetheless, in utilitarian terms, a timber frame structure destined for full fit-out with modern subsystems has little going for it. Plumbing, electric wiring, and heating installation require more time, labor, and finish detailing in timber framing than within conventional stud framing. In this case, the social body sustaining the system is motivated primarily by aesthetics and social valuation, rather than by economic or technical efficiency. Applied research to rationalize production followed increased demand. Timber frame housing has consequently become a laboratory for systems integration.

## Hassan Fathy and the Mud Brick House

A technical system that is arguably superior to common practice can conversely be rejected for reasons beyond the practical or function. A striking example is found in Hassan Fathy's account of his attempt to revive in modern times the ancient Egyptian mud brick vaulting system.[2]

As a young architect, Fathy came to admire the traditional mud brick buildings of by-gone eras in his native Egypt. He found them not only beautiful but also well suited to the climate and the light of the Nile region. Their vaulted and domed spaces remained cool even in the late afternoon. Light admitted by the small, deeply recessed windows lost its harshness and became imbued with many shades of color. At night, the massive walls slowly released heat stored throughout the day, protecting inhabitants from chill desert winds.

Fathy initially sought in vain to reinvent mud brick building. He could neither prevent dried mud from cracking nor erect barrel vaults without centering. Finally, he discovered that this building tradition survived in small southern villages, near what is now Lake Aswan. Every villager knew how to build a vault. The technique was surprisingly simple. Fathy soon set out to reintroduce this way of working to other architects and engineers, whose concrete boxes were hot inside, ugly outside, and expensive all around.

Others seeking to promote inexpensive ways for the poor to shelter themselves subsequently joined in his efforts to preserve and extend mud brick technology. Attempts were made to improve it with admixtures to make the walls more resistant to moisture, diminishing maintenance requirements. State-of-the-art supply systems were incorporated to demonstrate the system's compatibility with modern lifestyles and environmental requirements.

Fathy's proposals were rejected wholesale—by fellow architects, engineers, and administrators. Although the arguments were framed in technical jargon, technology was not the issue. Economic, functional, and technical rationale aside, there was simply no conceptual space for mud brick in the modern world. The new professional class steeped in Western ways was not prepared to abandon Western knowl-

265

edge, and attendant prestige and power, in favor of technology properly owned and executed by peasants.

The forces united in opposition were formidable: reintroducing this abandoned technical system would require that society entirely reorganize its culture of building, cooperating in specific new ways. A web of interrelated activities, based on given assumptions and beliefs, and substantial economic interests, would have to change. Adopting mud brick would require that construction workers and architects reskill. Building codes needed to be changed. Banks had to be persuaded to underwrite the funding of mud brick projects. Public bodies had to accept low-rise high-density environment, in place of the freestanding blocks compatible with concrete construction.

Fathy's quest, stubbornly and arrogantly sustained over a lifetime, tragically illustrates how socially rooted a technical system ultimately becomes. In jointly building, we interweave local social fabric with other networks. The result cannot be unraveled by rational and technical arguments.

Followers of Fathy still create beautiful architecture in mud brick. But their clientele—for the moment—is limited to independent souls, intellectuals and artists who not only appreciate the environmental quality of this architecture but also adopt its symbolism, frequently to distance themselves from modernism and Western values.

## General Panel Corporation

Fathy's generation of architects was obsessed with technical systems. While his peers rejected the past, they dove head first into pursuing the "dream of the factory-made house," as carefully documented in Gilbert Herbert's book of that title.[3] For a period of ten years, from 1942 to 1952, Walter Gropius and Konrad Wachsmann led the search to develop a "fully industrialized house," which was to be produced by the newly founded General Panel Corporation.

General Panel's integrated system, from which walls and roofs could be assembled, boasted beautifully conceived details. It was an exercise in pure ideology. To industrialize building, a limited number of standardized elements were designed and produced. By merely combining these, an unlimited number of different dwellings would then be erected—swiftly, easily, and with a precision intended to equal that of the motor car and other mass-produced factory products.

But in disregarding the house as a combination of autonomous subsystems, Wachsmann and Gropius betrayed their impatience with complex organization and revealed an ultimate yearning for singular systems control. At the wellspring of unified control, the enlightened architect would then cause marvelous variation to flow.

The General Panel story stands for many. As Herbert notes,

*This is the period when European architects of standing in the modern movement (Martin Wagner and Ernst May, Hans Poelzig and Hans Scharoun, Josef Hoffmann, Max and Bruno Taut, Otto Bartning) engaged with enthusiasm in designing prototypes for industrial production or even total systems of prefabrication, developing them in*

16.2 **The Dream of the Factory-Made House**

*the greatest of detail. In this crusade they were joined by Richard Neutra, Lawrence Kocher, Albert Frey, Barry Byrne, Buckminster Fuller, and many other notable architects in the United States. Their efforts, it must be conceded, were rarely brought to practical fruition; successes in the field were limited, disappointments frequent. Yet despite the lack of tangible results, the experiments continued and hopes were high.*[4]

The total number of integrated factory-made dwelling units actually produced through various incarnations remained insignificant. Their long-term ideological impact clearly overshadowed their minimal environmental presence. Eventually, in the heyday of mass housing, the leading ideas behind the American integrated prefabricated panel system were applied in Europe as well, but this time in concrete. Yet these highly compromised systems never gained the initial market share anticipated by their supporters. Absent government subsidies, they could not survive. Such hopelessly adulterated interpretations of the initial idea would surely have been dismissed out of hand by Gropius.

## Ideology and Reality

To develop the new way of thinking behind the dream required a priori rejection of all traditional ways of building, and of all history. Neither precedent, nor the past, nor contemporary practice could inform architecture or urbanism: henceforth, the built environment was to be reinvented. No sooner had the European intellectual diaspora brought Gropius to Harvard than he reportedly sent the school's premier architectural historian packing. Ideology remained the central force compelling so many of Gropius's peers to reinvent the house: as a factory product, it would unlock the door to a shining future in which all building would be radically different from the past, or the war-torn present.

Clearly, housing has always resulted from collective understanding expressed in form and systems, as well as in building technology. Vernacular and traditional buildings as complex artifacts embody the efforts and inventions of untold actors over a sustained period. The vernacular house combines a number of subsystems, each under control of an artisan following a particular trade: carpenter, mason, thatcher, plumber, and so forth. By the nineteenth century, the introduction of new materials and new utilities had dramatically increased the number of actors and decision makers.

This increasing social complexity and sophistication was disregarded by Gropius and others. The intricate social choreography by which houses are actually built was never seen as a point of departure. Instead, the house was recast as a product to be professionally redesigned. To render its many subsystems controllable, they would be unified, reduced to one. All enclosures would utilize a single type of panel. The ideal panel would accordingly integrate everything: structure, sheathing, window, insulation, cabling, and any other conduits.

In short, the dream of the factory-made house amounted to a coup intended to seize and centralize technical control. This may explain why, in spite of all good intentions, concrete panel systems proved sustainable on a large scale only in totalitarian Eastern European regimes. Where central control was solidified, "integrated" building systems did indeed result—and they were every architect's nightmare. Instead of streamlined, well-detailed industrial products available in a great variety of combinations, these systems produced lum-

**16.2**  *Daly City, California—Tract houses.*

**16.3**  *Dammam, Saudi Arabia—Manufactured aluminum prefab elements. Modern materials and technology are ubiquitously applied in informal, small-scale settings throughout the world.*

bering, standardized, monotonous housing barracks.

Yet the dream persisted. In the late 1960s, notably, the American government sponsored a national competition to defeat the housing shortage. The entries in "Operation Breakthrough" illustrated that the dream was still very much alive.

No submission even remotely approached large-scale implementation.

## Silent Industrialization

More than half a century after Gropius's failed attempt, housing construction is almost fully industrialized. Each subsystem of the stud-framed house is now subject to large-scale industrial production. Sheathing and wall surfaces have become panelized, windows and doors are fully systematized factory-made components, and so on. This trend was already well under way by the time Gropius's General Panel Corporation came into existence. The gradual shift has gone largely unremarked, perhaps because it happened in the context of common residential building.

Although the move toward industrialization appears stagnant in the United States, it continues unabated in Europe and Japan. More and more subsystems—from façade systems and roof systems, to heating, ventilating, bathroom, and kitchen equipment, to drainage systems and water and gas lines—have fully factory-produced components. Specifically designed for automated production, they arrive on site in increasingly customized subassemblies. The value added to the house by systems manufacturers is steadily increasing; value added by the local contractor is steadily decreasing.

Such "silent" industrialization has finally gained recognition. Advocates of Open Building have begun to study the theoretical and methodological principles on which it rests. As the sophistication of industrially produced residential subsystems increases, components become simpler, perform better, and are combined in smarter ways. Open Building now seeks to improve subsystem autonomy and coordination. The contemporary house is understood to result from complex dynamics, as individual acts of technical design and manufacturing constantly shift, innovate, and recombine.

Industrialization has ultimately succeeding by doing exactly the opposite of what advocates of integrated system design sought to achieve. True to the nature of the built environment as a largely implicit phenomenon, this ongoing process was not professionally planned. Nor was it predicted or sanctioned by any government or professional body. It has been neither widely documented nor researched, and to date, its ubiquitous existence has not significantly informed architectural practice or education.[5]

271

## 16.3 Repetition and Uniformity

### Eliminating Individual Action

Initial confusion regarding the "industrialization" of building systems led to a further misconception, as industrial production became synonymous with uniformity, with endless grid repetition of reductive standardized building forms over a large field. That misconception arose from a misapplied analogy: because the industrial age mass-produced identical commodities by machine, mass-producing large numbers of identical dwellings would somehow make them industrial products.

A uniform character was thus insinuated by association with the inevitability and prestige of industrial production. In reality, uniformity resulted solely from centralized decision making and execution: by military bureaucracy, by aggressive entrepreneurs like Levitt in postwar America, by subsidized housing corporations in Western Europe, and by outright government control of production in Eastern Europe.

Form repetition is not an invention of modernism: identical columns and capitals graced Sumerian, Egyptian, Greek, and Roman architecture.[6] It is also apparent, in less visually compelling ways, in colonies like Olynthus, which comprise many houses built as a large single project. In all cases, uniformity results from removing personal initiative from the creation of the artifact.

To achieve uniformity requires awesome discipline: humans by nature explore thematically, understanding a thing by variation. We find unmistakable minor variations in each piece of mass-produced domestic pottery exported from China, not only because workers' hands adjust the uniform mold but also because individual workers paint the standard decoration. No two specimens are ever exactly

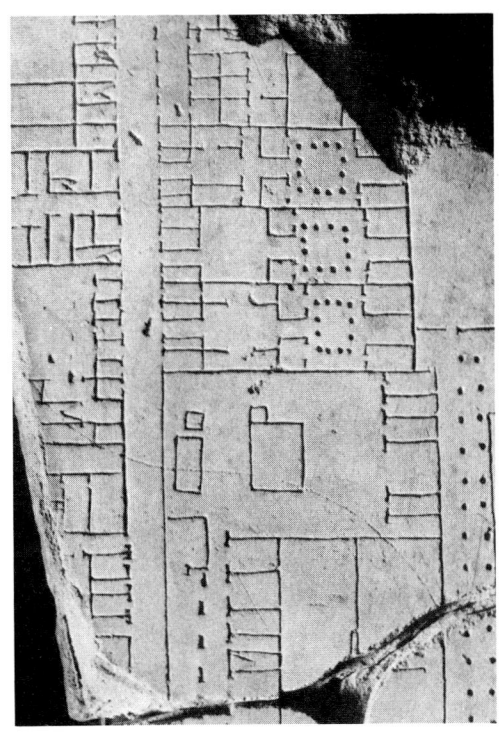

**16.4** *Luxor, Egypt—Columns: an ancient example of uniformity in production.*

**16.5** *Fragment of the Forma Urbis map of imperial Rome, ca. 200 A.D.—A detail of the etched marble shows three identical houses, suggesting that the small builder/ developer familiar today was already operating in classical times. Courtesy of the University of Michigan Press.*

the same. To make two capitals of columns indistinguishable, human effort must focus on becoming machinelike. While automation can effectively eliminate any human impact, uniformity is not simply an inherent by-product of machine production: it results from centralizing design control. Thus, a fragment of the Forma Urbis, a marble map of imperial Rome, reveals three identical houses with atrium and peristyle: the cookie-cutter imprint of the small-scale builder/developer is no modern phenomenon.

Leaves, waves, and wind patterns traced in sand dunes repeat endlessly, but without cloning or uniformity. It is unnatural, in the literal sense of the word, to produce identical things. Clinical uniformity signals an artificial condition resulting from a uniquely human intervention, in which production has been systematically cleansed of individual impact. For that reason, uniformity has always symbolized the presence of a "higher authority," be it human or divine.

## Sekisui

The ravages of the Second World War, combined with rapid population increase, produced a desperate need for shelter throughout postwar Europe. A world in transition from wartime to civilian culture quickly fixated on centralized control and management to marshal and deploy the forces necessary to defeat the problem. Design was standardized; assembly line production was imitated. Uniformity was simply accepted without question as the price to be paid for "efficient production."

At the same time, citizens throughout Japan also desperately needed shelter. Many had access to modest plots of land, whether left vacant following the destruction of the original house or acquired during the redistribution of private property. A different model emerged as the fledgling Sekisui Company industrialized housing production.

Sekisui's founders realized that any uniform house design could only suit so many individual clients. The housing problem to be solved was differently stated than it had been in Europe: how could Sekisui develop a way to offer many different houses to many different clients? They eventually developed a light system of cold-rolled steel frame components. By combining standardized profiles and joints, they easily created many shapes. Simple detailing systematically affixed "off-the-shelf" floors, walls, and roofs to this steel skeleton. Modularized dimensions simplified prefabrication.

This approach was firmly rooted in the local house building tradition, according to which a timber frame is quickly erected and then receives all other parts of the house. The new steel frame system joined together all conventional components of the house; and it also enabled strategic sequencing of prefabrication, which immediately followed custom design. Design was performed by a network of local architects contracted by the company, and the houses were built by similarly engaged local contractors. Employing off-the-shelf materials and

components allowed Sekisui Company to keep current and take advantage of new products on the market. By the early 1990s, Sekisui was producing and erecting more than sixty thousand custom units per year, all individually designed and erected. This is an astonishing and unprecedented production total; not even in standardized mass housing has it been approached elsewhere.

Comparing Sekisui with the producers of European mass housing illustrates more than just diametrically opposed ideas about industrial production, or an ability and willingness to recognize and harness existing social structures for building. The core of the difference regards control. Sekisui decided to recognize the design role of the individual user/client; European professionals assumed this was impossible. Technical differences ultimately reflected social patterns of control relative to the making of environmental form, which determine the consensus reached among those exercising that control. Both solutions no doubt reflected deep-seated historical differences in the role of professional designers and of government, as well as in land use.

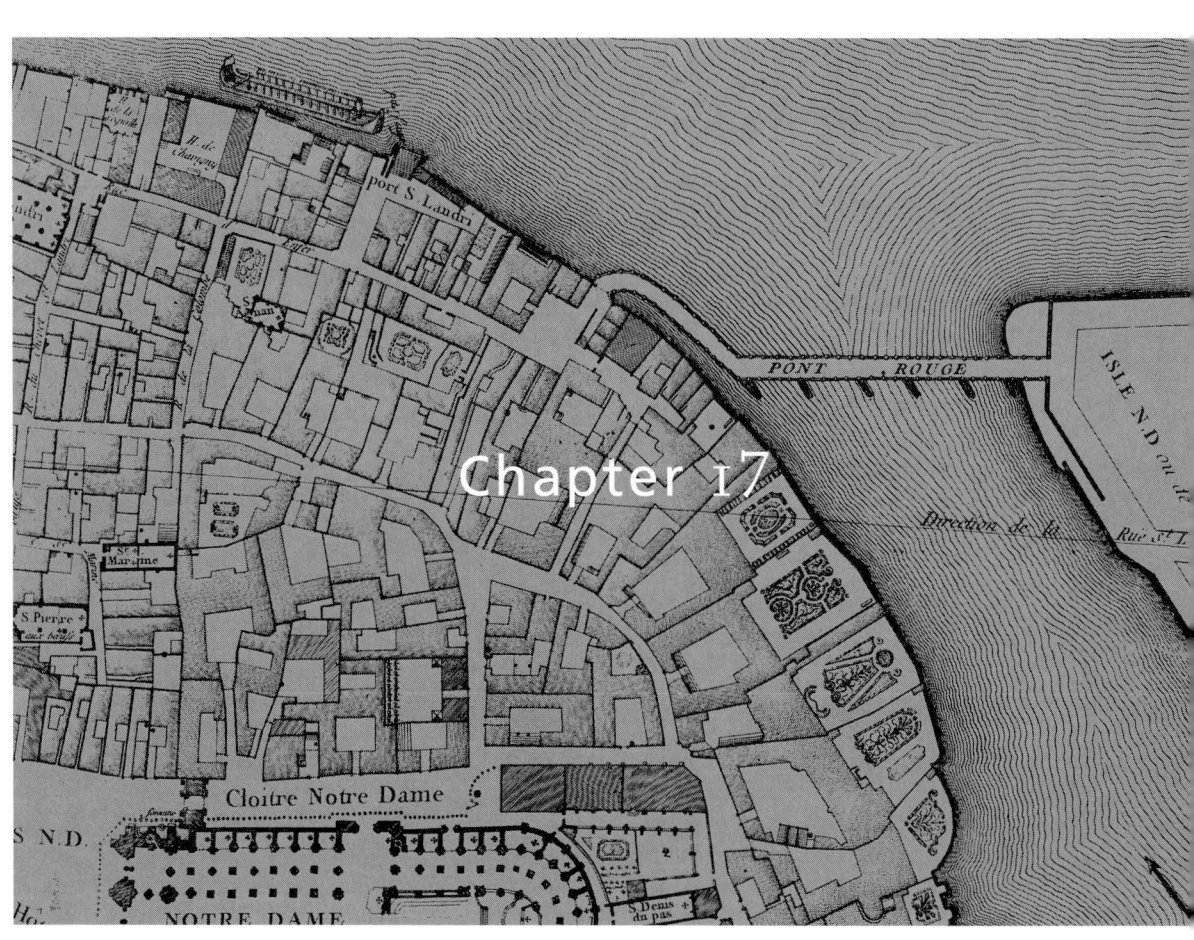

Chapter 17

Type

## 17.1  Environmental Types

### The Holistic Environmental Type

To define the Pompeiian house type, we may describe its spatial system: *atrium and peristyle, spaces open to the sky, are surrounded by rooms varying in size and function.* We may alternately describe it by material system: *masonry bearing walls pargeted with plaster carry wooden floors and roofs.* Or we may describe it as a system of representations, as convincingly done by Andrew Wallace-Hadrill. The description of a type generally combines observed patterns and systems. We may apply what Clifford Geertz calls "thick description."[1] The environmental type constitutes a comprehensive environmental world unto itself.

Environmental types recognize complex and multifaceted unities within the built environment. The house is a prime example, but rooms, neighborhoods, and towns similarly constitute environmental types, subsuming all kinds of material parts and spaces. The room as a type may include characteristic windows and lighting, but also furniture arrangement. The street, as a type, includes a physical system on a certain level, as discussed in part I, but it also implies a spatial entity that includes trees, sidewalks, streetlights, and the façades of buildings that line it.

This conception of environmental type further clarifies figure 3.5. Here, too, in the right-hand column, we found "wholes." The house, as a type, belongs to the "built spaces" of that chart, while the "room" is a combination of furniture and partitioning. The "street" as a

**17.1**  *Paris, 1754—Environs of Notre Dame, with typical Parisian private courtyard houses, some with formal gardens in the back. Detail from the map by Abbé Jean Delagrive (page 276).*

whole is on a par with the "block," similarly composed of roads and buildings. Thus the type typically straddles two levels in the order of form.

But combined elements represent a type only when particular constraints are added. Four walls may abstractly define a room, but it becomes a bedroom or kitchen only when inhabitation arranges furniture and equipment in a certain way. The house, as a type, is not just any selection of building parts and infill: its typological form derives from combining specific elements in a a socially determined fashion.

## The Type Defies Total Description

Given full documentation of an established house type—for example, the Venetian Gothic palace, baroque Amsterdam canal house, or Georgian terraced house—humans reveal a remarkable capacity to grasp the complexity of the type as a whole, even creating successful variants without much difficulty.

On the other hand, it proves exceedingly difficult to achieve a working definition for any given type. Within any group, individual definitions informed by experience will differ broadly. Some may define "typical" aspects: subsystems or patterns recognized within the type, its spatial organization or façade. Yet others will focus on the building system itself. More impressionistic narratives may describe the experience of entering the type and exploring its interior, focusing on how the type relates to its context.[2]

Each individual description may prove both reasonable and factually accurate, yet the essence of the type ultimately defies exhaustive description and cataloguing: there always remains more to point out. It likewise defies

systems definition, as the whole manifestly exceeds the sum of its parts.

Environmental types exist to be made, then appropriated. The daily rhythm of ongoing inhabitation links them to social bodies, shaping our movements, habits, and social relations. The experiential relationship between type and inhabitant transcends function. It is existential, encompassing all that surrounds us. The act of inhabitation reaffirms type through daily interaction, just as such continuity and repetition over time initially create the type.

## A System of Smaller Unities

In a phenomenon susceptible of only partial description, which system or pattern we choose to see in the type becomes a matter of preference and purpose. Spatial and physical systems represent but two among many possible dimensions in which typological description can occur. Clearly, the inherent implicitness of the type makes discussion problematic.

It is here that environmental names (see chapter 13.4) link language to form: *atrium, porch, iwan,* and the like denote utterly familiar units of space and form, obviating further description. Such names lend themselves to the description of types. Let us take once more a familiar seventeenth-century example.

The *canal house* is entered along the *sidewalk* via a *stoop,* bypassing the protruding *pothuis* (basement extension). The front door opens into the *voorzaal* (literally, "front salon"), a high space with stairs leading up to the *opkamer* (literally, "up room"), a low mezzanine space in the back of the house. Some rooms have a *schouw* (open fireplace), built-in *bedsteden* (sleeping alcoves), and so on.

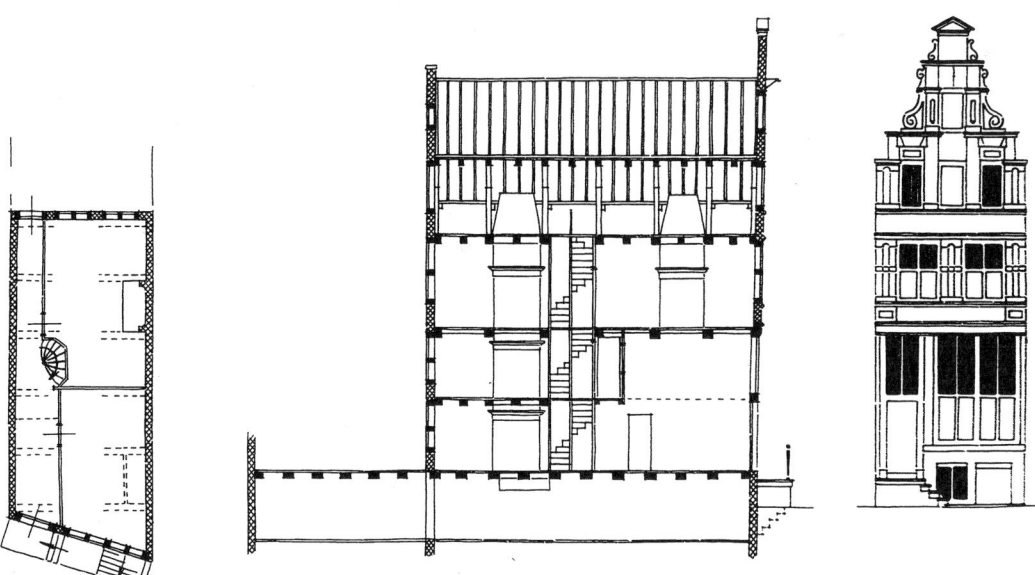

**17.2** *Amsterdam—Canal house plan, section, and elevation. Courtesy of H. J. Zantkuijl.*

Thus, the house type combines other, smaller entities, each with its own established identity. Each particular instance of the type may be described by conveying these component "typological parts" and their relative position. Such description and vocabulary reflect most naturally, if not most clinically, how the environment of rooms and houses, neighborhoods and streets, is built, inhabited, and shared.

A given type may also demonstrate significant range in size. Comparing large and small instances reveals much about the understanding embodied in the type. Such a comparison is best made in the context of an urban fabric, because it gives us a large number of instances sharing not only type but social, economic, and technical context as well.

Lastly, similar typological parts may be found in distinct, but related, types. For instance, a number of distinct Middle Eastern house types feature *iwans*, though other parts may vary.

Future environmental research may demonstrate systemic kinship between different types composed out of a similar set of typological parts. But the field of study may prove complex. Similar kinds of form may be linked to different words; and the same word may be linked to a wide range of form variations.

## 17.2 Variation within a Given Type

### Sizes of Component Parts Remain Consistent

In observing the Pompeiian house, we had opportunity to note a wide range in size among the variants. Courtyard sizes vary predictably: the large house has a large atrium. Rooms cluster about every larger space, public street as well as private courtyard. But room size displays a remarkably narrow range of sizes, lending scale to the fabric as a whole. The larger courtyard is consequently lined with more rooms, rather than larger ones.

Dimensions in the Pompeiian fabric relate to available length of spanning timber or to practical vault size. Both determine bay size, which, in turn, limits room size. Dining halls, workshops, and modest bedrooms alike are limited by the same structural spans. Larger spaces accordingly multiply and combine bays, as evidenced by columns or piers.

The same space-making strategy is evident in the Gothic palazzo of Venice (see figure 7.2), where rooms are arrayed along a long central hall, shunting canal breezes through the house toward the courtyard beyond. The central hall functions like the communal courtyard or atrium space around which smaller private spaces are arranged. But because the covered central hall is a single bay spanned by wooden beams, it is substantially larger only in length.

The act of building brings consistency in size. The limited span within the Pompeiian fabric conforms to normal room size. Almost universally, in the domestic vernacular, a normal room is very roughly about ten to twelve feet. That dimension combines reasonable use size with a reasonable wall-to-wall span. Larger spans create bays, which therefore allow partitioning. The contrapuntal relationship between use size and technical constraints defines much variation within type.

As one consequence, the big house is seldom a small house blown up; the small house is never a miniaturization. In seventeenth-century Amsterdam canal houses, sizes of windows, doors, and stoops are similar. The size of the façade itself and the number of windows may vary. But the similarity of spatial dimensions inside houses is striking. The structuring dimension is determined by the normal house lot, typically about six meters (18–20 feet) wide. This allows for three generous windows, or two windows and a door. Rooms are then sized to accommodate two or three windows. When the room is two windows wide, the remaining space may accommodate a corridor, built-in beds, or storage. When building width is one and a half or two lots, positioning more than three windows becomes possible. Thus several rooms are easily accommodated behind the façade.

Consistency of size in the basic parts with which we build—room, door, window, beam—establishes a base scale by which things are measured. The size of a building and of the spaces inside may vary by combination or subdivision of such parts.

In the Chinese traditional house, courtyard size is a function of the number of pavilion bays. Bay size, the distance between columns, is the module by which the whole compound is governed. Spans may vary somewhat between the urban aristocrat's house and artisan's, but there is a remarkable general consistency. Prestige was measured not in exaggerated scale but in the number of courtyards and pavilions, as well as in the articulation and number of bays. Three bays was the norm, and the very powerful were permitted five bays; only the emperor could build a seven-bay pavilion.

Technical span and human body combine to set parameters for room, window, door, and stair sizes. But those constraints neither prede-

termine nor explain the form. The constraints are merely systemic. The description of the type tells us about the disposition of these parts and explains the consistency in their deployment. Why it is one particular disposition and not another remains a matter of convention, reflecting the social body that promulgates the type.

## Stages of Growth

Given constants of size for basic units—span, window, door, and room—the variations in house size reveal qualitative priorities. The Pompeiian house again demonstrates this (see figure 15.2).

The humblest house has only a single central space, partially completed by a few rooms in rudimentary, asymmetrical form. There is no secondary larger space. It seems that the most primitive central space in the humblest house had no impluvium. We do not know how it was illuminated, or how it was roofed at all. But it is nevertheless the embryo that produces the atrium when house size increases.[3]

Next, a peristyle may be found in addition, with only a few columns on one side. If more space is available, columns will surround it. The back garden, however, is entirely optional: it may comprise no more than a few yards of open space between house and garden wall, or it may be absent entirely. Occasionally, the peristyle is missing while atrium and backyard are in place. Often the peristyle is incomplete due to lack of space.

Eventually, there is accommodation for an extended house with a generous garden behind a large complete peristyle. This full-blown version is ordinarily referenced when we speak of the Pompeiian house type, but it may be bet-

283

ter to see it as one extreme in a broad spectrum for which the type stands.

Houses within known typologies manifest characteristic stages of growth and development toward increasingly elaborate forms. The Gothic Venetian palazzo widens, centering and double-loading its spine. The two-room-deep Amsterdam canal house widens and lengthens. Eventually, it acquires a central light well and a "back house."

The narrow and exceptionally deep Taiwanese vernacular shop house first has a roofed central space between front and back rooms. A courtyard then separates the front house from a back house. This pattern often repeats with a second courtyard. Such growth by addition of open spaces and buildings clearly echoes the general layout of the Chinese courtyard house.

It should be noted that in all the examples cited—Chinese, Taiwanese, Dutch, and Pompeiian—the sequence of growth is not one of repetition. The secondary courtyard and the back house are somewhat different from those built first, most likely reflecting differences in use and degree of privacy, as is apparent in the Pompeiian house.[4] Growth always adds new elements that could not be accommodated in the smaller version. This may be a universal characteristic of environmental typology, witnessed on all levels and in all manner of buildings and urban organization.

Stages of growth are not stages of completion. All instances, small and large, represent integral wholes. Thus the common image of the type, as it resides in the social body that inhabits and creates it, is remarkably sophisticated. The shared image is not a template to be applied; instead, it reflects understanding of an organic process, in which the most primitive example contains the germ of the most elaborate one.

## Typology as Dialogue

It is tempting to derive a single form that summarizes the defining "essence" of a type. But typology is never an image of form only. The range of permissible variations and permutations within the type is socially determined and expressed each time an instance is made. The implicit underlying understanding is demonstrably real, as long as it continues to allow such action, thereby uniting the actors.

Thus a type may be compared to an ongoing musical improvisation. As the music continues, each musician plays his or her part. The theme is shaped and clarified by variation: it is not necessarily conclusively summarized in any single passage. While transcription can illuminate our understanding of the performance, recapitulation would be, of necessity, reductive. To understand is to be able to meaningfully participate in the ongoing performance. By analogy, to understand a type is not to summarize its meaning, poetry, and form but to creatively participate in the society which brings forth that type. The act of building demonstrates understanding. Although we have dwelt mainly on spatial organization, in typological variation all aspects of the whole carry significance: materials used, color, detailing, ornamentation, proportions, and so on are as many voices in the composition.

This way of knowing type blocks any attempt to make a definitive "prototype." Each variation is valid only in the context of its formulation. Subsequently, it may lose its power to clarify the type. Eventually, another statement seems to sum things up much better. Each iteration, when successful, constitutes one episode in the ongoing life of the type.

## Typology of Urban Tissue

To navigate in the city, recognition of urban tissue must be joined with higher-level knowledge of urban structure: we must be able to recognize familiar landmark buildings and spaces. Individual mental schemata for orienting ourselves within the city at large, as explored by Kevin Lynch, Donald Appleyard, and others,[5] do not include the knowledge by which we recognize the fabric itself. Urban fabric is knit from elements at the human scale: doors, windows, gables, trees, the profiles of canals and streets. We immediately and intuitively recognize the environment of unique cities like London, Venice, Amsterdam, and Bologna by the way these elements are knit into familiar patterns, systems, and building types.

Recognition of urban tissue can also be typological. There exists, for instance, kinship among seventeenth-century Dutch towns. Detailed observation of Utrecht, Delft, and Amsterdam reveals that they are thematic variations woven of a single urban fabric. Likewise, the Georgian squares and façades of London, Bath, and Dublin are closely related. The urban fabric of each furthermore displays internal consistency among certain unique thematic variations. Kinship is visible in urban typologies throughout the Veneto, although the fabric of Venice proper is quite distinct from that of Burano or other island towns.

Among North American suburbs, we find important local and regional variations, together with amazing consistency over sweeping territorial extents. Similarly, Mediterranean hill towns clearly exhibit a common foundation, although we cannot fail to register the significant differences between Italian, Greek, and Spanish versions.

## 17.3  Type without Shape

Whereas house type and street type weave themselves into a coherent whole, urban fabric has no form; it is mainly a structure of interrelations and continuities. The house may project a distinct exterior shape, but urban fabric is all internal experience: as perpetual inhabitants, we may view it only from within.

## Urban Structure

Familiarity with kinds of urban space—street, alley, square—is no less important for recognizing urban fabric than familiarity with house type. The two define one another to a significant extent. Streets in the traditional Tunisian fabric cannot be conceived apart from the courtyard house. Similarly, the Georgian square cannot be separated from the terrace house by which its space is defined. But street, alley, and square are also elements in a higher-level urban structure with its own typology. Among their combinations we find distinct hierarchies and interrelations.

Urban type is often characterized by linear spaces established in a directional field. The combination of the major Amsterdam canals arranged in their sweeping concentric semicircles with secondary perpendicular canals and streets, and tertiary parallel streets, displays a unique geometry adjusted to local geography as well as a hierarchical structure common to other canal cities.

Topography relates to urban typology. The directional properties of rivers inform the disposition of urban waterways. Major streets in hill towns more or less follow undulating slope contours, while secondary streets and alleys run up and down by way of flights of steps and meandering paths. The structure of old Edin-

burgh (see figure 18.1) is a prime example of a generalizable road hierarchy—a central axis feeding alleys that branch off into the landscape—that acquires special meaning because of adjustment to topography: its main artery forms the sole spine atop a craggy ridge, from which steep alleys thread downward. (San Francisco, where the grid extends uninformed by topography, is an obvious exception.)

Knowing such structures, it seems, requires a more abstract understanding than does recognizing patterns and systems on the building level. The hierarchy of streets, with its fractal landscape geometry, is not generally observable from any single point within an urban environment. When sixteenth-century cartographers like Joan Blaeu drew urban bird's-eye perspectives, citizens saw as a whole for the first time the structure they always had known from within.

Within their own typology, instances of urban structure, with their constant array of spaces, may also vary within the same city. The concentric canal extension of seventeenth-century Amsterdam, inhabited by rich traders, was followed by an orthogonal second extension intended for the artisan class. The latter has canals of far more modest proportions. Both hold their structure in common with the medieval core of Amsterdam, which has no dominant geometry: canals follow the river. Streets perpendicular to them run diagonally down the slope of the dikes. While the difference between the three variants is striking in plan, formal analysis and pedestrian experience alike confirm their common structure. Thus the same model was followed for centuries, guiding each successive extension.

287

**17.3**  *Amsterdam—Schematic exposition of three historic variations of the same basic urban fabric. The seventeenth-century extension (*top and right*) follows the same disposition of urban elements as the medieval core (*bottom*): major canals run parallel, and streets run perpendicular to them. Secondary streets may once again run parallel to the canals. Fabrics differ in size and geometry.*

**17.4**  *Tunis Medina—Detail of the urban block shown in fig. 8.4, highlighting one dead-end street together with the houses abutting it. In the Tunisian house, rooms cluster around courtyards. Three shallow niches or recesses in turn cluster about a central space to form a room in the shape of a shallow tee. Storage then fills in the remaining corner spaces of the rectangular bay. Base map courtesy of the Association Sauvegarde de la Medina, Tunis.*

288

## Conventions of Action and Control

The precise mechanism by which knowledge of urban structure is maintained and transmitted among inhabitants remains unknown. Yet evidence suggests that this deeply implicit knowledge must be highly sophisticated. The question is compounded by the fundamental differences in structures found. Compare the Western fabric, based on the urban block, with the traditional Middle Eastern urban fabric, where street and dead-end alley do not reflect any predetermined layout.

The two urban fabric typologies embody very different abstractions. The Western model allows for all manner of geometric formations: it is basically a web without beginning or end. The Middle Eastern model, which lacks a pre-

defined geometry, has a clear hierarchy from dead-end alley to street to major artery. Although interconnections can render the latter more weblike and differences between alley and street may make the former hierarchical, there seem to be two fundamentally different concepts at play. Must we therefore assume an innate abstract knowledge among inhabitants about such complex configurations?

Knowledge by abstraction may play a role, but observing or directly participating in hands-on control of form may be the more direct and common way of gaining knowledge. Western urban structure is a stable container accessible to all individual action. As long as predetermined public space is not invaded and territorial boundaries with neighbors are respected, one may act in freedom and anonymity. Middle

Eastern structure is based on neighbors agree-
ing: it results from a social contract without
predetermined form. As long as consensus is
obtained, most moves are possible. The first is
a form allowing play, the second a play producing form.

   Thus conventions of behavior may be the
key. The two models suggest quite different
rules determining environmental play. In one,
public space is predetermined. Within it, we
make our spatial claim, such that we may leave
one another alone. In the other, interaction by
consensus and agreement is constant and mandatory. Public space subject to change is the
result.

   In all cases, rules of play must be known
and understood. They, ultimately, produce the
form and do not require abstraction.

## 17.4 Emergence of New Types

### Duration of Types

We have observed (see chapter 15.3) how technical and stylistic systems may travel when the values they contain are adopted in other localities. When this happens, an international social network of parties sharing similar values is in evidence. The Palladian style, as a system of strong formal content, is a prime example. Urban building types like the British terraced house, the Venetian palace, and the Dutch canal house are more holistic. They apparently remain firmly tied to a local urban culture.

The classicistic style systems in particular, so clearly congruent with an intellectual and economic international elite, were often applied to local building types, without altering their spatial organization or way of building. The addition of classicistic façades to barnlike New England buildings illustrates the relative tenacity of local typology against the adaptability of an international style.[6]

Nevertheless, there is evidence of types traveling. Axel Boëthius argues that the Roman *taberna* evidenced in Pompeii and Ostia—a hole-in-the-wall shop with a loft reached by wooden stairs—traveled northward as far as France, where it persisted with gradual variations and developments throughout the Middle Ages.[7]

Building and urban typology might be transported wholesale when members of the social body sustaining them moved as well. This was the case when Greeks, Romans, and subsequent colonizers built their Miletuses and Timgads, their Djakartas and Bostons. Inevitably, in such cases transformations took place over time, eventually resulting in new types or clearly distinct variants on the initial typology.

Classicistic architecture, as we have observed, became international not because of wholesale population displacements, but because people from different locations and cultures came to subscribe to its values. Such networks of values, relating people in dispersed places, could also distribute building types internationally. The basilica, a place of worship for the faithful of the early Roman church, spread as a spatial and technical whole, together with the social network of the Catholic church. Local transformations occurred, and we witness, in the Romanesque and Gothic churches, how local elaboration and interpretation could ultimately create wholly new architectures.

International dispersal of local building types, revealing networks with distinctly global value systems, can be witnessed today as well. There now exists, for instance, a powerfully iconic "California bungalow" type. It is a low, sprawling building with tile roof, pastel stucco walls, driveway, carport, and patio, surrounded by informal plantings. That conceptual bungalow's formal imagery is expressed in suburban neighborhoods throughout the world. It combines with local preferences, frequently presenting, for instance, walled territorial boundaries. The bungalow's intended expression of stereotypical lifestyle values of California—affluence, freedom, and informal living—is unmistakable. Even a recently founded Israeli kibbutz has adopted this typology, deviating from the spartan modernism historically associated with such pioneer settlements.

The more superficial and stylistic imagery of the type can also be found applied to buildings that are no longer bungalows. Apartment buildings several stories high display similar roofs, stucco walls, and shuttered windows. (In such cases, it is a stylistic system that travels, not a type.)

## The Skyscraper

291

Another current example of a type adopted by an international network is the skyscraper. The

**17.5** *Manhattan—Cityscape with skyscrapers.*

forces accompanying its rise have been extensively documented.[8] Market demand for floor space in crowded downtown business districts and technological developments—in steel frame construction, electricity, elevators, and curtain walls—all accompanied the rise of the skyscraper as a North American institution.

The high-rise tower as a type, if not the skyscraper proper, soon came to reside in a network culture. Its widespread distribution cannot be fully explained in economic or technical terms. From the beginning, it is associated with compelling dreams of power and prestige. Lincoln, Nebraska, for instance, had Bertram Goodhue's State Capitol Building (1932), whose 400-foot tower is visible for miles from the surrounding plains, by the early 1920s. Similar visions propelled the appearance of this building type in cities and in rural and provincial communities throughout the industrialized and third worlds, independent of local conditions.

Those who build and use these buildings subscribe to a particular system of values and behavior. They are built by agents who take part in an international professional community, or who want to establish their credentials or become eligible for local participation or civic leadership within that community.

## Localized vs. Delocalized Types

High-rise culture relies on highly specialized technical and professional expertise. It is so thoroughly internationalized and networked that local typological variations are scarce. Consequently, the tall building is delocalized to an unprecedented extent.[9] Worldwide, relative uniformity of values exists among professionals who design and build tall buildings and clients who occupy them. Variations witnessed in tall buildings are not inspired by local conditions. They broadcast the personal idiosyncrasies of designers and clients—their signatures. Variations result from an essentially internal dialogue among members of an international network, delocalized investors, and local authorities.

By comparison, local variation is far more apparent in the medium- or low-rise apartment building. It remains a predominantly local interpretation of an international type. Developers, renters, or buyers all operate within the complicated local dynamics of values, customs, and fashion. For most of these buildings, the relationship between those who initiate building and those who inhabit remains close-knit, both pressured by market forces. In observing variations, we therefore learn about local preferences and lifestyles. Apartment buildings in Miami differ from those in Rio or Nice, although they manifest strong typological kinship.

By contrast, the emergence and development of the various public housing typologies was not shared by those who built and those who inhabited. Controlled by professional designers, builders, and civil servants who formed an international network by dint of education and access to information, these projects are designed to house those who, by definition, are not players.[10] Their typology therefore reflects very few local differences and a high degree of uniformity. Indeed, it was long impossible to distinguish between designs from Eastern or Western Europe, from North or South America. In terms of typology, high-rise public housing is mainly of interest because never before has any residential type been a purely professional (architectural, bureaucratic, and technical) product.[11]

## New Local Types

The variety of building types born out of international networks is limited, compared to the variety of those emerging locally. Ubiquitous local developments, however, occur quietly within ordinary environments. They therefore tend to go unnoticed: environmental observers, like most other professionals, operate within the familiar frame of reference of international networks, by virtue of their education and inclination.

Informal housing in developing countries consistently shows rapid growth and change rooted in strong local typologies. For instance, variation on the vernacular courtyard house, a Spanish tradition formalized and transplanted according to the Laws of the Indies, has been perpetuated in extensive informal communities ringing almost every Latin American city.

In Cairo, local residential builders now erect concrete frames up to five stories high, as well as traditional masonry walls supporting prestressed concrete floors. Another common feature is the shallow balcony, often extending along the entire façade. Windows and doors produced as commodities by local shops reveal a common typology. We lack documentation and study of such informal development. Yet preliminary observation reveals that there is always strong typology, driven by local customs of construction and manufacturing, and by the preferences of those who invest in houses and live in them.

In more formal circumstances, we also find new types, resulting from the private initiative of local builders and clients wherever cities

293

**17.6**  *Dammam, Saudi Arabia—Private residence within an emerging typology.*

expand and economies develop. In Tainan, Ming Hung Wang has documented the emergence of a building type wherein ground-floor workplaces, often extending the full depth of the lot, combine with a residence on the second and third floors.[12] This type reflects the family-based entrepreneur, a major force within Taiwan's economy.

Venturing off the beaten path in large cities—Tokyo, Seoul, Tainan, Djakarta, Dammam, Riyadh, Cairo—one finds local types emerging in small-scale, high-density places. Inspecting the local neighborhoods immediately behind the hotels, office buildings, and shops of the major arteries, one finds environments that reinterpret traditional features to accommodate the need to park a car, to possess a modern kitchen, to enhance security and protection.

In all parts of the world, at all levels of income, local dwelling types constitute an unfamiliar but vast and ever-growing field.

**17.7**  *Cairo, Egypt—Informally erected buildings reveal a clear typology.*

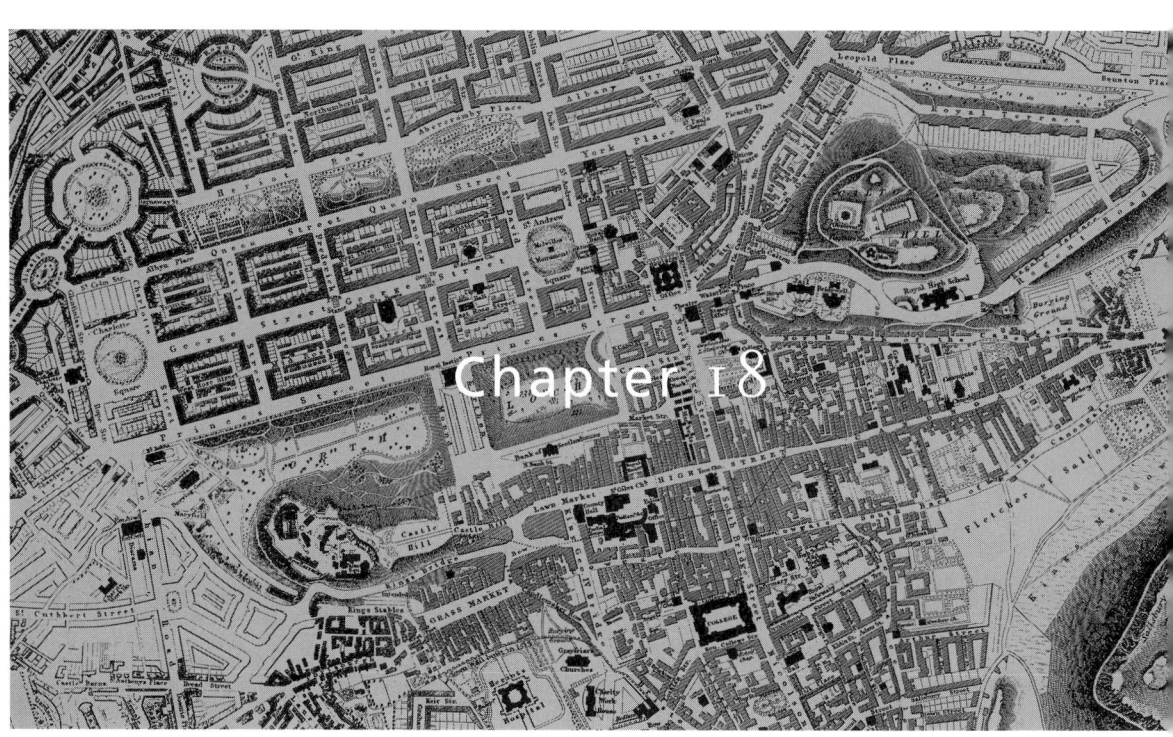

Chapter 18

# The Uses of Understanding

## 18.1 Understanding between Specialist and Layperson

### Limiting Need for Explicit Agreement

Forms of understanding diminish the need for more explicit agreement. What is already understood requires neither negotiation, nor confirmation, nor documentation. What needs to be written down, to be drawn or otherwise put on record, is only what is not yet clear.

Which particular variant to create must be decided anew with each intervention. Significant discourse and invention occur during design of the configuration. Once a system is selected, a host of details, specifications, and clarifications logically follow without further invention. Specific in-system solutions are inferred from what is already understood: for example, once a steel structure and its overall configuration are selected, professional construction practice follows a regular, rule-bound, and verifiable path.

Likewise, the decision to work within a certain architectural style system sets the scope of the task. Determining the particular configuration demands creativity, taste, skill, and knowledge. Once the general character and form are established, detailing and production again follow a rule-bound course. In designing a traditional classically proportioned Ionic colonnade in wood, one reinvents neither the classical system nor the production process. Yet each instance is unique.

The living type offers a kind of understanding to be shared by all: there are no experts specializing in typological knowledge. In understanding the type, all parties within the

**18.1** *Edinburgh—The old town on the ridge of the hill. To the north, Craig's New Town is ringed by subsequent extensions (page 296).*

culture are equal. The urgent primary question—what kind of environment will we create?—has already been answered in the choice of type. Holding its particular realm in common, the principals involved need consider only questions of interpretation that arise from site, program, and individual preferences.

## Meaning As Shared Decision

As John Onians explains, a good deal of meaning was implied within the vocabulary of the classic orders.[1] At Alberti's Palazzo Rucellai, orders present in the façade projected the relative importance of each floor. Doric was reserved for the utilitarian ground floor. The two floors above received Corinthian capitals on pilasters, because they were used by the family. Of the two, the main floor was more important than the top floor, a difference expressed by giving the small columns in the windows a composite shape in the former, but a Doric shape in the latter.

Application of a classicistic thematic style system served a dual function. It allowed specialist and layperson to settle issues of values and meaning. It then allowed the specialist to efficiently execute and interpret agreed-upon meaning. The participation of other specialists, draftsmen, technicians, and builders required relatively little additional specification, once a shared system was in place. The intent of a Corinthian capital required neither discussion nor explanation: the mason who cut the capital from the stone had made many similar forms before, albeit not exactly like those designed by Alberti at Rucellai. Only the specifics needed designing.

As we also learn from Onians, the meaning and thus the application of the orders shifted over time. Meaning is attached to form by convention. The issue here is not the particular meaning of any particular classical order, but the very existence of a system of form common enough to designer, client, and craftsman that it imparts shared meaning.

The same mechanisms work within thematic technical systems. Steel construction also offers a two-tiered understanding, enabling architect and structural engineer to negotiate the design of a particular configuration. The balance between architectural and technical creativity and innovation may vary widely from one instance to the next, but in all cases there exists a common structure within which the intent of the configuration is clear. Once the configuration's design is settled, the system allows for efficient conventional detailing and specification, as all parties involved share knowledge.

299

## The Tatami

Common understanding for making value judgments by means of type, system, and pattern is shared among all players. However, specialized knowledge, craft skills, and professional expertise remain the province of specialists.

In the traditional Japanese house as described by Heino Engel,[2] all parts of the wooden frame are known by name and function; and all joints between them fall within the domain of specialized carpentry. The technical system is further governed by sophisticated dimensional organization, based in part on a module of about 90 cm. This module also determines the size of tatami mats with which floors are covered.

Inhabitant and carpenter discuss house layout within the realm of the type, expressing

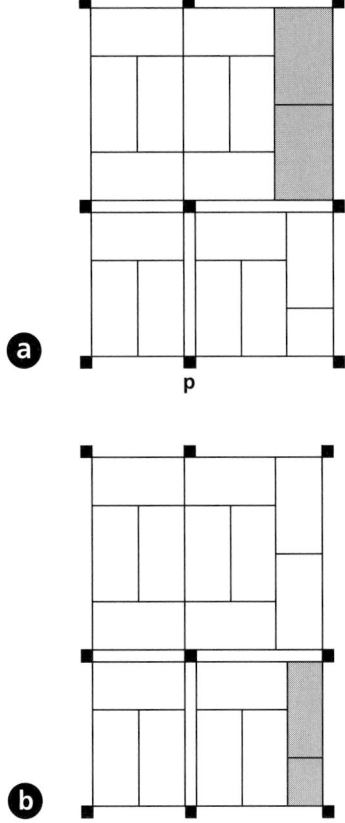

**a**

p

**b**

p

room sizes in terms of number of tatami mats needed to cover the floors. Although ceiling heights differ from room to room, a "four-tatami room" has quite specific and generally familiar proportions of length, width, and height. Hence the tatami is both a formal unit by which the variant can be described and a technical module for dimensioning wooden frame, screens, and partitioning. It epitomizes the link between typological knowledge shared by all and specialized technical knowledge.

The tatami as a unit for design and communication is an abstraction, not a consistent technical module. To ensure consistent systematization, exact tatami dimensions must vary with partition thickness. As figure 18.2 illustrates, modular sizing cannot prevail: either the large room must use extra large mats, or the smaller room must use smaller ones. In practice, the solution chosen is a matter of regional preference. In one part of the country, tatamis are cut smaller when needed, in another part wider tatamis are available when needed.

The tatami's function, as a module, is thus not to set dimensions or standardize parts. It is, above all, a tool for communication about the whole. It also links typological decisions directly to the intricate wood frame system. Carpenters then translate this information into decisions about sizing parts.

**18.2** *Modules as a means of communication. Employing them neither implies nor requires standardized elements. The length of a large tatami room adjoining two smaller ones must necessarily equal the sum of the two smaller ones plus the thickness (p) of the partitioning between them.*

*(a) Some elements are larger than the module.*

*(b) Some elements are smaller than the module.*

## 18.2 The Image Precedes the Form

### Informal Settlements

Observing seventeenth-century London expanding in the direction of his estates, the duke of Bedford had his lands subdivided and built upon. He became one of the largest real estate holders in the city. Two centuries later, Marx and Engels decried the notorious "jerry-building" at the fringes of the world's largest city. In creating shelter for the tens of thousands arriving in search of work, landowners built in defiance of law. The result of such initiatives would today be categorized as "informal settlement."

These processes are now ongoing throughout rapidly growing cities of the third world. In defiance or absence of formal planning, landowners typically subdivide their holdings, have streets and plots laid out, and provide an infrastructure sufficiently attractive to lure buyers. This process works only when there exist sufficient numbers of citizens capable and desperate enough to purchase lots in such informal subdivisions.

Often the initiative is reversed, as when no profit is to be had from would-be settlers. Declining private estates and unguarded public lands may be taken by force, subdivided by those who invade it: *parachutistas* in Latin America, *geocondu* (mushrooms) in Turkey, *squatters* in English-speaking countries. Settlers have often been urban renters, who previously lived with entire families huddled together in one room or part of a room. They share in common the aspiration of joining the middle class, having resources just sufficient to escape, to strike out on their own.

Appearing overnight, settlers pitch tents and makeshift huts. When acting in open defiance of local police as well as the law, they arrive in groups to gain strength from numbers. Landowners will typically vie to have the invaders evicted, sometimes successfully. But, as of-ten as not, municipal politicians refuse to alienate potential voters. There may also exist "squatter's rights" in codified law and in recog-nized precedent. In the meantime, feverish transformation of the site continues. Settlers dig trenches, build makeshift sheds, and lay the first course of a first masonry wall, asserting control. Police may be bribed or won over through other social processes or linkages. If the owner cannot get his land cleared in the first few weeks, he will generally never succeed (see figure 12.1).

There are many gradations of compliance with rules. Between patent invasion of property and the fully formalized professional project, there exist many processes involving small builders, small developers, self-help organiza-tions, institutions to help shelter the poor, and myriad other parties. But the driving force re-mains the settlers themselves.

It is through informal processes that the majority of the world's population now find shelter. The resulting settlements, poor and makeshift though they be in the beginning, are not slums or signs of social pathology. They represent urban environment emerging in spite of ineffective laws and administrative procedures.

Most of Mexico City has sprung forth in this way. The same holds true for virtually all Latin American towns and for cities in the Middle East, on the Indian subcontinent, and elsewhere. In most cases, the environmental processes are quite well organized and coordi-nated. The invaders lay out their streets and lots in orderly fashion, organize themselves politi-cally and socially, and wholeheartedly set about creating a middle-class urban environment.

The results are not always successful. De-velopment often stalls, then stagnates. Slums may ultimately result. Yet, over a number of

decades, informal settlements usually do suc-ceed in becoming fully enfranchised urban environments.

## Colonia Santa Ursula

The growth and development of the (informal) Colonia Santa Ursula neighborhood of Mexico City has been studied in depth by Jorge An-drade.[3] This extensive neighborhood was ini-tially subdivided illegally by an enterprising clerk of the municipal authority. Exploiting ex-tensions of transportation and services that ac-companied the Olympic stadium then under construction, he proceeded to sell neighboring allotments of land that had remained unculti-vated, because it was rough and stony, pock-marked with fissures and escarpments.

Unfortunately, the land was not his to sell, and he landed in jail for his efforts. None-theless, once started, the neighborhood grew steadily, always adhering to the original urban layout. First, perimeter walls were built to pro-tect the newly occupied territory. Houses then began to grow, room by room. A marketplace and a church were established. Over the years, the growing population also gained political clout. Eventually, the municipality brought in a sewage system and water mains. Finally, paving appeared on the roads.

Santa Ursula's buildings are now two sto-ries high. It would be hard for the casual ob-server to believe that this substantial settlement, the size of a small town, was created from the bottom up.

## The Invisible Plan

Santa Ursula is by no means the largest infor-mal settlement in Mexico City: it is merely

303

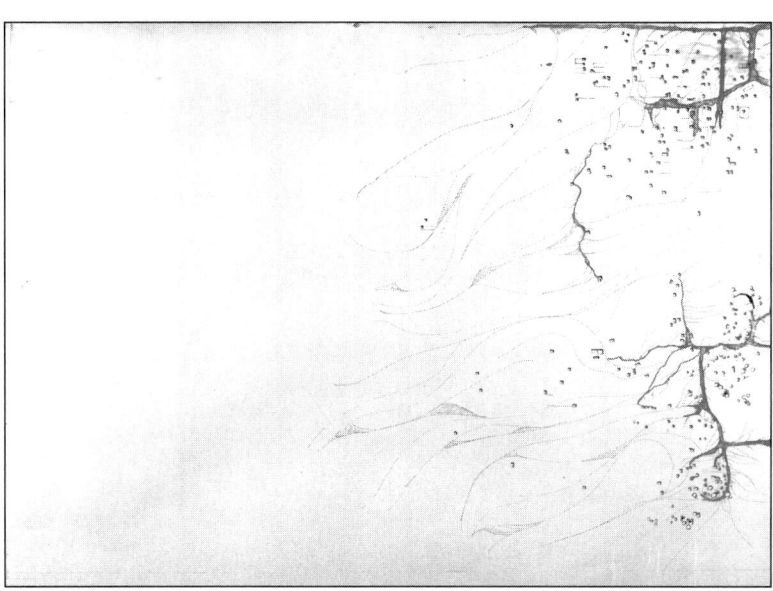

a

b

where the process of emergence has been most carefully documented. Thousands of similar environments have grown throughout Latin America.

Nevertheless, it remains difficult to accept that an environment of such regularity and coherence could come about without profes-sional intervention, in a bottom-up process. Such occurrences suggest a powerful implicit covenant among a dynamic and only gradually emerging population. Even where a formal sub-division plan existed, implementing it required spontaneous concerted action by thousands of individual citizens. Clearly, this could only

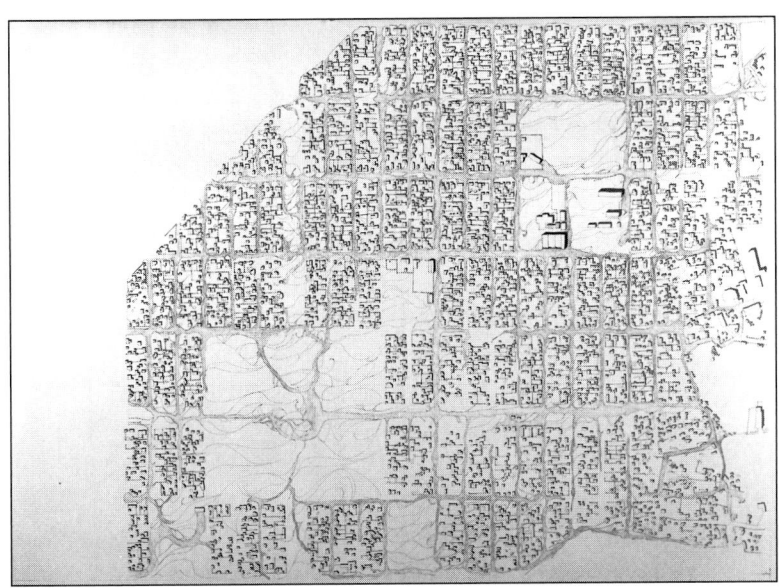

**c**

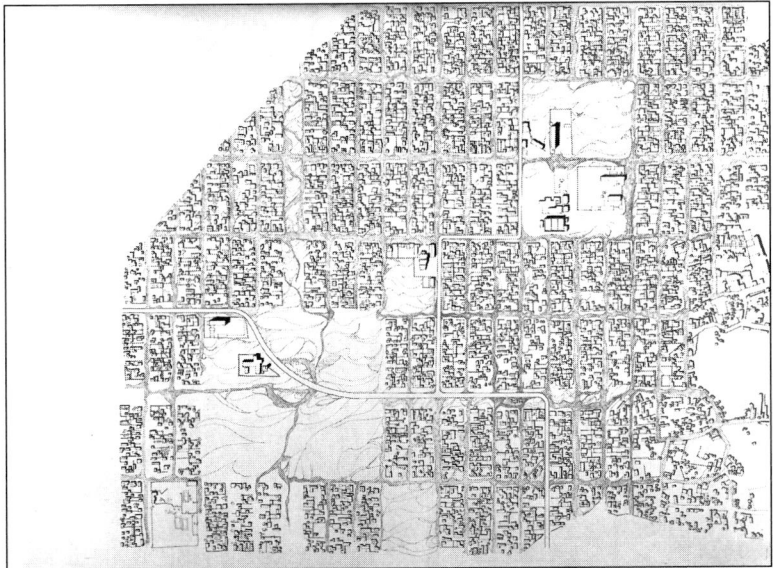

**d**

**18.3** *Colonia Santa Ursula, Mexico City—Successive stages of the informal settlement showing the gradual emergence of a well-defined urban structure, as drawn from aerial photographs by Andrade and his team. Courtesy of Jorge Andrade, Rodolfo Santa Maria, and Alfonso Govela.*

*(a) 1954.*

*(b) 1963.*

*(c) 1970.*

*(d) 1974.*

succeed where the plan represented a clear and generally understood spatial organization, whose implications and values all subscribed to. Such settlements evince detailed common knowledge of an environment not yet in existence. The informal settlement comes into being in tandem with a social body that is itself only gradually emerging.

Santa Ursula did not grow from a single access point or central region, expanding gradually toward the periphery. Instead, the earliest settlements were scattered throughout its ultimate territory. Watching the documented emergence of formal urban structure is like watching a grainy photographic image slowly appear. Development occurs everywhere at once, until the whole preexisting image is fully articulated.

There were initially no roads, only pedestrian paths. Yet, to judge by the final result, the layout of the streets was adhered to before they existed. In later stages, the walls surrounding the private lots are well aligned, the streets straight and wide.

## The Oklahoma Land Rush

What is happening now in Latin America happened in the United States a century earlier. The gridded towns of the Midwest are testimony to that period. Although towns in the Midwest by and large were laid out by surveyors, the strict adherence to their orthogonal structure in dynamic and unruly times can only testify to a common image honored by all participants. Spectacular confirmation of the built environment as collective image, guiding the action of hundreds of individual citizens, appears in John Reps's account of the Oklahoma land rush and the founding of Guthrie.[4]

Although the Oklahoma Indian Territory was initially granted in perpetuity to the "five Civilized Tribes," Congress soon began to capitulate to political pressure from land-hungry settlers. As a result, treaties were abrogated; tribes were summarily removed, with great loss of life.

On April 22, 1889, at noon, the borders of the "Unassigned Lands" were opened. Preceded by a number of "Sooners," prospective settlers rushed in—in trains, carts, and carriages and on foot. On the first day, the town of Guthrie was no more than a field. Hundreds of individuals literally squatted on the ground, having staked their claims. Foresighted settlers huddled in makeshift tents. Streets were already laid out and regular geometrical blocks indicated. Within a year, evidence of informal settlement had vanished. With respect to character of formal structures, Guthrie and similar "overnight cities" could not be distinguished from other midwestern towns.

**18.4** *Guthrie, Oklahoma, 1889—Settlers sitting in the prairie of what will become the town of Guthrie, on the day that the great Oklahoma land rush began. Engraving by Davies from* Harper's Weekly *(May 18, 1889).*

## 18.3 Harvesting Forms of Understanding

### Nash in London

The design of Regents Park and Regent Street in London demonstrates the power of conventional form. John Nash's scheme gave structure to central London. At the end of his long and productive life, he introduced the idea of the wide urban park bounded by monumental crescents, applying it with admirable ease and grandeur.

Most elements marshaled in Nash's grand scheme were "borrowed," having first been developed elsewhere, by others. The Georgian terraced house, which first emerged in the late seventeenth century, had been in widespread use for over a century prior to Regents Park. John Wood, Sr., Robert Adams, and others had already employed the unified façade shared by a row of houses to shape new urban spaces. Similar façades appear around the squares of the Bedford estate in London. Although Nash's interpretation was decidedly new, the classicistic style was quite familiar to professionals and laypeople alike.

Nash's achievement is neither diminished nor denied by observing his borrowings. He employed the familiar device of the monumental façade across a number of terraced houses to create giant screens. It was a given that state-of-the-art screens could be built, such that houses following a familiar typology could subsequently be built behind them, keying in the façades. Integrating known typologies allowed him to focus on urban space and the façades that formed it.

Familiarity of style and typology made it possible for citizens to invest with confidence in the scheme, knowing that their houses, shops, and offices could be properly and functionally built behind the monumental façades. The same familiarity allowed contemporaries to broadly appreciate the qualities of his particular vision, as well as to criticize occasionally hasty or haphazard detailing.

Nash's design, which combined sweeping grandeur and dexterous structuring of urban environment, created a form not witnessed before. This originality was achieved not in spite of home-grown typology and heavily systematized form, but because of it. This was no avant-garde invention rejecting the past and blazing a new path to the future, but an apotheosis of the familiar, utilizing potential developed over a long time. It was executed within forms and types well known to the citizens of London, albeit not in this grand manner. Like the arcade that processes from the city gates of Bologna to the shrine of San Luca (chapter 14.2), Nash's work achieved the ultimate expression of the customary. In both cases, the monumental and explicit act of design was made possible by the powerful presence of the traditional and the implicit.

Nash's opportunity was born of beau geste. Wealth, power, and royal patronage conjoined with traditional craftsmanship, allowing a single individual to lift an established architectural system to the level of urban infrastructure, then play with it. But that individual had become an old man. Nash consequently did not produce more than the principal sketches, confident that they could be developed in detail and coordinated with state-of-the-art understanding by others with more energy, patience, and time remaining.

A general can marshal thousands of troops and machines because training and discipline imprint every player with the rules of the game. Just so could this seasoned, talented, and well-placed designer marshal the skill and industry of a city, transforming it almost overnight.

Type, style, and pattern had come to full fruition. In Regents Park and Regent Street, Nash reaped a harvest that had grown over generations. His was the power of the conventional, on which the architectural profession ultimately depends. In Nash's achievement, we cannot also fail to recognize how society's collective environmental knowledge establishes both context and limits of design.

## The Familiar Replaced

The shared types that fuel concerted action need not derive from local convention. This is demonstrated in the remarkable extension of the city of Edinburgh, half a century before Nash designed Regent Street. The decision to build a "new town" across the North Loch was the result of a long process of deliberation. But once decided, the subsequent design process was swift. Architects were invited to submit plans in March 1766. In August of that year, James Craig was selected by the city's provost and John Adam. There then followed a year of further exchange between Craig and the town council, during which time "Mr. Craig by their direction made out a new plan."[5]

Pointing to town planning in England and in France preceding Craig's, A. J. Youngson judges this urban layout "painfully orthodox."[6] He also makes it clear that Craig had nothing to do with the buildings themselves. It is the very conventionality of the plan and its buildings that is of interest, for it stood in stark contrast with the extant medieval plan of Edinburgh, the only local alternative.

The new town reflected the values common among a ruling class in close contact with London and familiar with prevailing classicistic tradition. As the quality of the final result dem-

309

onstrates, type need not be local, but it must, at all times, be shared by those who will take action.

The strength of a shared urban form is best appreciated on the building level. In Edinburgh, the amazing consistency and regularity of the street walls and house types built along the newly laid-out streets resulted purely from convention. That convention, to be sure, developed in response to what was new as much as it had to what was familiar. The houses of Edinburgh could consequently be built by citizens and their architects without benefit of regulation.[7]

## Haussmann in Paris

In Paris, feudal urban mansions for nobles featured *cours d'honneur* accessible from the street. The main house sat between that court and the formal garden. Its wings afforded quarters for servants, staff, and artisans, as well as stables and storage. Eventually, this form was adapted to a more democratic society, providing apartments around a common courtyard. The transition is described by Marcel Proust:

*It was one of those old town houses, a few of which for all I know may still be found, in which the main courtyard was flanked—alluvial deposits washed there by the rising tide of democracy, perhaps, or a legacy from a more primitive time when the different trades were clustered round the overlord—by little shops and workrooms, a shoemaker's, for instance, or a tailor's, such as we see nestling between the buttresses of those cathedrals which the aesthetic zeal of the restorer has not swept clear of such accretions, and a porter who also did cobbling, kept hens, grew flowers—and, at the far end, in the main house, a "Countess" who, when she drove out in her old carriage and pair, flaunting on her hat a few nasturtiums which seemed to have escaped from the plot by the lodge . . . dispensed smiles and little waves of the hand impartially to the porter's children and to any bourgeois tenants who might happen to be passing and whom, in her disdainful affability and her egalitarian arrogance, she found indistinguishable from one another.*[8]

Remnants of this earlier type can still be seen in the Left Bank, the Marais, and the Île Saint-Louis, in older parts of the urban tissue (see, for example, figure 17.1).

Eventually, buildings around a courtyard accessible from the street were specifically built as apartments. They frequently retained work-

# 18.4  The Power of Conventional Form

places and shops on the ground floor, surmounted by five or six floors of residential space. The vigilant concierge stationed at the entrance of the courtyard henceforth became a Parisian institution.

The model is extremely efficient in terms of public/private land use. The mass of built space behind the street façades is dense enough to support continuous ground-floor commercial activity along the streets. The pedestrian population makes the boulevards social spaces, rather than massive traffic arteries. Such communal living was already highly compatible with French urban culture. Integral to the type was the entresol (see figures 14.3, 18.5–18.7). Continuous use of this pattern on the building level contributed substantially to urban structure.

The courtyard building and associated patterns were firmly in place when, under the prefecture of Baron Georges Eugène Haussmann, monumental restructuring of central Paris began. The recent cutting of Regent Street into London's urban fabric had been a modest enterprise by comparison. Haussmann's urban intervention on the grand scale, innovative both in form and in financing, effected profound and radical changes in historical urban structure.

Yet the urban fabric witnessed profound continuity of types, patterns, and materials. Haussmann's engineers and architects did not try to reinvent; rather, they built from a collective image. Use of the courtyard building, including the entresol pattern, continued. Now optimized for speed and efficiency, its construction was institutionalized and standardized. Floor heights became almost uniform. Windows with their wrought-iron banisters were mass produced. The interplay of ground floor and entresol in the façade injected life and vari-

ety into the zone of pedestrian experience, saving the boulevards from utter monotony.

## Harnessing the Power of Convention

It was easiest to experiment or innovate on one level only. To rebuild a city by changing the configuration on the level of urban structure, while simultaneously reinventing urban fabric on the level of the building, would have been too difficult and disruptive. But limiting innovation to the level of the urban structure, and systematically adapting from precedent whatever had to be done on the building level, made the transformation of central Paris possible. Haussmann's use of levels was both rational and successful. Of course, these choices were not explicitly made: no alternative ever seemed possible.

The success of Haussmann's ambitious scheme was therefore due to the marriage of innovation (financial and managerial) with tradition (typological). Forms built to shape the new boulevards were, to a large extent, based upon a shared image. Exactly what was to be built was known by all players, from the construction worker to the developer and the bureaucrat.

Many discussions, explanations, and deliberations that we would now consider essential prior to implementing a project of such scale were simply dispensed with. Because self-evident forms evincing shared value required little planning, they allowed immediate action. The design process, on the level of the building, was accordingly short and simple. Common understanding greatly facilitated coordination between all parties involved in its execution.

The transformation of Paris demonstrates the tremendous power of the shared image; its extent cannot be fully appreciated

313

**18.5** *Paris—Entresols.* Top, *avenue de l'Opéra;* bottom,
*side street viewed from avenue de l'Opéra.*

**18.6** *Paris—Entresols*. Top, *rue Royale;* bottom: *rue de Rivoli.*

316

***18.7*** *Paris—Entresols.* (Clockwise from upper left) *The Left Bank, Place Dauphine, the Marais, Île Saint-Louis.*

without asking what process would ensue if this project were undertaken today. Throughout all of the stages—feasibility studies; traffic, environmental impact, and engineering studies; preprogramming, programming, and each successive phase of design—different proposals by a variety of design teams would be solicited, then evaluated. Each might well articulate a vastly different conception.

To stand out in a crowded field, the winning design scheme would certainly not just extend existing typology, nor would it merely reinvent at the urban scale. It would also intervene on other levels of the form in innovative ways, reinterpreting or reinventing, seeking to engage the existing fabric in a memorable dialectic at every opportunity.

By comparison, Haussmann virtually designed Paris by imperial decree. Yet the absence of alternative proposals was not a result of heavy-handed top-down decision making. The belief which holds that radically different proposals for an urban environment can be entertained, that the urban form appropriate to a people can be debated, or that the environment constitutes a commodity to be selected from among available options or styles is a (post-) modern idea. In nineteenth-century imperial France, it remained unthinkable.

Haussmann's intervention to renew the city of Paris was immune to neither architectural nor social criticism, which was at times quite fierce. But from our current perspective, we must marvel at the degree to which questions were not raised. Convention and consensus were harnessed to glorious effect, ultimately re-creating Paris in one powerful (and efficient) intervention.

## A New Game

Historically, professional intervention always evidenced the use and adaptation of existing forms of understanding. The Bolognese portico and the Parisian entresol exemplify the formal use of patterns. In the cases of Regent Street in London, New Town in Edinburgh, the Parisian courtyard apartment building, and ancient Olynthus, commonly held types were put to large-scale use. An existing common understanding allowed the emergence of new forms by transformation. Most nineteenth-century instances of formalization may have been without precedent in size, but they still continued the historic relation between professional innovation and common forms of understanding.

However, in the development of recent building types such as the office tower and the apartment block, the role of existing understanding in providing continuity could not be sustained. Professional initiative and invention had to venture forth on their own, under pressure from new circumstances and ambitions. This represented a move into uncharted terrain. The conditions and rules of the game have been fundamentally altered.

The city of Amsterdam as it grew over the course of seven centuries provides an insight into gradual transformation. Within that historic context, we may witness the introduction of the new professional game and identify some of the new and often bewildering problems arising from it.

## The Great Extension of Amsterdam

The bold sweep of Amsterdam's three monumental canals around the medieval core of the city forms the major part of what became

# 18.5  The Point of No Return

known as the Great Extension of the seventeenth century. It suggests the hand of a master urban designer, someone with a sure sense of scale and drama, with a refined sensibility—a feeling for proportion and for the hierarchical arrangement of civic space.

Minutes of city council meetings in which the new extension was debated and decided upon record protracted deliberations about property, about the cost of land and infrastructure, about establishing priorities of action: *Should we build the ramparts before the canals are done, or later on?* The decision was to

first build the defenses: a good deal of politics was involved.

There was an even more fundamental question: *Is the extension large enough?* Small merchants and guilds put pressure on the council to allocate more land for their benefit, lest the new infrastructure to which their tax moneys contributed benefit only the rich families who controlled the council. The pressure worked, and an additional, smaller-scale neighborhood was added (see figure 18.9, right-hand side). This was subject to land speculation and subsequent scandals.

319

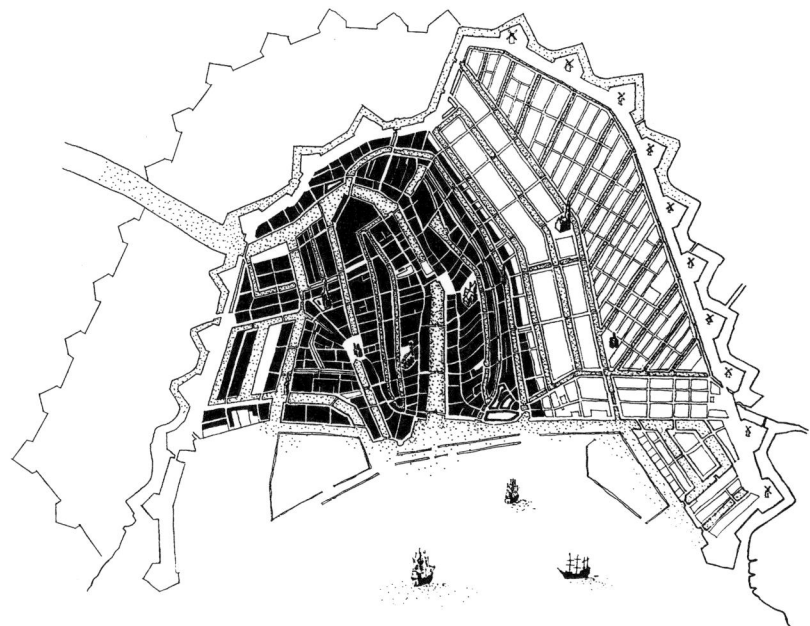

**18.8** *Amsterdam, ca. 1650—Map following completion of the Third Extension. The older town is shown in black. The extension begun in 1613 is shown in outline. The subsequent extension, begun in 1660, would ultimately bring the urban fabric out to the banks of the Amstel River. The future extension of the ramparts is also indicated. After Joan Bleau.*

**18.9** *Amsterdam, end of the nineteenth century—One of the major seventeenth-century canals, photographed by Jacob Olie. Several centuries later, the view remained very much as it had been just after completion.*

## An Absence of Design

In short, the Great Extension of Amsterdam followed an economic and political process familiar to us. However, among the records of all the deliberations carefully preserved in municipal archives, the name of the designer is never revealed. There is no mention or record of designs for the extension.

In fact, there are no designs for the extension. There is no mention or evidence of any design process whatsoever—at least, not in the way we understand that process today.[9]

At various stages, layouts of parts, such as the ramparts or some portions of the major canals, were submitted to and discussed by the council. But such evidence only reinforces the hypothesis that the scheme as a whole was a continuation of a way of working already followed by earlier extensions: Amsterdam would simply dig concentric canals and lay out streets between them.

When we compare the seventeenth-century urban fabric with that of the historic center, we find exactly the same urban typology. Most important, no new house type was applied. To be sure, there is an evolution of house plans. New styles are applied, buildings tend to be larger, and, indeed, in later stages the double lot house did emerge as a new type. But the basic type that drives the new plan was a direct continuation of the one that had developed together with the medieval core.

The way the new extension had to be built was thus already known to all. It was the way of the old city, simply larger. It differed primarily in being laid out in straight geometry, whereas the old center followed cow paths along the dikes of the Amstel river, its meandering canals dug incrementally over time (see figure 17.3).

Hence available collective knowledge concerning the new extension made design unnecessary. The idea, so familiar to us now, that a new environment had to be conceived anew, that one could or should generate alternative "solutions" to be considered and debated, was unheard of. Issues of dimensions and numbers, issues of occupancy and costs, certainly—but questions of concept and form? Decidedly not.

## Berlage's Environment

We can accurately pinpoint just when Amsterdam's built environment in its entirety became a professional design problem: with the Berlage plan.

Under pressure from a burgeoning economy and changing demographics, stimulated by new laws for public housing, the city had to expand once more. This time, the municipal powers did not know what the new extension should be like. There appeared to be a variety of ways to build it. In 1901 H. P. Berlage was asked to submit a design.

The process was slow. A first plan, produced in 1904, was mainly used as basis for consolidating land by right of eminent domain. A second plan, commissioned in 1914 and accepted in 1917, formed the basis for the Amsterdam South neighborhood as we know it.

Defining an appropriate building type had become a crucial prerequisite for any proposal that might be made. This, in turn, depended on developing a concept for the dwelling itself. The new building type that emerged was basically a four- to five-story walk-up apartment. It allowed for high-density stacking of small dwelling units for nuclear families. Based on it, Berlage designed an urban fabric of great coherence, to be filled in by his peers.

In essence, Berlage's plan was implemented. The celebrated "Amsterdam School" architecture was the result. Apart from the building heights, there is little borrowing from the past, other than perhaps a continued affinity for the palette of materials and their detailing. There are new patterns, a new typology, new systems both stylistic and technical, new details. As already touched on in chapter 4.3, great coherence resulted from close collaboration among designers. Guidelines for street and building profiles were proposed and accepted by peer committees, and building plans had to be approved by peer review.

Amsterdam South provides a remarkable instance of professional conduct and cooperation, seldom matched later on. And for the first time in the city's history, the process of reaching an understanding took place among a purely professional and interdisciplinary social body sustained by architects, their institutional clients (in the form of subsidized housing corporations), their builders, and a sensitive municipal bureaucracy. All of these actors shared similar values, ideals, and pride in what was to be achieved.

## A Line Crossed

Amsterdam South was one of those rare occasions when all conditions were ripe for excellence. Still extant traditional craftsmanship and materials were made to serve newly unleashed creative power in search of a new task. Sufficient public funds, readily available as the city's

321

**18.10**  *Amsterdam South extension—Perspective drawing by H. P. Berlage, illustrating his urban design (1915).
Photograph of original from the Gemeentearchief Amsterdam. Reprinted with permission.*

commerce prospered, were dispersed in a most remarkable display of cooperation among professionals. Experiments in architectural form-making were conducted in the framework of well-defined urban spaces. Amsterdam South's outstanding architectural and urbanistic qualities remain undisputed after three-quarters of a century.

To all appearances, it was an auspicious beginning. Yet there were inherent difficulties—veiled, subtle, or dormant—in the new order. In later extensions, these would come to dominate the urban fabric.

Many of these factors have already been identified. Where agents were exclusively professional and institutional, decision making was centralized, making units of intervention large and control distribution coarse. In Amsterdam South this circumstance was still combined, in many cases, with well-conceived and varied interior layouts. But within the com-

mercial projects and public housing alike, the uniformity of floor plans so characteristic of unified control quickly resulted.

In all cases, the same unified control patterns coupled with state-of-the-art technology made interior fit-out rigid and subsequent small-scale renovation or transformation impossible. Block-size buildings were still constrained by well-defined urban space. But in later extensions, they would become increasingly autonomous, resulting in a fundamental change of environmental structure (see chapter 4.3). We also noted an emerging lack of territorial expression in spite of the exuberant architecture (see chapter 10.2) and an increasing tendency for control over exterior space to be exerted by public authorities, both inside and outside urban blocks (see chapter 12.2).

In short, the stage was set for the succeeding twentieth-century urban fabric. All aspects typical of that environment, already in

323

**18.11** *Amsterdam, 1928—Bird's-eye view of part of Amsterdam South, just after completion. Photo by KLM.. Reprinted with permission.*

place but obscured by the magnificent façades and powerful urban concept, would subsequently unfold. For the first time in the city's history, a totally new environment was professionally created and designed on all levels, demonstrating a new environmental process. Propelled by forces beyond human control—economical, technological, and ideological—a line was inevitably crossed. Henceforth, environment as a design problem would be the working model.[10]

**18.12** *Amsterdam, ca. 1990—Composite aerial photo. In the lower right-hand corner is the historic town, with the seventeenth-century extension of concentric canals; above it, in the middle, Berlage's Amsterdam South; directly above that, part of the van Eesteren extension of the era immediately after the Second World War. Hexagonal residential building complexes at the top left are part of the infamous Bijlmermeer extension of the 1960s and early 1970s. At its lower right-hand corner, a subsequent return to the closed block concept is observed.*

324

## Epilogue

Built environment develops and extends in fields: urban, suburban, rural. Built fields retain their identity for centuries, continually transforming while remaining faithful to the relations of their constituent parts. They are sustained by local and incidental acts of architecture and urban design: variations on environmental themes that rejuvenate extant fabric.

Built environment has always been self-organizing. As professionals, we intervene in a natural, ongoing process. Despite our increasing ability to effect large-scale change and our escalating ambitions, built environment follows its own laws. That reality renders our practice thoroughly thematic. Eventually, we must engage the environment's terms, not just our own intentions. Deep currents of form, place, and understanding flow, determining how professional practice will function.

They may, for instance, cause us to abandon the idea of vertically integrated design control in favor of a mode of dispersed responsibilities. The big building, like older urban fabric, will become susceptible of fine-grained transformation, reinterpreted through its own internal patterns of public space and private settlement.

They may challenge us to once more articulate territorial reality, so persistently ignored in (post-)modernist free-flowing space— to deal substantively with the ancient presence of boundaries, gates, and territorial depth in a new way.

Most difficult of all for environmental professionals may be learning to use forms of understanding and to speak of them freely. To find words suitable for naming thematic qualities. To find pride in continuity, in variation on a common theme.

Human creativity is irrepressible. The desire to invent, renew, and reinterpret makes environments bloom. But the new can only be identified against what is held in common. Now that we are responsible for the well-being of the common as well, it must be discussed. Thus a fresh vocabulary is in order.

We tend to record the innovative while discounting the familiar. But the former, which initially depends on the latter, may eventually transform it. We should therefore seek to understand our present environments, so radically different from those in the past, as the result of a collective search for new thematic knowledge.

We may begin by reexamining what, in an age of invention and revolution, has eventually become conventionally accepted, and is now taken for granted in practice. We might then discover a rich ore of already common forms, spaces, and patterns of control, brought to light in modern times by experiment and innovation.

The idea that a living environment can be invented is outmoded: environment must be cultivated. This requires proper use of levels, judicious articulation of territory, and creative application of types, patterns, and thematic systems. It must also ensure well-modulated distribution of control, compatible with an increasingly mobile and informed humanity.

After all, it is by the quality of the common that environments prosper and by which, ultimately, our passage will one day be measured.

**19.1**  *Venice—View from the Doge's palace.*

**Notes**

## 1. The Physical Structure of the Built Environment

1. N. J. Habraken et al., *Concept Design Games*, 2 vols. (Cambridge: MIT Department of Architecture, 1987).

2. N. J. Habraken, "The Uses of Levels," paper presented at the UNESCO Regional Seminar on Shelter for the Homeless, Seoul (1988).

3. N. J. Habraken, "Control Hierarchies in Complex Artifacts," in *Proceedings of the 1987 Conference on Planning and Design in Architecture*, ed. J. P. Protzen (New York: American Society of Mechanical Engineers, 1987), pp. 75–84.

## 2. Recognizing Levels

1. See also D. E. Boas-Vedder, *Het Dynamisch Groeiproces* (The Hague: Vuga Boekerij, 1974), a study of the economics of bottom-up urban growth.

2. Fernando Domeyko's survey (unpublished study) of the Islamic medieval tissue of Córdoba documents a street that runs now in a staggered fashion, having been diverted across old courtyard spaces. Conversely, the earlier street may be traced in the courtyards of other houses.

3. The behavior of these forms also reveals a balance of power not seen in the Western model. Public space is often changed by bottom-up initiative while remaining under communal control. See Jamel Akbar, *Crisis in the Built Environment: The Case of the Muslim City* (Singapore: Concept Media, 1988), pp. 118–124. See also S. al-Hathloul, "Tradition, Continuity, and Change in the Physical Environment" (Ph.D. diss., MIT, 1981).

4. D. M. Robinson, with J. W. Graham, *Excavations at Olynthus*, vol. 8 (Baltimore: Johns Hopkins University Press, 1929–1946).

5. Jerzy Wojtowicz, *Illegal Facades* (Hong Kong: privately published, 1984).

6. Michael Dennis, *Court and Garden: From the French Hôtel to the City of Modern Architecture* (Cambridge: MIT Press, 1986), p. 82.

7.   Hillary Ballon, *The Paris of Henri IV: Architecture and Urbanism* (Cambridge: MIT Press, 1992), chap. 2, "The Place Royale," p. 71.

8.   Kramer, quoted in Bernhard Kohlenbach, *Pieter Lodewijk Kramer, 1881–1961: Architect van de Amsterdamse School* (Naarden: V+K Publishing, 1994), p. 106.

## 3.   Hierarchies of Enclosure

1.   Taking into account the first four levels, the chart presents all possible instances. Because the first level is always in place, there exists only one way to span a single level (*H*). There is also only one way to span all four (*E*). There are three possible alternatives spanning two levels (*A, C, G*); and three as well comprising three (*B, D, F*). This makes for a total of eight modes of inhabitation, given levels as defined in this model.

## 4.   Changes in Enclosure Hierarchy

1.   The practice of putting containers filled with night soil on the street every morning used to be universal. In Delft in the late 1940s, wastes in containers with wooden lids were still routinely collected door-to-door by horse-drawn cart.

2.   Stephen H. Kendall has reported repeatedly on residential fit-out development in both Europe and Japan, recently in "Open Building for Housing," *Progressive Architecture*, November 1993, pp. 95–98, and *Developments toward Open Building in Japan* (Silver Spring, Md.: Technology and Economics, 1995).

3.   N. J. Habraken, "Reconciling Variety and Efficiency in Large Scale Housing Projects," in *Large Housing Projects: Design, Technology and Logistics*, ed. Margaret Bentley Sevcenko, special edition of *Designing in Islamic Cultures*, no. 5 (Cambridge: Aga Khan Program for Islamic Architecture, 1985), 46–53.

4.   This reality has been recognized by the Open Building movement, which brings together designers, builders, manufacturers, wholesalers, managers, and financiers. Each player seeks clearer distinction of levels for his or her own reasons.

5.   Issues of technology and control relating to the modern movement's failure to recognize levels, and its generally uneasy relation with them, remain largely unexplored. For Rietveld, the Schröder house represented an exception, its flexible partitioning no doubt a response to specific client demands. Its uniform detailing on all levels clearly also reflects Rietveld's background as a furniture maker. The architecture, while setting a standard for integral coherence while maintaining level distinctions, is not an unqualified exemplar of such coherence.

6.   Next21, Osaka, client: Osaka Gas. Design by professors Yositika Utida and Kazuo Tatsumi et al. See *Next21*, special issue of *SD*, no. 25 (Tokyo: Kajima Institute Publishing Company, 1994); and also Utida et al., "Osaka Gas Experimental Housing Next21," *GA Japan*, no. 6 (1994): 60–95.

7.   In affluent countries, furniture is still a symbol and means of identification, but its mere presence no longer signifies a class distinction.

## 5.   The Act of Building

1.   "Two Step Housing" was a phrase first coined by Tatsumi in describing his infill housing projects. The term is apropos in a broader context as well. See Kazuo Tatsumi and Mitsuo Takada, "Two Step Housing System," *Open House International* 12, no. 2 (1987): 20–30.

2.   H. J. Zantkuijl, *Bouwen in Amsterdam: Het Woonhuis in de Stad* (Amsterdam: Architectura & Natura, 1993); see esp. chap. 3 and p. 66.

3.   Abbott Lowell Cummins, *The Framed Houses of Massachusetts Bay, 1625–1725* (Cambridge: Harvard University Press, Belknap Press, 1982), p. 64.

4.   See Thomas C. Hubka, *Big House, Little House, Back House, Barn: The Connected Farm Buildings of New England* (Hanover, N.H.: University Press of New England, 1984).

5.   Doo-Ho Sohn, "Design Rule-Making: A Study of Hawhoe Houses in Korea" (master's thesis, MIT, 1989), p. 35.

6. Bainbridge Bunting, *Houses of Boston's Back Bay: An Architectural History, 1840–1917*. (Cambridge: Harvard University Press, Belknap Press, 1975).

7. J. J. Coulton, *Ancient Architects at Work: Problems of Structure and Design* (Ithaca: Cornell University Press, 1977), p. 97.

## 6. Other Forms at Play

1. See also Stephen H. Kendall, "The Entangled American House," *Blueprints* 12, no. 1 (1994): 2–7.

2. E.g., the porticoes of Bologna were uniformly set at 2.66 meters to accommodate a mounted rider; see Spiro Kostof, *A History of Architecture: Settings and Rituals* (New York: Oxford University Press, 1985), p. 360. To cite another example, Besim S. Hakim notes, "Seven cubits [was] the minimum width of public thorough-fares. . . . The basis for this width is to allow two fully loaded camels to pass. The cubit ranges from 46 to 50 cm. The width, therefore, ranged from 3.23–3.50 m. From my research, I found that the minimum vertical height of a public through street is also 7 cubits. This corresponds to the maximum vertical height of a camel with the highest load" (*Arabic-Islamic Cities: Building and Planning Principles*, 2nd ed. [New York: Routledge and Kegan Paul, 1988], p. 20).

3. While touring the town walls of Xi'an, I was informed that twenty soldiers could march abreast on them.

4. The car is an extraordinary artifact: it can be domesticated to share space with people in their homes and yards as well as in the residential street. But once any need for coexistence is obviated, the vehicle is observed to quickly take over. Accommodation to increase vehicular flow then creates forms that do not safely admit the unencapsulated human body.

5. Locating the point of transition from secondary to tertiary scale is not a simple matter of density: it varies greatly. We observe it in Amsterdam between the prewar fabric of Berlage (fig. 4.4d) and the postwar fabric of van Eesteren (fig. 4.4f). Manhattan presses the limits of the enclosure hierarchy at the secondary scale, Singapore tends toward the tertiary scale. Most large cities will combine two scales, or, like Tokyo, all three, depending on local conditions.

## 7. Territory

1. See Edward T. Hall, *The Hidden Dimension* (New York: Doubleday/Anchor Books, 1966), pp. 113–148.

2. In many cases, this similarly occurred each night, when predatory hunters—bandits, poachers, and wild beasts—could no longer be kept out of outlying fields.

3. Louis de Rouvroy, duc de Saint-Simon, *Memoires*, vol. 1, ed. Yves Coirault (Paris: Gallimard, 1990).

4. This duality holds for all but the deepest territory in the hierarchy: with no included territory, it is undivided space and entirely private, unless personal space is taken into account.

## 8. Observing Territorial Structure

1. Jamel Akbar, *Crisis in the Built Environment: The Case of the Muslim City* (Singapore: Concept Media, 1988), pp. 87–92, argues that prior to the Muslim era, towns were conglomerates of tribes, settling by themselves. This tradition was subsequently retained during Muslim expansion and town building.

2. Ibid., pp. 149–150, 186.

3. This impression was reinforced by observing ancient models in the Musée des Plans-Reliefs, Paris. For example, in the scale model of the town of Maastricht originally made for Louis XIV, following detailed survey sketches by his spies, two- and three-story houses again press up to the street edge. Quite extensive green spaces behind remain invisible from the public space.

4. This has been observed and documented by John F. C. Turner, Horacio Caminos, and Jorge Andrade, among others.

5. Judging from extant photographs of the historic city, Beijing street gates were often ceremonial and could not be closed. However, residential streets may well have been locked at sundown.

6. The example is cited out of many in an extensive three-year study conducted by Fernando Domeyko (unpublished).

## 9. Territory and Buildings

1. Bainbridge Bunting states that a regulation of 1873 restricted bay windows to project no more than five feet. That maximum quickly became the norm. A mandatory setback of twenty feet was also established. This simple pattern ensured the coherence of the street walls of the Back Bay. See Bunting, *Houses of Boston's Back Bay: An Architectural History, 1840–1917* (Cambridge: Harvard University Press, Belknap Press, 1975), p. 253.

2. See A. Boeken, *Amsterdamse Stoepen* (Amsterdam: Van Saane, 1950). Boeken details how elaborate steps, ironwork, and other architectural elements installed in front of the houses actually occupied public space. Such customary occupation was already a well-established pattern before the seventeenth century. It ultimately became an unquestioned right.

After the Second World War, the Amsterdam municipality began to widen streets in response to car traffic. Owners were initially compelled to clear the stoop zone of steps and other obstructions. Court battles ensued. Ancient surveys laying out house lots along the canals confirmed that property lines coincided with façades. Nevertheless, home owners won, and territorial custom prevailed over restricted land titles.

In many parts of North America up to the present time—notably in Texas—it is a serious invasion of turf to park one's car in front of someone else's home, particularly in "their" spot. These parking disputes, according to anecdotal reports, have sometimes led to gun battles. The particulars of such histories provide valuable insight into the difference between legal property and territorial claim.

3. *Mews* formerly referred to stables grouped along an alley or around a courtyard, a usage still encountered. Eventually, the alleys that provided access to such groups of stables came to be so named. The term now frequently refers to back streets with small houses. In the United States, it has further been appropriated to clustered or courtyard multifamily residences not directly accessed from a main street.

4. In what follows, I use the word *gate* broadly, with considerably liberty. The term *gate* here connotes a present control boundary. It need not be a physical gate.

5. Even the urban variant is not incompatible with private yards, as we know from certain Dutch examples, notably the Begijnhof in historic Amsterdam.

6. Introducing the principle of territorial continuity invariably triggers a search for a case that disproves it: to date, the closest thing to an exception remains the condition of segregated women in Arab towns who communicate via the roofs of their houses, thereby creating virtual public space that is isolated within private domains. The case is real and of great interest; nonetheless, it is obviously weak as a rebuttal of the continuity principle.

## 10. Gates

1. Clearly, not every doorway is a gate. Unfortunately, more nuanced and precise terminology quickly becomes cumbersome, if not pretentious, in exploring the relation between forms of passage and their territorial meaning.

2. Amsterdam School architects designed for both public agencies and private developers. Accordingly, this poverty of territorial expression is not observed where they designed areas under the control of public agencies or managers: e.g., at public entrances like open communal stairs leading to private houses.

3. Herman Herzberger, notably in De Drie Hoven, a housing and care center for the elderly in Amsterdam, made a serious effort to provide inhabitants some territory immediately beyond the apartment door.

4. Screens are also a vehicle for architectural play. Edwin Lutyens, born in the Victorian age, possessed a postmodern sense of irony. In the main hall at Little Thakenham in Sussex (1902), he created a gate whose form fairly broadcasts territorial meaning. In fact, Lutyens's gate stands squarely in the middle of the space, to screen the stairs. See David Dunster, *Architectural Monographs 6: Edwin Lutyens* (New York: Rizzoli, 1979), p. 49.

## 11. In and Out of Territory

1. It is also routine for home owners in most countries to extend short runs of wiring in their own homes, to hardwire dishwashers and microwave ovens, and also to freely split and reconfigure incoming cable TV. This

is a case apart from wholesale ad hoc wiring, which occurs throughout informal settlements in the third world.

2. Although the spatial relationship is vertical, the territorial relationship is horizontal: the two neighboring apartments occur at the same territorial depth.

## 12. Shifts in Territorial Structure

1. Johannes Adolf Overbeck, Plan der Stadt Pompeii, endpaper of *Pompeii in seinen Gebauden Alterthumen und Kunstwerken, für Kunst- und Alterthumsfreunde* (Leipzig: W. Engelmann, 1866).

2. This occurrence was not restricted to Europe; it can be found in nineteenth-century North American urban fabric as well.

3. Already in chapter 8.1, reference was made to backyard houses with a slender path, drive, or alley accessing the street. This is a variation of the same pattern, known as the "flag lot" in the United States.

4. Bainbridge Bunting and Robert H. Nylander, *Survey of Architectural History in Cambridge*, report 4, *Old Cambridge* (Cambridge, Mass.: Cambridge Historical Commission, 1973).

5. See Jamel Akbar, *Crisis in the Built Environment: The Case of the Muslim City* (Singapore: Concept Media, 1988), particularly the case study on Taif (pp. 191–196).

6. Such moves resemble the takeover of abandoned city lots in North American cities, which we sometimes observe subdivided into a number of private gardens. This is not invasion of public space but a deepening of territory: the original house lot is still private, but it now features communal paths connecting a number of small gardens.

7. According to Akbar (conversation with author), cleaning responsibilities had formerly rotated among neighbors who shared the space. In the ensuing confusion about responsibility, dead-end streets were no longer kept clean.

8. Akbar, *Crisis*, pp. 171–172, refers to H. al-Wahhab, *Takhtit al-Qahirah wa Tanzimaha* (Dar an-Nashr: Lil-Jami', 1977).

9. Bernard Stoloff, *L'affaire Claude-Nicolas Ledoux: autopsie d'un mythe* (Liège: Pierre Mardaga, 1989).

10. See Joseph Masheck, "Bentham's Panopticon: An Architectural Perpetration," in *Building-Art: Architecture under Social Construction* (Cambridge: Cambridge University Press, 1993), pp. 6–28.

11. Bentham's first proposal was written in 1787, thirteen years after the design of the Salt Works. Bentham saw his building type as useful not only for prisons but for all kinds of institutions—schools, hospitals, and accommodations for the destitute included. Neither the building nor its attendant utilitarian theory is incidental to the rise of modernism.

12. The duc de Saint-Simon describes his own apartment in Versailles as a corridorless procession of five connected spaces, whose middle room connects to a palace corridor via an entrance room. Between the rooms and the corridor is a zone with an entresol. Beneath this mezzanine is Saint-Simon's private work space and, most likely, additional service space. These receive light only indirectly, via shuttered partitions from the major rooms. Louis de Rouvroy, duc de Saint-Simon, *Mémoires*, vol. 1, ed. Yves Coirault (Paris: Gallimard, 1990), pp. 264–265.

13. The most dynamic architectural forms proposed in postmodern times tend to restore the complexity of public space in buildings. But this does not necessarily increase territorial depth. The issue is not one of architecture but of mode of inhabitation, and hence of control.

## 13. Common Understanding

1. Amos Rapoport, *House Form and Culture* (Englewood Cliffs, N.J.: Prentice-Hall, 1969). See particularly chap. 2, "Alternative Theories of House Form" (pp. 18–45).

## 14. Patterns

1. Christopher Alexander, *A Pattern Language* (Oxford: Oxford University Press, 1973).

2. Christopher Alexander, *The Timeless Way of Building* (New York: Oxford University Press, 1979).

3.   Ground-level arcades supporting houses above with cyclopic pointed arches rather than columns frequently ring bastide *cornière* market squares. Their consistent recurrence among scores of towns planted within a century suggest that the pattern was already well accepted by the twelfth or thirteenth century.

4.   Anna Maria Matteucci, *Carlo Francesco Dotti e l'architettura bolognese del Settecento* (Bologna: Alfa, 1969).

## 15.   The Systemic Environment

1.   The smallest units exhibit no atrium proper, but they do have a central space. Whether this was roofed is unclear. See Andrew Wallace-Hadrill, *Houses and Society in Pompeii and Herculaneum* (Princeton: Princeton University Press, 1994), p. 81. There are also many *tabernae*, hole-in-the-wall shops with a loft above for living. Such minimal houses for the poor are also indicated in figure 15.2.

But as Axel Boëthius has shown, these form a different type altogether and cannot be classified as a variant of the Pompeiian courtyard house. See Boëthius, *The Golden House of Nero: Some Aspects of Roman Architecture* (Ann Arbor: University of Michigan Press, 1960), chap. 4, "The Domestic Architecture of the Imperial Age and Its Importance for Medieval Town Building."

## 16.   Systems Misunderstood

1.   For a thorough discussion of the history and current development of the timber frame home, see Tedd Benson, *The Timber Frame Home*, 2nd ed. (Newton, Conn.: Taunton Press, 1997).

2.   Hassan Fathy, *Construire avec le peuple* (Paris: Jerome Martineau, 1970).

3.   Gilbert Herbert, *The Dream of the Factory-Made House: Walter Gropius and Konrad Wachsmann* (Cambridge: MIT Press, 1984).

4.   Ibid., p. 5.

5.   However, the International Council for Building Research Studies and Documentation (CIB) has recently formed an Open Building Implementation task group.

In so doing, they have thus begun to formalize what was previously an informal network.

6.   Form repetition is not found, however, in Romanesque churches, where each capital is an individually designed and executed sculpture.

## 17.   Type

1.   "Thick description" is an anthropological method of illuminating a given cultural phenomenon by combining a number of (inevitably partial) different views, from different angles, of the same phenomenon. See Clifford Geertz, "Thick Description: Toward an Interpretive Theory of Culture," in *The Interpretation of Cultures: Selected Essays* (New York: Basic Books, 1973), pp. 3–32.

2.   I first observed this in an MIT workshop. After studying examples of a given type, architecture students could produce an instance with no difficulty. Nonetheless, when subsequently asked to define the type, they clearly found consensus impossible. Subsequent research verified the implicit nature of typological understanding.

3.   These observations result from scrutiny of Johannes Adolf Overbeck's map. Andrew Wallace-Hadrill's study, supported by data on house size and statistical occurrence of atrium, peristyle, and garden, appears to confirm these impressions. Wallace-Hadrill's statistics also make clear what is *not* so immediately obvious: "embryonic" occurrences of the house typology, in which the central space is not yet an atrium proper, together with *tabernae*, constitute more than half the number of identified units. The lesser portion, those within which the type is clearly recognizable, represent by far the larger percentage of built surface. A remarkable range of unit sizes may also be found in a single urban block: Roman society manifestly did not separate incomes by location. See Wallace-Hadrill, *Houses and Society in Pompeii and Herculaneum* (Princeton: Princeton University Press, 1994), pp. 79–81, 86, and Overbeck, end paper, *Pompeji in seinen Gebauden Alterthumern und Kunstwerken, für Kunst- und Alterthumsfreunde* (Leipzig: W. Engelmann, 1866).

4.   Wallace-Hadrill, *Pompeii and Herculaneum*, chap. 2, "The Language of Public and Private," pp. 17–37.

333

Wallace-Hadrill's reflections on the publicness and privateness of spaces in the Pompeiian house are particularly helpful to understand the social forces behind the type.

5.    For a more thorough discussion, see Kevin Lynch, *Good City Form* (Cambridge: MIT Press, 1984).

6.    Evidence generally points to stylistic systems changing while spatial organization remains constant. John McAndrew asserts that "Renaissance palaces are no bigger and showier than the preceding late Gothic ones . . . and the difference is only skin deep" (*Venetian Architecture of the Early Renaissance* [Cambridge: MIT Press, 1980], p. 195). Baroque and classicistic canal houses in Amsterdam are no less similar behind markedly different façades.

7.    Axel Boëthius, *The Golden House of Nero: Some Aspects of Roman Architecture* (Ann Arbor: University of Michigan Press, 1960), chap. 4, "The Domestic Architecture of the Imperial Age and Its Importance for Medieval Town Building."

8.    See especially Carl W. Condit, *The Rise of the Skyscraper* (Chicago: University of Chicago Press, 1952).

9.    Clear emergence of local high-rise typologies may only be a matter of time. Many Asian architects are now deliberately seeking to define a high-rise architecture more compatible with local culture. The key question remains the extent to which the resulting differences will reflect socially adopted structures.

10.    We cannot assume that the uniformity evident in the public housing typology results solely from shared information among an international professional class. Similar rules of play and ideology may produce a similar typology even in isolation, as occurred in the People's Republic of China, during an era when professionals in China were virtually cut off from their peers elsewhere.

11.    Historical examples of stylistic systems that existed solely within a purely professional context are equally rare. Classicistic architecture as a style resided in a network culture that was elite but not narrowly professional. Therefore, Thomas Jefferson, employing classical elements in his design of the University of Virginia,

could situate it more broadly within classical education. The International Style, by comparison, was a far more proprietary system, whose values were initially nurtured and championed largely, although not exclusively, by architects. Its narrow base eventually became a liability for the profession that generated it.

12.    Ming-Hung Wang, "Factory-Villa: A Case of the emergence of type," paper submitted to the IAPS 12 International Conference on Socio-Environmental Metamorphoses (*Proceedings* IV), July 1992, Marmaras, Chaldiki, Greece.

## 18.    The Uses of Understanding

1.    John Onians, *Bearers of Meaning: The Classical Orders in Antiquity, the Middle Ages, and the Renaissance* (Cambridge: Cambridge University Press, 1988), pp. 183–185.

2.    Heino Engel, *Measure and Construction of the Japanese House* (Rutland, Vt.: C. E. Tuttle, 1985), pp. 35–42.

3.    Jorge Andrade's extensive studies have not been published in depth, although they have been occasionally exhibited and referred to. I draw from his original material.

4.    John W. Reps, *Cities of the American West: A History of Frontier Urban Planning* (Princeton: Princeton University Press, 1979), p. 642.

5.    A. J. Youngson, *The Making of Classical Edinburgh* (Edinburgh: Edinburgh University Press, 1975), p. 71.

6.    Ibid.

7.    Acts were passed to regulate the proper alignment of houses and the laying out of "areas," thus assuming a shared typology. "There is no record of any more detailed regulations being passed until 1781, by which date St. Andrew's square had been entirely built and building was going on as far west as Hanover Street." Included among those new regulations were others to constrict building height to a maximum of three floors, and to disallow storm or other windows in front of the roof (ibid., p. 81.).

8.    Marcel Proust, *Remembrance of Things Past*, vol. 2,
*The Guermantes Way. Cities of the Plain*, trans. C. K. Scott
Moncrieff and Terence Kilmartin (New York: Random
House, 1981), p. 10.

9.    Contemporary historians had widely assumed the
existence of a lost master plan for the extension, even
obliquely referring to it. But in "Derde Vergroting van
Amsterdam" (The third extension of Amsterdam), in
*52nd Yearbook of the Amstelodamum Society* (Amsterdam:
J. H. de Bussy, 1959), L. Jansen gives an almost canal-by-
canal and street-by-street account of council deliberations. He concludes: "It is almost certain that the
famous three-canal-plan in fact never existed. The Town
Carpenter's design of 1610 was no more than a plan for
new ramparts around the whole town." Moreover, "The
. . . extensions of Amsterdam followed each other so
quickly, that . . . no other method could have been
adopted" (p. 88). The conventional way of building concentric canals or canals and roads that followed already
existing ditches and paths was merely adapted. This is
not to say that the town council did not discuss plans,
but the discussions were always partial, intended to
decide on the next street or canal to be done. In Jansen's
account, there is one instance in which an alternative to
convention is discussed. On September 2, 1614, with digging already under way, there was a proposal "to make
the middle canal not into a canal but into a wide avenue,
a 'bel vedere,' in the style of the Voorhout of the Hague.
For reasons not further explained, it was judged better
not to follow this proposal" (p. 62).

10.    Indeed, the Dutch housing law of 1901, possibly
the first in modern history to make funds available for
public housing, stipulated among other things that
municipalities exceeding a certain population size
should have an urban development plan, to be updated
periodically. Berlage's first commission coincided with
the establishment of this law. The law can be seen as a
formalization of the understanding that urban extension
had become a design problem after a period of
nineteenth-century laissez-faire expansion.

335

This book came about not as a result of traditional schol-
arship, but rather through a process of reflection, synthe-
sis, and distillation of approximately four decades of
writing, teaching, research, consulting, and practice. The
sources that have ultimately informed this work are consequently quite varied, broad in scope, and numerous.
This bibliography, of necessity, lists only those printed
sources that have been of immediate and primary importance as references in the creation of this text. Regretta-
bly, the list is by no means comprehensive, let alone
exhaustive. Nonetheless, I hope it proves convenient as a
point of departure for the reader.

## Selected Bibliography

Akbar, Jamel A. *Crisis in the Built Environment: The Case
of the Muslim City*. Singapore: Concept Media, 1988.

Alexander, Christopher. *A Pattern Language*. Oxford:
Oxford University Press, 1973.

———. *The Timeless Way of Building*. New York: Oxford
University Press, 1979.

Anderson, Stanford. "People in the Physical Environment: The Urban Ecology of Streets." In *On Streets,* ed.
Stanford Anderson, 1–11. Cambridge: MIT Press, 1978.

Andrade, Jorge, with Rodolfo Santa Maria and Alfonso
Govela. "Transformación de un entorno urbano: Santa
Ursula, 1950–1977." *Architectura y Sociédad* 1, no 10.
(1978): 27–31.

Babelon, Jean-Pierre. *Demeures parisiennes sous Henri IV
et Louis XIII*. Paris: Editions Le Temps, 1965.

Ballon, Hillary. *The Paris of Henri IV: Architecture and
Urbanism*. Cambridge: MIT Press, 1992.

Benson, Tedd. *The Timber Frame Home: Design, Construction, Finishing*. 2nd ed. Newtown, Conn.: Taunton Press,
1997.

Boas-Vedder, D. E. *Het Dynamisch Groeiproces: een nieuwe
wijze van stads-centrum-ontwikkeling*. The Hague: Vuga
Boekerij, 1974.

Boeken, A. *Amsterdamse Stoepen*. Amsterdam: Van
Saane, 1950.

Boëthius, Axel. *The Golden House of Nero: Some Aspects of
Roman Architecture*. Ann Arbor: University of Michigan
Press, 1960.

Boudon, Françoise, André Chastels, Hélène Couzy, and Françoise Hamon. *Système de l'architecture urbaine: le quartier des Halles à Paris.* Vol. 1, *Texte;* vol. 2, *Atlas.* Paris: Editions du Centre Nationale de la Récherche Scientifique, 1977.

Bruneau, Philippe, and Jean Ducat. *Guide de Delos.* Paris: Editions de Boccard, 1983.

Bunting, Bainbridge. *Houses of Boston's Back Bay: An Architectural History, 1840–1917.* Cambridge: Harvard University Press, Belknap Press, 1975.

Bunting, Bainbridge, and Robert H. Nylander. *Survey of Architectural History in Cambridge.* Report 4, *Old Cambridge.* Cambridge, Mass.: Cambridge Historical Commission, 1973.

Carp, John C. *Keyenburg: A Pilot Project; Frans van der Werf, Architect.* Eindhoven: Stichting Architecten Research, 1985.

Casciato, Maristella. *De Amsterdamse School.* Rotterdam: Uitgeverij 010, 1991.

Chen, Li Xian. *Art and Architecture in Suzhou Gardens.* Nanjing: Yilin Press, 1992.

Clarke, John R. *The Houses of Roman Italy, 100 B.C.–A.D. 250: Ritual, Space, and Decoration.* Berkeley: University of California Press, 1991.

Condit, Carl W. *The Rise of the Skyscraper.* Chicago: University of Chicago Press, 1952.

Coulton, J. J. *Ancient Greek Architects at Work: Problems of Structure and Design.* Ithaca: Cornell University Press, 1977.

Cummings, Abbott Lowell. *The Framed Houses of Massachusetts Bay, 1625–1725.* Cambridge: Harvard University Press, Belknap Press, 1982.

Dennis, Michael. *Court and Garden: From the French Hôtel to the City of Modern Architecture.* Cambridge: MIT Press, 1986.

Depaule, J.-Ch., ed. *Espace centré.* Les Cahiers de la Recherche Architecturale, nos. 20–21. Paris: Editions Parenthèses, 1987.

Derwig, Jan, and Erik Mattie. *Amsterdamse School.* Amsterdam: Architectura & Natura, 1991.

Dietz, Albert G. H. *Dwelling House Construction.* Cambridge: MIT Press, 1977.

Domeyko, Fernando, with A. Pedraza, R. Suarez, P. Salzberg, A. Herrera, J. Schochting, A. Wreighton. *Tissue urbain San Pablo, Santiago de Chile.* Special issue of *A+ Architecture, Urbanisme, Design,* no. 7. Brussels: CIAUD, 1974.

Dunster, David. *Edwin Lutyens.* Architectural Monographs 6. New York: Rizzoli, 1979.

Engel, Heino. *The Japanese House: A Tradition for Contemporary Architecture.* Rutland, Vt.: C. E. Tuttle, 1964.

———. *Measure and Construction of the Japanese House.* Rutland, Vt.: C. E. Tuttle, 1985.

Fathy, Hassan. *Construire avec le peuple.* Paris: Jerome Martineau, 1970.

Geertz, Clifford. *The Interpretation of Cultures: Selected Essays.* New York: Basic Books, 1973.

Geist, Johann Friedrich, and Klaus Kürvers. *Das Berliner Mietshaus, 1740–1862.* Munich: Prestel Verlag, 1980.

Gemeente Archief Amsterdam. *Berlage en Amsterdam Zuid.* Rotterdam: Uitgeverij 010, 1992.

Habraken, N. J. "Control Hierarchies in Complex Artifacts." In *Proceedings of the 1987 Conference on Planning and Design in Architecture,* ed. J. P. Protzen, 75–84. New York: American Society of Mechanical Engineers, 1987.

———. "Cultivating the Field: About an Attitude When Making Architecture." *Places* 9, no. 1 (Winter 1994): 8–21.

———. "Forms of Understanding: Thematic Knowledge and the Modernist Legacy." In *The Education of the Architect: Historiography, Urbanism, and the Growth of Architectural Knowledge,* ed. Martha Pollak, 267–293. Cambridge: MIT Press, 1997.

337

———. "Reconciling Variety and Efficiency in Large Scale Housing Projects." In *Large Housing Projects: Design, Technology and Logistics*, ed. Margaret Bentley Sevcenko, 46–53. *Designing in Islamic Cultures* No. 5. Cambridge: Aga Khan Program for Islamic Architecture, 1985.

———. *Supports: An Alternative to Mass Housing.* Trans. B. Valkenburg. New York: Praeger; London: Architectural Press, 1972.

———. "Type as a Social Agreement." Paper presented at the Third Asian Congress of Architects, Seoul, Korea, 1988.

Habraken, N. J., and Mark D. Gross. "Concept Design Games." *Design Studies* 9, no. 3 (1988): 150–158.

Habraken, N. J., et al. *Concept Design Games.* Book 1, *Developing;* Book 2, *Playing.* Principal investigator with Mark D. Gross and James Anderson, Nabeel Hamdi, John Dale, Sergio Palleroni, Ellen Saslaw, and Ming-Hung Wang. Report submitted to the National Science Foundation. Cambridge: MIT Department of Architecture, 1987.

———. *The Grunsfeld Variations: A Demonstration Project on the Coordination of a Design Team in Urban Design.* Coauthor with J. A. Aldrete-Haas, R. Chow, T. Hille, P. Krugmeier, M. Lampkin, A. Mallows, A. Mignucci, Y. Takase, K. Weller, and T. Yokouchi. Cambridge: MIT Laboratory of Architecture and Planning, 1981.

Hakim, Besim S. *Arabic-Islamic Cities: Building and Planning Principles.* 2nd ed. New York: Routledge Kegan Paul, 1988.

Hall, Edward Twitchell. *The Hidden Dimension.* New York: Doubleday/Anchor Books, 1966.

Hamdi, Nabeel, and Brad Edgerly. *Bath: A Topographical Study.* Cambridge: MIT Department of Architecture, n.d.

al-Hathloul, S. "Tradition, Continuity, and Change in the Physical Environment." Ph.D. diss., MIT, 1981.

Herbert, Gilbert. *The Dream of the Factory-Made House: Walter Gropius and Konrad Wachsmann.* Cambridge: MIT Press, 1984.

Hubka, Thomas C. *Big House, Little House, Back House, Barn: The Connected Farm Buildings of New England.* Hanover, N.H.: University Press of New England, 1984.

Hwang, Ming Chorn. "A Study of Urban Form in 18th Century Beijing." Master's thesis, MIT, 1986.

Jansen, L. "Derde Vergroting van Amsterdam." In *52nd Yearbook of the Amstelodamum Society,* 42–89. Amsterdam: J. H. de Bussy, 1959.

Kendall, Stephen H. "Control of Parts: Parts-Making in the Building Industry." Ph.D. diss., MIT, 1990.

———. *Developments toward Open Building in Japan.* Silver Spring, Md.: Technology and Economics, 1995.

———. "The Entangled American House." *Blueprints* 12, no. 1 (1994): 2–7.

———. "Open Building for Housing." *Progressive Architecture* (November 1993): 95–98.

Kendall, Stephen H., and S. Sawada. "Changing Patterns in Japanese Housing." In *Changing Patterns in Japanese Housing,* ed. Stephen Kendall. Special issue of *Open House International.* No. 12 (Eindhoven: Stichting Architecten Research, 1987): 7–20.

Kohlenbach, Bernhard. *Pieter Lodewijk Kramer, 1881–1961: Architect van de Amsterdamse School.* Naarden, the Netherlands: V+K Publishing, 1994.

Kostof, Spiro. *A History of Architecture: Settings and Rituals.* New York: Oxford University Press, 1985.

Laprade, Albert. *Croquis Paris: quartiers du centre, les Halles, le Marais.* Paris: Vincent, Fréal, 1967.

Liang Ssu-ch'eng. *Annotated Construction Methods. (Ying-tsao fa-shih chu-shih.)* Vol. 1. People's Republic of China: Chinese Architectural Industry Publishing, 1983.

———. *A Pictorial History of Chinese Architecture: A Study of the Development of Its Structural System and the Evolution of Its Types,* ed. Wilma Fairbank. Cambridge: MIT Press, 1984.

Lukez, Paul. *New Concepts in Housing: Supports in the Netherlands.* Cambridge: MIT Department of Architecture, Design and Housing Program, 1986.

Lynch, Kevin. *Good City Form.* Cambridge: MIT Press, 1984.

———. *The Image of the City.* Publication of the Joint Center for Urban Studies. Cambridge: MIT Press, 1960.

Maretto, Paolo. *L'edilizia gotica veneziana.* Venice: Filippi Editore, 1978.

Masheck, Joseph. "Bentham's Panopticon: An Architectural Perpetration." In *Building-Art: Architecture under Social Construction,* 6–28. Cambridge: Cambridge University Press, 1993.

Matteucci, Anna Maria. *Carlo Francesco Dotti e l'architettura bolognese del Settecento.* Bologna: Alfa, 1969.

McAndrew, John. *Venetian Architecture of the Early Renaissance.* Cambridge: MIT Press, 1980.

Nieuwenhuijzen, Kees, comp. *Jacob Olie: Amsterdam Gefotografeerd 1860–1905.* Amsterdam: Van Gennep, 1974.

Onians, John. *Bearers of Meaning: The Classical Orders in Antiquity, the Middle Ages, and the Renaissance.* Princeton: Princeton University Press, 1988.

*Open Housing.* Special issue of *Toshi-Jutaku* (January). Tokyo: Kajima Institute Publishing, 1979.

Overbeck, Johannes Adolf. *Pompeji in seinen Gebauden Alterthumern und Kunstwerken, für Kunst-und Alterthumsfreunde.* Leipzig: W. Engelmann, 1866.

Palladio, Andrea. *The Four Books of Architecture* (1570). New York: Dover, 1965. Facsimile of the 1738 edition published by Isaac Ware.

Pehnt, Wolfgang. *Lucien Kroll: Buildings and Projects.* New York: Rizzoli, 1987.

Periánez, Manuel. *L'habitat évolutif: du mythe aux réalités.* Paris: Ministère du Logement, 1993.

Perocco, Guido, and Antonio Salvadori. *Civiltà di Venezia.* Vol. 1, *Le origine e il Medio Evo.* Venice: La Stamperia di Venezia, 1977.

Philippides, Dimitry, ed. *Greek Traditional Architecture,* trans. Philip Ramp. Book 1. Athens: Melissa Publishing House, 1983.

Pinkney, David H. *Napoleon III and the Rebuilding of Paris.* Princeton: Princeton University Press, 1972.

Proust, Marcel. *Remembrance of Things Past.* Vol. 2, *The Guermantes Way. Cities of the Plain,* trans. C. K. Scott Moncrieff and Terence Kilmartin. New York: Random House, 1981.

Rapoport, Amos. *House Form and Culture.* Englewood Cliffs, N.J.: Prentice-Hall, 1969.

Reps, John W. *Cities of the American West: A History of Frontier Urban Planning.* Princeton: Princeton University Press, 1979.

Richards, J. M., Ismail Serageldin, and Darl Rastorfer. *Hassan Fathy.* Singapore: Concept Media, 1985.

Rietveld, Gerrit. *Rietveld, 1924. Schröder Huis.* Text and drawings by Gerrit Rietveld; typographic design by Pieter Brattinga. Amsterdam: Steendrukkerij de Jong, Hilversum, 1963.

Robinson, D. M., with J. W. Graham. *Excavations at Olynthus:* Part 8: *The Hellenic House.* Baltimore: Johns Hopkins University Press, 1938.

Saint-Simon, Louis de Rouvroy, duc de. *Mémoires,* vol. 1. Ed. Yves Coirault. Paris: Gallimard, 1990.

Santelli, Serge. *Medinas: Traditional Architecture of Tunisia.* Tunis: Dar Ashraf Editions, 1992.

Shen, Wa. *Shanghai Urban Vernacular Architecture.* Beijing: Chinese Architectural Industry Publishing, 1993.

Sohn, Doo-Ho. "Design Rule-Making: A Study of Hawhoe Houses in Korea." Master's thesis, MIT, 1989.

Spencer-Brown, G. *Laws of Form.* New York: E. P. Dutton, 1973.

Stoloff, Bernard. *L'affaire Claude-Nicolas Ledoux: autopsie d'un mythe.* Liège: Pierre Mardaga, 1989.

Summerson, John. *Georgian London.* London: Penguin Books, 1978.

339

Tatsumi, Kazuo, and Mitsuo Takada. "Two Step Housing System." In *Changing Patterns in Japanese Housing*, ed. Stephen Kendall. Special issue of *Open House International*. Eindhoven: Stichting Architecten Research, 1987. 20–30.

Trincanato, Egle Renata. *Venezia minore*. Venice: Filippi Editore, n.d.

Turner, John F. C. *Housing by People: Towards Autonomy in Building Environments*. New York: Pantheon Books, 1977.

Turner, John F. C., and Robert Fichter, eds. *Freedom to Build: Dweller Control of the Housing Process*. London: Collier-Macmillan, 1972.

Utida, Y., K. Tatsumi, S. Chikazumi, S. Fukao, and M. Takada. *Next21*. Special issue of *SD [Space Design]*. No. 25. Tokyo: Kajima Institute Publishing, 1994.

———. "Osaka Gas Experimental Housing Next21." *GA Japan*, no. 6 (1994): 60–95.

van der Werf, Frans, with Hubert-Paul Froyen. "Molen-vliet-Wilgendonk: Experimental Housing Project, Papendrecht, the Netherlands." *Harvard Architectural Review* 1 (Spring 1980): 161–169.

———. *Open Ontwerpen*. Rotterdam: Uitgeverij 010, 1993.

Venturi, Robert, Denise Scott Brown, and Steven Izenour. *Learning from Las Vegas*. Rev. ed. Cambridge: MIT Press, 1977.

Vitruvius Pollio, Marcus. *The Ten Books on Architecture*, trans. Morris Hicky Morgan. 1914. Reprint, New York: Dover, 1960.

Wallace-Hadrill, Andrew. *Houses and Society in Pompeii and Herculaneum*. Princeton: Princeton University Press, 1994.

Wojtowicz, Jerzy. *Illegal Facades*. Hong Kong: privately published, 1984.

Wood, Margaret E. *The English Mediaeval House*. London: Bracken Books, 1983.

Yagi, Koji, ed. *Collective Housing in Holland*. Special issue of *Process Architecture*. No. 112. Tokyo: Process Architecture Publishing, 1993.

Youngson, A. J. *The Making of Classical Edinburgh 1750–1840*. Edinburgh: Edinburgh University Press, 1975.

Zantkuijl, H. J. *Bouwen in Amsterdam: Het Woonhuis in de Stad*. Amsterdam: Architectura & Natura, 1993.

## Maps

Georg Braun and Frans Hogenberg, *De Hollandse Steden* (1574). Facsimile reprint of *Civitas orbis terrarum*. Groningen: B. V. Foresta, n.d.

Bretez, Louis. *Le plan de Paris (dit "Plan de Turgot"): Edition de Jubilé 1739–1989*. Nördlingen, Germany: Verlag Dr. Alfons Uhl, 1989.

Comune di Venezia. *An Atlas of Venice: The Form of the City on a 1:1000 scale photomap and line map*, ed. Edoardo Solzano. Princeton: Princeton Architectural Press, 1989.

*Complete Map of the Capital City during the Qianlong Era* (Qianlong jingcheng quantu). 18 vols. Beiping: Asia Development Board, 1940. Photolithograph of the original map, ca. 1750, in the Palace Museum, Beijing.

Dancersz, Danckert. *Map of the City of Amsterdam*. Amsterdam: Danckert Dancersz, 1662.

Delagrive, Abbé Jean. *Plan détaillé de la Cité*. Paris, 1754.

Florisz van Berdkenrode, Balthasar. *Map of the City of Amsterdam, 1625*. Amsterdam: Balthasar Florisz van Berdkenrode, 1625.

*Historische Plattegronden van Nederlandse Steden*. Book 1, *Amsterdam*. Introduction by W. Hofman. Alphen aan den Rijn: Canaletto, 1978.

Nolli, Giambattista. *Pianta grande di Roma, 1748*. Highmount, N.Y.: J. H. Aronson, 1984.

## Illustration Credits

Except as noted, photographs, drawings, and diagrams are by the author.

Figures 0.2 and 18.14 © KLM Luchtphotographie. Reprinted with permission.

Figures 2.2, 8.4, and 17.4 Composite images drawn over a base map courtesy of Association Sauvegarde de la Medina, Tunis.

Figure 2.3 Based on the Olynthus plan drawing published in D. M. Robinson with J. W. Graham, *Excavations at Olynthus,* Part 8: *The Hellenic House.* (Baltimore: Johns Hopkins University Press, 1938).

Figure 2.4 Photograph courtesy of Jerzy Wojtowicz.

Figure 2.5 Place Louis-le-Grand, Paris, etching by Pierre Aveline, Illustration Number BNCE VA-234A (Cl.85.C.17109), Service Photographique, Bureau des Estampes, Bibliothèque Nationale de France. Reprinted with permission. Photo courtesy of Michael Dennis.

Figure 3.1 Detail of Georg Braun and Frans Hogenberg map in *De Hollandse Steden* (1574), facsimile reprint of *Civitas orbis terrarum* (Groningen: B. V. Foresta, n.d.).

Figure 4.2 Drawing by Projjal K. Dutta, based on a floor plan drawing in Gerrit Rietveld, *Rietveld, 1924. Schröder Huis* (Amsterdam: Steendrukkerij de Jong, Hilversum, 1963).

Figure 4.3 Rembrandt (?), *The Women at the Fireplace at Rembrandt's House,* Coll. no. Tu57b,6. Reprinted with permission of the Royal Museum of Fine Arts, Copenhagen.

Figure 4.4 Composite image of aerial photographs © KLM Luchtphotographie. Reprinted with permission.

Figure 5.6 After a drawing in Liang Ssu-ch'eng, *Annotated Construction Methods* (*Ying-tsao fa-shih chu-shih*), vol. 1 (People's Republic of China: Chinese Architectural Industry Publishing, 1983).

Figure 5.7 After a photograph by Chrysavgi Arnaoutoglou, in Dimitry Philippides, ed., *Greek Traditional Architecture,* trans. Philip Ramp, book 1 (Athens: Melissa Publishing House, 1983).

Figures 5.8 and 8.5 Photographs of the *Complete Map of the Capital City during the Qianlong Era* (Qianlong jingcheng quantu), facsimile reproduction of 1935. Reproduced courtesy of the Harvard-Yenching Library.

Figures 5.9, 18.3, 18.4, 18.5, and 18.6 Courtesy of Jorge Andrade, Rodolfo Santa Maria, and Alfonso Govela, previously published in "Transformación de un entorno urbano: Santa Ursula 1950–1977," *Architectura y Sociedad* 1, no. 1 (December 1978): 000–000.

Figure 5.10 After a drawing in Doo-Ho Sohn, "Design Rule-Making: A Study of Hawhoe Houses in Korea" (master's thesis, MIT, 1989).

Figure 6.4 Illustration by Age van Randen, reprinted courtesy of OBOM Research Group, Delft University of Technology.

Figures 6.5, 18.12, and 18.13 Reprinted with permission of the GemeenteArchief Amsterdam.

Figure 7.2 By Projjal K. Dutta, after a drawing in Paolo Maretto, *L'edilizia gotica veneziana* (Venice: Filippi Editore, 1978).

Figure 8.1 Detail from *Le plan de Paris de Louis Bretez* (Nördlingen: Verlag Dr. Alfons Uhl, 1989).

Figure 8.6 After an unpublished drawing of the "Cité Knossos" by Fernando Domeyko.

Figure 9.1 Detail of Jacopo de Barbari map of Venice.

Figure 9.7 After a drawing in Nabeel Hamdi and Brad Edgerly, *Bath: A Topographical Study* (Cambridge: MIT Department of Architecture, n.d.).

Figure 10.1 Photograph reprinted courtesy of Zhu Jia-Bao.

Figure 11.1 Photograph © Landslides. Reprinted with permission.

Figures 12.2 and 15.2 After the Plan der Stadt Pompeii, endpaper of Johannes Adolf Overbeck, *Pompeii in seinen Gebauden Alterthumen und Kunstwerken, für Kunst-und Alterthumsfreunde* (Leipzig: W. Engelmann, 1866).

Figure 12.3 Drawing by H. Reijenga, courtesy of SAR.

Figure 12.4 Drawing by Projjal K. Dutta, after a drawing by Susan M. Fogel in Bainbridge Bunting and Robert H. Nylander, *Survey of Architectural History in Cambridge*, report 4, *Old Cambridge* (Cambridge, Mass.: Cambridge Historical Commission, 1973).

Figure 12.5 Reprinted courtesy of Jamel Akbar.

Figure 16.5. Photograph detail from Axel Boëthius, *The Golden House of Nero: Some Aspects of Roman Architecture* (Ann Arbor: University of Michigan Press, 1960), © The University of Michigan. Reprinted with permission.

Figure 17.1 Detail of *Plan detaillé de la Cité*, by Abbé Jean Delagrive (Paris, 1754).

Figure 17.2 Reprinted from H. J. Zantkuijl, *Bouwen in Amsterdam: Het woonhuis in de stad* (Amsterdam: Architectura & Natura, 1993), courtesy of Vereniging Vrienden van de Amsterdamse Binnenstad.

Figure 18.1 Detail of undated map of Edinburgh showing Craig's 18th-century New Town extension. Publisher unknown.

Figure 18.7 Photograph detail of OHS# 20656.89.393.T, "Laying out Town Lots in Guthrie, twenty minutes after the arrival of the first train," *Harper's Weekly*, 18 May, 1889. Reprinted with permission of the Archives and Manuscripts Division of the Oklahoma Historical Society.

Figure 18.11 After a map by Joan Blaeu at the Amsterdam Municipal Archives cat. d'Ailly 133, ca. 1650. Also published in a portfolio of maps by W. Hofman, *Historische plattegronden van Nederlandse steden*, book 1, *Amsterdam* (Alphen aan de Rijn: Canaletto, 1978).

Figure 18.15 Composite image aerial photographs © KLM Luchtphotographie. Reprinted with permission.

Index

351

353

357

358